RAISING
Wildflowers

Homeschooling
at Ease in a Frantic Culture

EMILY B. RIFFE

Raising Wildflowers
Homeschooling at Ease in a Frantic Culture
Emily B. Riffe

Copyright © 2020 Emily B. Riffe. All rights reserved. Except for brief quotations for review purposes, no part of this book may be reproduced in any form without prior written permission from the author.

Published by

Mary Ethel

Mary Ethel Eckard
Frisco, Texas

To contact the author
emily@raisingyourwildflowers.com

ISBN (Print): 978-1-7338233-5-7
ISBN (Ebook): 978-1-7338233-6-4

All Scripture quotations, unless otherwise indicated, are taken from the Holy Bible, New Living Translation, copyright © 1996, 2004, 2015 by Tyndale House Foundation. Used by permission of Tyndale House Publishers, Inc., Carol Stream, Illinois 60188. All rights reserved. Scripture quotations marked ESV are taken from the ESV® Bible (The Holy Bible, English Standard Version®). ESV® Text Edition: 2016. Copyright © 2001 by Crossway, a publishing ministry of Good News Publishers. The ESV® text has been reproduced in cooperation with and by permission of Good News Publishers. Unauthorized reproduction of this publication is prohibited. All rights reserved. Scripture quotations marked NIV are taken from the Holy Bible, New International Version ®, NIV ®. Copyright © 1973, 1978, 1984, 2011 by Biblica, Inc. Used by permission. All rights reserved worldwide.

DEDICATION

This book is dedicated to Charlotte Mason: Simply, thank you.

SPECIAL THANKS

A huge thank you to Kristi for the initial editing of this book. It is a difficult task to tie this tongue down. You have made me a better writer. Thank you.

To my husband Darren. Thank you for listening to me as I argued with myself about many aspects of this book. For not only your support, but your wisdom and engagement with me throughout this process, for recommending books and articles, and for your love.

CONTENTS

Dedication v
Special Thanks v
Preface xi

SECTION I | WINTER 1

Chapter 1   Our Story 3
Chapter 2   Foundations 9
Chapter 3   A House of Prayer 13
Chapter 4   Your Home 19
Chapter 5   Reasons 25
Chapter 6   The Letter 29
Chapter 7   Image 37
Chapter 8   Socialization 43
Chapter 9   View 49
Chapter 10   Time 55
Chapter 11   Change 59
Chapter 12   Living Stories 61
Pondering Winter 68

SECTION II | SPRING 71

Chapter 1   Attention 73
Chapter 2   Nature 79

Chapter 3	Nothing	93
Chapter 4	Habits	99
Chapter 5	Technology	103
Chapter 6	How Much?	109
Chapter 7	What Kind?	113
Chapter 8	Smartphones and Social Media	119
Chapter 9	What Message?	131
Chapter 10	Beautiful Words	139
Chapter 11	Fairest Lord Jesus	143
Chapter 12	Living Stories	147

Pondering Spring 155
Resources for Spring 158

SECTION III | SUMMER 161

Chapter 1	Who Am I?	163
Chapter 2	Your Advisers	167
Chapter 3	Your Need to Know	175
Chapter 4	Your Value	179
Chapter 5	Your Friendships	185
Chapter 6	Your Boundaries	193
Chapter 7	Your Helicopter	201
Chapter 8	Your Voice	209
Chapter 9	Your Enjoyment	223
Chapter 10	Your Individuality	227
Chapter 11	Your Failure	231
Chapter 12	Living Stories	235

Pondering Summer 243

SECTION IV | FALL 247

Chapter 1	Full Circle...	249
Chapter 2	Philosophy	253
Chapter 3	Schedules and Routines..	271
Chapter 4	A Sample Schedule	289
Chapter 5	Saplings..	295
Chapter 6	College	305
Chapter 7	Adventure	311
Chapter 8	Working Hands	315
Chapter 9	Reviving the Renaissance......................................	319
Chapter 10	Seasons Beyond	327
Chapter 11	Living Stories..	333
Chapter 12	The End	339

Pondering Fall 343

About the Author... 347

Notes 349

Works Cited.. 359

PREFACE

*"Consider how the wildflowers grow. They do not labor nor spin.
Yet I tell you, not even Solomon in all his splendor was dressed like one of these."*
~ Luke 12:27 NIV ~

Little Marigold Mae steps lightly through the tall green grass of what seems to be Texas prairie land. She's viewed these long stretches of land from her Mom's car window many times her whole eight years. But this time, she's walking through it. She sees it up close and personal. Little blades of Bermuda grass stick under her worn but still white sandals. The weight of the world looms deep in her heart, but a warmth lifts her eyes and turns her head. Something so bright she must shade her eyes until He comes into view…and she runs.

She seems to be moving in slow motion, but her pace quickens, and her lavender eyelet dress brushes the wildflowers, making a small path through the bright yellows, pinks, and blues. He runs too. He runs to meet her, and His smile is like pure honey, brighter than the sun. When they embrace, He's more than the Father she never knew, He is God. And her pain and shame seem to be from some make-believe time and place, some fantasy world that never existed, and the real is here and now in this thicket of wildflowers, and she wakes.

Every young girl loves wildflowers. Though well-meaning adults tell her otherwise, all girls know the secret that many a weed is a wildflower. It all depends on your perspective. Why else would all the little girls pick them and make baby bouquets. They are like a procession of little bridesmaids lovingly handing them to their teachers and mothers.

In her book, *The Teeth of the Lion,* Anita Sanchez says, "Only in the twentieth century did humans decide the dandelion was a weed. Before the inventions of lawns, the golden blossoms and lion-toothed leaves were more likely to be praised as a bounty of food, medicine and magic. Gardeners used to weed out the grass to make room for the dandelions."[1]

I guess even weeds across a west Texas schoolyard were trying to symbolize something to me as a young girl.

Current cultural thoughts impact what we see as true, and cultural perspective changes as fast as a paratrooper dandelion through a spring breeze. But, long ago, as light and darkness were separated and life breathed into man, the Creator made an order and a plan and the truth. Yet just like Adam and Eve, we are easily deceived by what seems, and we are not satisfied by what is. We don't trust Him; we dethrone Him because it's just easier to trust bone and flesh. We wee weeds.

Maybe that's one of the reasons I noticed sunflowers everywhere that summer. Sunflowers, crazy sunflowers! Rows and rows of chocolate centered lollipops, golden arms outstretched to the sun above. As I zoomed past in my car, I wondered if anyone else noticed them. Then I started to think, perhaps to make sure, I could gather them, tame them, and somehow yell out for everyone to put their phones down and see something! But I sighed and took a deep breath. I simply get to be an observer, a witness.

And so, on a hot July afternoon, Deer, Blondie, Blue Eyes and I put on our big boots. We walked to where the sunflowers bloomed. Hair stuck to foreheads with sweat. Boots suctioned into deep brown mud across the small ditch. Arms stretched out like airplanes, fingertips gliding across the tops of delicate petals. At our eye-line, we could not see where the bushels of the flower families ended. That's what they looked like to us. Little family clusters. "There's Uncle Sun, Aunt Sunny, and Little Sunshine." Way, way across the way, we see the highway. So fast, so hurried. In this present moment, I am thankful to be here. I just long for other families to feel what I feel. I want others to join me. I'm just grateful. Because it's been a long road for us. My children are still growing and so am I.

The Wildflower's Story

Only the Lord really knows the wildflower's story. He watches the first bud appear. He sees the flash floods and thunderstorms, the scorching heat, and feels the spring breeze. He knows them before they grow to be anything that would catch the eye of a passerby on a lonely country road. Some may only ever truly be seen by Him. Yes, there is something about flowers that grow uncultivated, freely, without human intervention.

And so it is with these beautiful babies, children, teenagers, and young adults He has gifted us. Will you grow boxed flowers? Roses clipped to perfection and seated in a beautiful vase? Or, will you have wildflowers? Crimson clover, purple coneflower, evening primrose, cultivated by the Lord?

Can you let go of your control, your plan, your expectations, and trust in the Master Gardener to raise these seedlings to full bloom? Will you let them weather the inevitable storms, heat, and wind that are part of being out in the open? Will you let them experience the uncommon and the vulnerable instead of safely tucking them away in a flower shop? For, in full bloom, in their season, there is nothing that points to God more beautifully than an authentic wildflower.

Families, like wildflowers, have their own unique stories. Five years ago, I began a quest to keep track of inspirational thoughts gained from literature and friends regarding the journey of homeschooling. It also became a personal journey to record what I was learning, the pitfalls taken, and observations of current culture. These were my novice first readings and baby steps into understanding the art of homeschooling. At the time, I was only in my second year of schooling at home, but God was kindling in me a desire to inspire others who were new to homeschooling.

This then, lead to the pleasure of interviewing 21 homeschooling moms to learn their stories. The core of this book comes from countless conversations and observations, the rumination of voices at playgrounds and on sofas, over coffee and make-shift tissues. Words shared through calls, emails, texts, inspirational books, random articles, laughter and tears. Voices calling back to the beginning, to the Word Himself, to Jesus, Creator, who made children and family and discovery. It was a call to the philosophies behind education and homeschooling and the way life was meant to be lived. In addition, I gained a keen recognition of the current culture and its impact upon it all.

But mostly, this book was inspired by moms. Sentences and paragraphs rolling off friends' tongues as they worked through first and second drafts, and back to first drafts, of their lives as homeschoolers. And here I am, through their eyes, watching their children pass from imaginary play to beautiful and independent youth. The fear, the excitement, the letting go. I watch from the backseat, the battle that is waged to protect innocence and faith in the face of a culture of fear and self-idolatry. And the feeling, that illusion, that we can control it all if we just try hard enough. Then, finding that we are not like those without hope, we place our children in the hands of the One who holds the tilt of the earth in His very fingertips. These bittersweet seasons, which change through passages of maturity and organic God-ordained processes, are not about school years and schedules.

Whether you are new to homeschooling or an old pro, I hope the thoughts brought forth through the topics within give you water for your journey and a sense that you are not alone. I will discuss practical day-to-day topics, but my first desire is that this book will speak more to holding on to the spirit of homeschooling in our current culture. Homeschooling is not just materials and routines, it's also about foundations and freedom to build and learn. Fear is not a viable or Biblical rock. We can't build our school or life upon worry.

This book is written from a Christian worldview. Like the wildflower has its seasons, this book, too, has its winter, spring, summer, and fall. I suppose it flows like a conversation, as conversations were the inspiration. Whatever brings you to this book, I pray the Lord will use it for some good. My heart is that I still have so much to learn, and I hope you'll join me on this journey.

A.R., age 7, and R.W., age 8

Living Stories

At the end of each seasonal section is a chapter called "Living Stories." This chapter shares how women, like yourself, answered questions related to the seasonal topic. The information is given in a way that is honest, clear, and spoken from the heart, and it is mostly given in simple qualitative grouped answers. I highlight a few specific quotes in each section. In this way, you hear directly from the women.

You will also notice, throughout the book, sketches created by children. I hope these will inspire you to see the importance of slowing down and including nature. Consider the drawings as a child's perspective on God and His handiwork. For me, they are vital in depicting in art what I hope to portray in words.

It seems natural to share some general facts about the women I interviewed. I live and homeschool in North Texas. It is not terribly hard to find other homeschooling families close by. Many of the people I interviewed were friends or friends of friends. So, yes, scientifically, this is a biased population. However, I do feel confident this data will still prove helpful to families starting their journey in homeschooling.

As I stated previously, 21 homeschool moms were interviewed for this book. Most of the interviews took place in North Texas. Eight of the women were Texas natives. Thirteen of the women were born in and grew up in another state or outside of the United States. Both large and small families were represented. Five of the families interviewed had five or more children. Similarly, five of the families had one or two children. Most of the families I interviewed had three or four children. I also aimed to speak to moms with younger children, as well as those whose children were off to college/work life. Seven out of the 21 moms had at least one child age 16 or older. Three out of the 21 women were non-Caucasian. More research is needed on the unique needs, joys, and challenges of women homeschooling from a variety of backgrounds.

How did I choose the questions asked?

After much reading, research and prayer, a framework formed as to what topics might be discussed. I knew there were wonderful and inspiring books on the "how-to" of homeschooling. But I thought readers might appreciate an authentic response from real moms living the daily homeschooling life. So, I created questions under the topics I wanted to explore. After completing the interviews, it became clear which topics mattered most to these homeschooling mothers. I have written more extensively in those areas. I felt it extremely valuable to share not only my thoughts, but to also glean from others. In addition, I considered doubts I had when I started homeschooling. These factors played into the questions asked. I also allowed time for women to share subject matters important to them. Some of my categories included: general routines, co-ops, special needs, teenage / college years, burnout, and inspiration.

Although I did my best to ask the same questions to each woman, if one topic needed more time and depth, I was okay with missing a question here and there. I wanted to respect the authenticity of their story. Generally, my hope was that these interviews would be more of an experience of sitting with a friend who was opening their "homeschool scrapbook" and sharing their story.

SECTION I

Winter

To my Mom: for when we had nothing, we had everything.

"I prefer winter and fall, when you feel the bone structure of the landscape. Something waits beneath it; the whole story doesn't show."[2]
~ Andrew Wyeth, painter ~

Two snow-covered lampposts sit in the strangest of places. One lamppost stands with a hazy amber light just on the other side of a wardrobe. Follow the path and it just might lead to an adventure.[3] Another lamppost sits in the middle of an icy front lawn in West Texas. The possibility here is smacking into the post while playing football with your brothers. But even an unknown lamppost, in a small corner, in the middle of nowhere, can lead to something unexpected. A pondering that brings a moment of clarity years later.

When I think back, I can still sense the joy as my brothers and I threw on mismatched gloves, stuffed somewhere at the bottom of our closets, when surprised with a "snow day." After we'd played every game imaginable

WINTER

before the snow melted, I would take a warm bath. I can still feel the burn of frost-bitten toes as I stepped into the steaming water. I was so cold that nothing seemed more soothing than the hottest bath imaginable. Oh, did it burn! Surely in that moment nothing could have been more comforting than warm water to freezing flesh, but it wasn't. I can still hear my mom's voice, "You might want to start the water a bit colder, then slowly turn the faucet warmer." I was hoping for instant relief, but first I needed to be content with the defrosting process.

It just might be there is a defrosting process that must take place in us before we can fully embrace this homeschooling life. A bit of unlearning must take place; a breaking down and building up. We feel frigid and scared, gripping for control of a path we cannot see. But it's the bare-boned tree and the lily-white snow-covered field where no boot has laid its print that shows us all that is possible. And there is *so* much that is possible! We must patiently wait for the picture to unfold. For deep inside that frost-covered soil a seed awaits. We clear out the roots of the dead and prepare for new life.

The clean canvas beckons us to start fresh.
So, take in the crisp clean January wind and let's begin.

K.C., age 11

CHAPTER 1

Our Story

*"Unless the Lord builds the house, those who build it labor in vain.
Unless the Lord watches over the city, the watchman stays awake in vain.
It is in vain that you rise up early and go late to
rest, eating the bread of anxious toil;
for he gives to his beloved sleep."*
~ Psalm 127:1-2 ESV ~

Our journey into homeschooling was not smooth. I never intended to be a stay-at-home mom, much less a homeschooling mom. My husband, Darren, and I have three children - two sons and one daughter. Before having children, my job was to help people stop smoking. It was a meaningful job.

Becoming pregnant was difficult for us, and that time changed my perspective. When I finally became pregnant there were complications. In the span of two hours, I went from being a working woman at the Texas Medical Center in Houston to a patient on six-weeks of bedrest. Morning after morning the nurses would bring my menu and I would circle pancakes, eggs, and hot chocolate. I tried to change it up now and again. I mean, it was the most exciting part of my day because I had a choice to make.

WINTER

There were no hurricanes that year, but I remember looking up at the tiny windows in my room as the spring rain of south Texas poured day after day. I remember thinking, if I ever got out, I would stop taking the sky for granted.

I thought when the baby was born, life would be easier. But William was born prematurely. Life got much harder, for years. It was the first time I remember feeling anxiety. I chose fear and doubted God's goodness. I had always been a positive Christian who trusted the Lord and believed everything happened for a reason. But this situation was beyond me. I was spent and my faith, which consisted of milk, wasn't ready for meat and bread - the meal of men and martyrs.

I distinctly remember walking into the NICU on week five after numerous hospital visits. I spoke plainly to the nurse, "I don't want to do this anymore!" What I wanted was an easy full-term pregnancy. I was discontent with what I had been handed. There is probably some good in being honest. But truthfully, being angry and seeping into feelings of unfairness, and wishing someone else had to do this job instead of me, made things worse. Sheer exhaustion and disrupted hormones overtook me. It's understandable. I can reason it now because I am older, and I no longer have crying babies and sleepless nights. But in that moment, I couldn't just be thankful that my son had not died. What was wrong with me?

Sadly, that statement of, "I don't want to do this anymore!" came in frequent bursts many times during those early child-rearing years. My sleep did not improve, and the expectation of what a great mom I would be could only be seen in glimpses surrounded in failures. Motherhood is much more difficult than anyone is willing to share. It seemed most of my friends and family had no difficulties with their pregnancies or with nursing. I felt like a failure. My standard of the ideal mom was not met. I felt insecure. Though I seemed to lose my faith during that time, I began to see it was faith in myself. I needed to have faith in God and trust and rest in His timing.

God is enduring and He allowed me to suffer for His greater plan, this story. He knows best. He was teaching me the lesson of being completely dependent upon Him, "We were crushed and overwhelmed beyond our ability to endure, and we thought we would never live through it. In fact, we expected to die. But as a result, we stopped relying on ourselves and learned to rely on God, who raises the dead" (2 Corinthians 1: 8b-9). This learned reliance took a long journey. It started with my shaky hands securing a 4-pound baby into a car seat, headed for home.

Night Terrors and Sleep Deprivation

I've heard that some people get a lot of sleep. I wonder what that must be like. Throughout my life, I never struggled with sleep issues. Little did I know so much of my character was dependent upon good sleep.

Because William was born prematurely, he had horrible acid reflux, and for a long period of time, we stopped sleeping. It wasn't just the not sleeping; it was the crying and not keeping food down, and 20 minutes later doing it all over again. I kept telling myself it was a phase, "everyone goes through this and one day this will end." But life hit a downturn that consumed much of my existence. William would wake up from his naps crying, and it could take an hour to calm him.

Then, at 3 years old, he started waking up with night terrors off and on, and he had tremendous difficulty falling back to sleep. He woke up screaming at midnight almost every night. He was always restless. We thought, with a little more time or a better routine, we would work through this, he was just a bad "sleeper." By ages 4 and 5, we decided it must be a behavioral problem. So we drew a line in the sand and walked him back to his room to sleep without our help. After multiple nights of this, taking up to 4 hours to put him back in his bed, we realized something was not "normal." By the

WINTER

grace of God, we discovered something else must be going on. So we slept on his floor and beside his bedroom door to help him fall asleep. Then, for a time, he slept in our bed. Of course, we felt guilt. What kind of parents sleep on their kid's floor? Any parent who has fed and comforted babies at night knows how exhausting it can be. But, when you are up at night with babies and toddlers for years, you feel like you are on a one-way trip to "Crazy Town" and there is no end.

Strangely, when we did the opposite of whatever we read in books, when we handled him with grace and peace and love, and when we stopped listening to "experts" and got on our knees, Darren and I were changed. Our circumstances were not changed. We, of course, knew something would have to improve. He could not sleep with us forever. But God would bring change about in His timing, though some of it took longer than we could have imagined.

As hard as that journey was, and as much as I did not respond like I should have many days, God allowed that difficult time for the greater good. He was building our household, not of my design or power, but His. He no longer wanted me to be that happy-go-lucky Christian who had never been on the anvil. It was time to experience the Refiner's fire. And, it was hot! But it gave me a perspective I would not want anyone to take away.

During those late nights laying in the hallway, the seeds of this book were planted. In fact, much of this book has been written lying on the carpet. Long before I ever thought I could or would homeschool, God had a plan for our family. He has one for yours, too. It was the acceptance that some things in life are just hard for a long time. But, if we let Him, these are also times when God teaches us the secrets of life. The books I read, the cries of prayer, the accepting of new answers or no answers, and the painful letting go, all the pieces of this jagged little puzzle will become a picture one day - a completed story.

The truth I can now see is, although lack of sleep is a terrible thing, often it was my anxiety and anger and living in the future that kept me from living at rest in the present. "It is in vain that you rise up early and go late to rest, eating the bread of anxious toil..." It does not say the faithful will receive the required 8 hours of sleep. Many people can get a full night's sleep and remain full of anxiety. It is the staying up late and rising early "filled of worry" that is the problem. When we worry, when we fret, we cannot rest. We let small, trivial things overwhelm us and we feel our feet frozen to the floor. And that, I have found, is far worse than lack of physical rest.

But a mind which stays on the Lord can be at peace and can sleep even amid difficulty. Most of it involves letting go of our expectations and living this one blessed day. So, will your vision for your children be carried out by your two strong shoulders and great will, or the Lord's? Staying your vision on the Lord means living in the present: praying about everything, seeking the good in a whole host of bad, taking account of the current moment, and being in real conversations and relationships with others. We must stop trying to escape or live in fast-forward. Sometimes, the best thing we can do is lay ourselves prostrate on the carpet. It's time to be vulnerable.

> *When we release to God the results, often, this is the beginning of change. Slowly, then more steadily. We lift one snow covered boot at a time.*

The Remedy: Homeschooling

So, how did we end up homeschooling? During my son's first grade year, we continued to be told he was a smart, sweet kid. But he was delayed in all subjects. At home he was difficult, and my husband and I didn't like who

WINTER

we were with him. For over a year, ideas were thrown around from anxiety to sleep issues, to OCD, to sensory processing disorder, to ADHD and learning disabilities. They all seemed to have some merit, and the solutions offered were more school and tutoring and therapy. Some of these helped. But nothing stuck.

After a few months of this schedule, we realized this could not continue. Even though we could not imagine how it would work, my husband and I prayed and realized the answer was clear: we needed to homeschool. In my heart, it was there all along. And not just for our one son, but for all our children. Neither was this decision to be for our family's academics only. It would be for the amazing group of friends and for the community He would place in our lives. It was for the moments, the sweet beautiful moments of discovery and learning, that would happen together. The Lord would bring joy. The details of what this would look like and how it would be done would unfold.

Five years later, I sit on a sandy step this cold November day and watch the seagulls fighting for a spot on the white buoys of Little Elm Beach. My kids, with rain jackets and rain boots, wade in the water and make sand angels. I catch William's deep brown eyes and we both smile. We both know something no one else knows. This day is to be embraced. The months leading up to this moment included sleep studies, surgery, and help from learning centers. In the end, though, we accept the boy in him. We daily die to the worlds standards and accept the plan we know God has for that little life. We hold character and kindness above test scores. It's a freedom we wash ourselves with because it's a treasure God gave us through pain. All I can do is look back in awe with gratitude.

We are still a work in progress. But, when you have lived in chaos and anxiety and begin to feel that burden lift, it's like Jesus whispering in your midst, and that great storm you thought might end you, becomes suddenly still. A ripple in a pond.

CHAPTER 2
Foundations

"...but the grand point remains undecided——how shall this heart, this head, these hands be employed? To whose service shall they be dedicated?"[4]
~ Charlotte Mason ~

A house cannot be built until a foundation is secure. No matter how clean or beautiful or fancy a home is, it will crack under a poor foundation.

So, what type of foundation are you building your life upon? The Bible tells us to build on the rock, Jesus Himself, "Though the rain comes in torrents and the floodwaters rise and the winds beat against that house, it won't collapse because it is built on bedrock" (Matthew 7:25). The storms will come, and your house will survive because it is founded on Christ. No other materials are stronger.

We may think we can keep our house secure by controlling the sea. We might think we can be smarter, stronger, or holy enough to stop the clouds from forming. We would be wrong. One person's house gets a little rain while others get hail, floods, and fire. We may never understand why one house gets more weather worn than another.

WINTER

God tells us to focus on making Christ our foundation. So, what does the architectural plan of foundation building look like? The Westminster shorter catechism asks, "What is the chief end of man? Man's chief end is to glorify God and enjoy Him forever."[5] How beautifully simple. Our number one goal is not to produce genius, all-star, perfectly well-behaved children. Our work is to wake up each morning and ask God to show us how to bring Him glory and enjoy Him. Everything else folds in behind.

The two greatest foundations we must build our lives upon are prayer and Scripture. You say, "That's it? I've been told that my entire Christian life!" We like to complicate the situation. We feel we should get some credit for how it all works out. Maybe we must do something special or be someone special and, if we do that, everything will work out in the end.

But we've been called first to worship because it puts us in our right position. I love the term "quiet time" because it is what I need. I need to be still before a Holy God who can move mountains. He will be my strength. Often, the mountain that needs to be moved is me.

As part of His creation, even if my day is horrible, does He not deserve praise for all things? Praise Him because He has given all things. Praise Him because of who He is. When it all seems wrong, He is still good. In my prayers, I find strength for this journey. In His Word, I am reminded I am not alone and others have walked this same walk.

Homeschooling will take perseverance, creativity, and a strong belief that God knows what is best for your family. The spirit by which you carry these days out is bound up completely in the power of God. You will need the power of God, through the work of His Holy Spirit, to continue this journey.

> *At the core, homeschooling starts with you. You must start with God. No philosophy or curriculum is higher than Him.*

The biggest temptation is to slowly rely on self. As pastor Chuck Swindoll says, "The beginning of pride is when you start seeing God as an option rather than essential."[6] Your relationship with the Lord is the foundation for which everything else will be built. It may seem simplistic to some. But we may find that prayer and Scripture are the first things to be pushed aside when we're overrun with other daily tasks.

Now of course, there are times when this is easier and times when this is harder. When we are up with babies all night or with toddlers who are struggling with discipline, it is understandable to fall asleep while reading our Bible. It might be that we set aside 10 minutes to thank the Lord for His blessings. We may fill the house with worship music while our children play. These are small choices made daily, even when we're exhausted. This makes a difference in our day because we put Christ first.

The reality is, when we have young children, it is both a beautiful and exhausting time. Someone always seems to be crying, hungry, or sleepy. Some children are more challenging than others. Indeed, we also live in a culture that fights hard for our time. Sometimes it's making the choice to listen to a devotional or read our Bible instead of checking social media or the news.

So how do we make time for the Lord? We talk with Him. We tell Him how worn out we are. We ask Him for help to set time aside. Some days a mom's prayers may be said through many tears. Don't give up seeking Him. We were created to worship Him. It is better to set aside time, small as it may be, to be in God's Word and in worship and prayer. During these overwhelming years, God understands our situation so graciously. I would

WINTER

have been calmer during the early child rearing years had I put Him first more often. Take one day at a time.

Look at each season. Ask the Lord, "What is best?" Listen to a devotional or worship music while cooking. Attend a Bible study or read one chapter of the Bible per day. Intentionally stop and pray at various points in the day or use a prayer list or app to help guide the time. We can write our struggles in a journal. We must not just let our days roll out repeatedly, trying to perform our life duties in our own strength. We must seek hard after the Lord and lean into Him. It doesn't have to look the same each day. But it must be each day.

CHAPTER 3
A House of Prayer

"Prayer; the key of the day, the lock of the night."[7]
~ Thomas Fuller ~

In the Bible, Jesus, so filled with righteous anger, turned over the tables in the temple. His house of prayer had been turned into a house of trade for thieves. That which was set out to be uncommon had been made common.

We, too, can easily turn our homes, which are to be places of prayer and devotion and beautiful pursuits, into places of idol worship. These idols creep in and are different for every family, such as activities, academic pursuits, entertainment, consumerism, comfort, and envy. We do not want to replace a Biblical mindset of what matters most with a cultural one. Indeed, we will wake up and pursue many wonderful academic and extra-curricular tasks. However, when we start with the Lord, He provides the atmosphere in which all other matters should be viewed.

Now that my children are older, I realize it's best if I wake up 30 minutes earlier and start with prayer and devotion before beginning our homeschooling. That extra time changes me and sets me before our Holy Lord in a way where I am ready to lead and guide, teach and love. It puts me in my proper order, under proper authority. I can become so stressed about getting the

WINTER

day going, and about the work to be done, that I lose sight of the Spirit by which I should be teaching. I may even think I've succeeded at the end of the day, but maybe God had a different way.

> *When we pray without ceasing, we teach our children we need God every moment.*

In the home, this is done with family reading of the Bible and prayer together. We teach them the beauty of God's truth. They hear stories of heroes and sinners and God's loving kindness. Discussions allow for pondering and connections. Questions arise in their young hearts. God kindles a fire within. They hear Mom and Dad pray and they learn to pray too.

As children age, we let go of our hold on their spiritual life and allow the Holy Spirit to make their relationship a priority. As they are able, we move Bible time and prayer to them in the mornings or evenings. Perhaps we teach them to write in their prayer journal, gently guiding them as needed. We are to let it be a creative process, not belabored. This helps them build their lives on Christ, the solid Rock. There is no more important gift we can give our children than to show them, by example, their need for the Lord.

Evaluate and Reevaluate

Every few months, reevaluate how this area is going for your family. Make changes as needed. Perhaps your family has four children under the age of 8. In the beginning, start by reading a storybook Bible in the morning. Share a brief discussion and prayer. As the older children begin to read and write independently, they may go into their own quiet places to read their Bible. They might write in a prayer journal or tell you verbally something they learned. This entire process might take between 10-20 minutes, depending on the age of the child.

It is possible your history curriculum will cover heroes of the faith. This is a great age to expose them to church history, leaders, and martyrs. Help them be creative. Teach them how to pray for themselves, their family, the church, and its mission to the world. They can ask friends and family how they can pray for them. All along, God is doing His work to build a beautiful relationship and areas of interest where they might serve.

While the older children have their quiet time, spend time with the younger ones. Read to them while they color, build, or play quietly. During other times of the week, you may still have a family Bible time, or discuss and pray for other communities, church, or cultural issues. As children get even older, help them pick out a Bible and devotional to read on their own.

Don't hover too much. Some might use this time to write prayers to the Lord and sketch what they've learned in the Bible. You may choose to use a homeschool Bible curriculum, but it's not a requirement. Again, it doesn't have to look the same each day or season. As the children grow, one child might enjoy more reading, while another enjoys more prayer and journal writing. Add variety to your spiritual routine. What a wonderful house of prayer!

The goal is complete dependence on the Lord. You want them to leave your home with firm foundations as they establish their own lives. Practically, all of this is counted as "schoolwork" as they read, write, and grow their spiritual education. This time is about a true life of discipleship and love for God and His Word. It's important that children do not see their Bible time as an academic pursuit, primarily, but as a relational life pursuit. Your desire is that they might willingly bow the knee to His teaching and wisdom and be convinced of His great love. Memorizing scripture and discussing theology with intelligence is a plus, but as you organize the subjects and materials for their learning, make sure the priority goes to making yours a true house of prayer.

Biggest Barrier to Homeschooling

As I've spoken with homeschool mom's over the years, worry seems to be the biggest barrier to homeschooling well. What is the antidote for worry? Throughout the day, constantly communicate with the Lord so that you are not held captive by worrisome thoughts. Instead, turn to Him with prayers of gratitude and trust. Have your morning devotion, but, as the day progresses, don't forget to keep praying and praising. Constant communication takes discipline.

Allow the Holy Spirit to direct your thought life and turn fearful thoughts into prayers. For example, you realize you are worried because you have not found the strength or routine to teach math well. The natural man's way is to ponder it over and over and make attempts to change the routine or curriculum. The spiritual man's way is to simply pray, "Lord, you know the importance of math for my child's life. You know our strengths and our weaknesses, and you know the best way to teach this subject to my child. I'm failing in this area; would you help us?"

Suddenly, it's not fear that guides how you teach math, it is faith. Though math may have caused you much consternation during your childhood, you don't have to teach it under stress. Indeed, you might bless your children with a new perspective on math. Though math might be difficult, it is a key from God that unlocks understanding to His universe. You might stop frantically changing materials, settle with the materials you have, and learn to change the WAY you teach.

Prayer in the Moment

I am getting to the place where I plan our routine, but I wake up each day and say, "Lord, help me leave room for You to guide this day."

In the middle of lessons, when I am frustrated or unsure, I say, "Lord help me do this Your way." When worry and fear want to consume me, I shut those thoughts. I shrink them between my index finger and thumb, and I say, "Lord, please help me!" I truly have no idea what plans He has for my children or what they may need in the future. But He does.

As Oswald Chambers, teacher and author of "My Utmost for His Highest," puts it, "Keep your life so constantly in touch with God that His surprising power can break through at any point. Live in a constant state of expectancy and leave room for God to come in as He decides. We plan and figure and predict that this or that will happen, but we forget to make room for God to come in as He chooses."[8]

Think of all God has done in your life. He doesn't ask for your permission. And so, the beautiful simplicity is that we must keep our eyes on Him. That is all He requires. We teach our children the same message. He is their Rock and the chief Cornerstone. When they have Him, they have it all. They may be as intelligent as Albert Einstein, but if they don't know the Lord and how to love others, they have nothing.

As followers of Christ, what matters most to Him is what should matter most to us. We still do the "hard work" of training and teaching. We still search for opportunities to help our children succeed. But this house is not to be built by our strong or weak hands, nor our child's great strengths or weaknesses. We don't know how to best carry out our teaching, so we place our lives in God's hands, we move our focus to Him, and we let the burdens fall upon Him. Maybe we find we are less reactive to our children's emotional ups and down. Possibly we experience new calm and wisdom in our daily dealings within our home. We let go of our expectations and fall to His plan.

WINTER

He will pick the design, the material, the colors, and the time frame for this house to be complete. We are free to live and teach moment by moment, day by day. It may be common that we function in our own strength, but we ask God to make us more aware of these tendencies. With His help we can learn to stop in our tracks and pray before we respond in word or deed.

One sure way to know we are trusting in Him more is when we go from, "I will be good when we get everything done in this school day" to "I am good now, before this school day ever begins, because God is with me."

> *We want them to leave our home with firm foundations as they establish their own lives. This time is about a true life of discipleship, dependence, and love for God and His Word.*

There is no "magic formula" to homeschooling. It is an organic process that will change year-to-year as our family grows and matures. The earlier we grasp this concept and give control of our children's future to God, the closer we are to the cusp of understanding the beauty of every day and every season. When our children leave our home, they will not have mastered every skill or piece of knowledge to get them through adulthood. But what kind of people will they be? How will they empathize with others, love God, be mentally and spiritually healthy? Will they be able to ride the inevitable waves of hardships and joys that are a part of jobs and relationships and church life? Will they be able to persevere and find joy each day of their lives? These are the real questions that should guide how we plan our homeschooling days.

CHAPTER 4
Your Home

"See, I lay a stone in Zion, a tested stone, a precious cornerstone for a sure foundation; the one who relies on it will never be stricken with panic."
~ Isaiah 28:16 NIV ~

The first and most prominent word in "homeschooling" is home. Once a home's foundation is set, construction can begin. Though blueprints are similar from one home to the next, what takes place inside the building is unique.

Although not all schooling will take place in the four walls of your home, a good portion of it will. Much of the schooling will not be in workbooks, but in conversations within the living spaces of your home. Every home is different. I think of the homeschooling community like the church itself. It includes families on the mission field, some tucked away in small apartments, others in suburban neighborhoods or on country farms. All are taking this beautiful and sometimes difficult journey called homeschooling. The atmosphere of these homes carries unique sounds and flavors. Some homes are boisterous and talkative, while others are quiet and contemplative. Some are bursting with colors and pictures on every wall, and others are streamlined with modern décor. Some homes have mud rooms full of dirty

WINTER

boots and last year's hand-me-downs. Other homes have closets with fancy jackets and shiny new gloves with matching hats for the coming winter.

The thing about home is, it is yours and there is not another one like it. Before you set out on your homeschooling journey, or even if you're already homeschooling, I encourage a "home review." Step back and see if your home represents you and the things that matter most to you as a family.

Whether you have a "school room" or do your work at the dining room table, do you feel inspired by your space? Do you love music and great artists, culture and geography, or math and science? How can you represent these individual interests in your home, in the corners, on tables or in bookshelves? Are you moved by nature and Scripture? Is this revealed in your home environment? Pray over your home space and ask the Lord to guide you in setting-up your entire home, as well as what seems like traditional places of learning.

Realize your whole home is your area of learning. Be prayerful about what needs to be thrown out or reorganized. Are your priorities and your family's heart easy to see by someone walking into your home? This is the basis for the atmosphere you want to create in your daily life. Get inspired by this powerful home where great things take place.

In my home, we started out, like many new to homeschooling, with a dedicated "homeschooling room." We had desks, a white board, and bulletin boards that would rival any public-school classroom. This was a natural part of our journey. You may have put creative energy into your homeschool classroom. That is fabulous. Over time, especially as kids get older, these spaces can and probably should change.

Using seasons of the year is a great timeline for reevaluating spaces. Each winter, spring, summer, and fall look at your locations for learning. If everything is working well, it might be that nothing needs to change. But you can decide to change the desks, move in a bookshelf, or find a new location for a picture.

We all need to be inspired anew, especially in our home which serves many purposes. Taking the time to create a home whose flow, colors, and organization represent your style will do your heart good. Our brains need to be stimulated with fresh wind under our wings. At times, these changes may be simple and understated. At other times, you may feel particularly bold and do your schoolwork outside or simply move out of the school room to the dining room table.

Minimalist Mindsets

Let's be clear, this re-organizing of your home does not mean you need to go out and buy new items. Use what you already have in new ways. In America, many of us are owned by our stuff. Our things are our identity and status. But what if we were freed of that? I am not saying we should not purchase special items or have a big home, but we should be thoughtful about what we buy and add to our homes. Every decision to purchase must be managed by our time and space. Eventually, much will be thrown away.

If our home is overrun by stuff, it can cloud our life. We need to be free to purchase without unnecessary guilt while removing the feeling that we must "keep up" with others. As minimalist and author Joshua Becker states, "Your life is far too valuable to be wasted on the life that everyone else is choosing."[9]

I fear we have all fallen into the trap of slowly acclimating to the idea that we need more than we do. Becker continues, "We were never meant to live life accumulating stuff. We were meant to live simply enjoying the experiences of life, the people of life, and the journey of life-not the things of life."[10]

WINTER

The more time we spend storing and managing, the less time we have for relationships and schooling. We learn to value what we already have. It might be a special letter, a piece of artwork, a book. But hanging on to everything can be unhealthy.

I am a minimalist, at least in "first world" terms. One day, my son found preschool papers he had just given me in the recycling bin. He asked, "What kind of mom are you?" When my husband got sick a couple of years ago, part of our healing process was decluttering our home. We eventually moved. We learned to live on less. It was an amazing journey.

Don't confuse decluttering with a perfectly clean home. I feel better thinking you have laundry piled up in your bedroom like me, even if you don't. But clear space seems to help clear our minds. Everyone is different. I came to the declutter idea easily, yet I know others hold more value in their things. Not from a materialistic heart, but because certain things hold memories. New purchases are made with an expectation of the experiences of togetherness they will give the family.

> *The Lord's presence is the most important "atmosphere" of your home.*

Of course, a clean table or a beautiful picture hanging on the wall will not add joy and peace to your home if the Holy Spirit is not dwelling there.

Pray about your home and decide if there are things to clear out. There may be areas to dust that reveal a special place to enjoy. Appreciate the past, homeschool in the present. As organization consultant Marie Kondo says, "The space in which we live should be for the person we are becoming now, not for the person we were in the past."[11] It's a process we should go through each season in our homes.

If you are starting your homeschooling journey, this is an exciting place to begin. If you have been homeschooling for years, stop and review your space. This allows you to give away those preschool books and toys your children have moved beyond. Perhaps it's time to trade out desks for cozy reading spaces or create that outdoor space.

CHAPTER 5

The spiritual foundation you build your life upon will shape the lens with which your child sees themselves and the world at large.

When we step out of our homes and have conversations with neighbors or church friends, we may find that the topic of homeschooling comes up more frequently. Why is this? The landscape of homeschooling has changed dramatically in recent years, and more families are considering it as an option.

According to the National Center for Education Statistics (NCES) in 2012, 3.4% of school-aged children were homeschooled, an increase from 2.9% in 2007. To give you a broader view, if we back up this statistic to 1999, 1.7% of school-aged children were homeschooled in the United States (NCES, Homeschooling in the U.S. 1999).[12] So, why the increase? Obviously, the reasons are different for every family.

According to the same study by the NCES, 91% of the homeschooled families surveyed said "a concern about the environment of other schools" (meaning safety, drugs, and negative peer pressure) was an important reason for homeschooling their child, which was a higher percentage than other reasons listed. Other reasons included: a desire to provide moral instruction, a dissatisfaction with academic instruction, and a desire to provide religious instruction. And then, suddenly in 2020 COVID-19 hit. Who could have predicted that all American families would be doing some form of homeschooling? There is an uncertainty amongst many parents as to what they will do when school returns. Should they take their children back to public school when the doors open? Many families will be pondering whether continuing to homeschool is the better choice. And now comes the opportunity. A whole new world and way of education can open to these families.

What are your reasons for homeschooling?

Many children have had difficulties in public or private institutions. Yet, it is important to make sure our main motivation to homeschool is not based in fear and isolationism. Fear is never a good foundation to build upon, "For God has not given us a spirit of fear and timidity, but of power, love, and self-discipline" (2 Timothy 1:7).

It is noble to want to protect our children from spending most of their days being influenced by peers or leaders who believe the opposite of what we want taught, and to keep them safe. However, let's not forget the garden. The sin is within our child, they are born that way. We all are born this way. It is Christ alone who will save us from ourselves, "For all have sinned and fall short of the glory of God" (Romans 3:23 ESV). Our children are sinners and surrounded by other imperfect, sinful people wherever they go.

A benefit to homeschooling is the ability to be a great source of influence to our children and slowly release independence to them in an age appropriate manner.

It is wise to have a goal for them to live and work in the culture without fear so they can bring others to the One who casts out fear. How will they be able to do this if they have been shielded from the way the world works, or instilled with such fear of the world they do not know how to relate in a meaningful way? "That you may be blameless and innocent, children of God without blemish in the midst of a crooked and depraved generation, among who you shine as lights in the world" (Philippians 2:15 ESV).

Homeschooling can be a big part of the life you are looking for and the environment for which your child can flourish. But it is not the answer to the fears and hopes of you or your child. Christ is. An important starting point is to pray and think carefully about your motivation to homeschool.

CHAPTER 6
The Letter

"Remember how the Lord your God led you all the way …"
~ Deuteronomy 8:2 NIV ~

When I first began homeschooling, some days were very hard. I was unsteady and unsure. There were periods when I was overwhelmed by the feeling that my children were not getting the best. I compared what my children could or could not do with others. I looked at the material we were "supposed" to cover and wondered how others got it done. I felt bursts of energy and excitement when things were going well. I could intellectually understand the goodness of homeschooling, but I couldn't keep my finger on the pulse of why "our" family was homeschooling, and I struggled to settle on a routine that was right for us.

At that point, my husband encouraged me to write a letter, listing the good reasons I wanted to homeschool, believing it would bring clarity to our routine. Initially, I saw this letter as something to read on days when things were not going well. It has served that purpose. However, it has become more than that. I write a letter once a year listing the things we've enjoyed and learned together. I include a note on how each child has grown, and I list our priorities as a family for the year. These priorities are the growth areas

WINTER

and topics that have the most importance. This letter helps me see, in the sea of doubt, what we learned over the last year. In addition, it gives focus to our family's goals for the next year. It keeps my mind in the present and helps me set clear boundaries between what our family's schooling looks like versus someone else's. It keeps me from forgetting and comparing.

Remember the Israelites during their desert sojourn, who suffered greatly from memory loss? "And the people of Israel wept again and said, "If only we had meat to eat! We remember the fish we ate in Egypt at no cost – also the cucumbers, melons, leeks, onions, and garlic. But now we have lost our appetite; we never see anything but this manna!" (Numbers 11:4-6 NIV).

> *It is amazing how one great day at home can have us soaring with the joys of homeschooling, and how one bad day can have us wondering where our brain was when we thought this was a good idea.*

What we once saw as a gift, we suddenly see as a curse. Many times, I have thrown the "baby out with the bath water" when things were not going smoothly. These large waves of doubt tend to lessen the longer you homeschool. However, it is not healthy for you or your children to constantly question and verbally ponder whether choosing to homeschool was a mistake. So, like the voice of Moses, be the voice that speaks truth to yourself through this letter.

Write Your Letter

Write your own letter! This letter will be written annually as you plan your next year of schooling. You will grow, your children will grow, and this letter will grow with each season. The letter starts as an opportunity to organize your thoughts and plan your routine around those areas essential to your family. Then it becomes a rock, a remembrance, for when times get tough or you feel yourself drifting. This letter is not your school schedule, but it's a guide to build your school schedule upon.

Guidelines for what to include in this letter:

1. <u>Introduction:</u> Include a scripture that speaks to your relationship with the Lord and inspires you for this year. Briefly discuss where you are as a family and evaluate the current state of schooling in your home. Look at what each child has learned or how they have grown and consider ways they might mature in the upcoming year. What good habits have grown? Are there bad habits that need to be uprooted?

   Please take account not only of academic growth but spiritual and emotional growth as well. Look at the same growth patterns for yourself. This is a chance to review and be grateful for the past year and set a compass for the next year.

2. <u>Priorities</u>: List your learning priorities for the new year. These priorities are the most essential educational topics for your family. These will guide in how you build your schedule and pick materials. When you hit a busy time and you can't get in a full schedule, the priority list tells you what must stay.

   I recommend a priority list of 10 items. If that is too many, depending on the age of your children, list 5 items. Beware: too many items might set you up for an overstressed schedule or false expectations. In setting this priority list, take into consideration your children's ages, learning capabilities, and what inspires your family. These may be based on your faith. They may also be areas you feel are essential to a well-rounded education; a well-rounded child.

When a topic comes off your list from one year to the next, this does not mean the topic is no longer of value. It might mean the topic has been accomplished. It might mean you've decided to wait another season to tackle that area. Or, the topic has taken a "basic" spot in your routine but is not emphasized as much. We know all children will need to study math and learn to read and write. Those areas will be represented when you make your schedule, but they don't necessarily need to be listed as a "priority" for this year.

Generally, we want to think bigger picture as we choose priority areas. They are what makes your family who you are. They are "first things," the "non-negotiables." They are the things that make homeschooling worthwhile and sweet. The subjects of greatest value. However, they can also be a topic you deem particularly important to learn this current year. Or a new topic you want to introduce for the first time. For example, spelling is on my list below. You discover in these priorities a balance between what your children need to be productive adults and the freedom to choose topics very different from what our current educational system deems valuable.

These areas give us the strength to work through the parts that are not our favorites. Your foundations are yours! You might have some values in common with others. But there are some priorities you may not have in common with anyone else. This is part of the beauty of homeschooling. Some of the topics on your priority list may stay year after year.

I've listed below an example of what our family priority areas were for one year versus two years later. I sometimes put more than one topic together. Generally, this is because they either go together or would be something we might cover at the same time, and they hold the same value for that year.

Year 2017/2018:

1. The Bible/Prayer and Spiritual Discussions
2. History/Geography/Culture Study and Discussions
3. Read Alouds
4. Outdoors/Exploring God's World
5. Persecuted Church Discussions and Actions through Letters and Support
6. Music
7. Child Independence in Schoolwork and Self-Management
8. Working as a Family in Chores, Cooking, and Schoolwork
9. Spelling
10. Service

Year 2019/2020:

1. Nature
2. Independence/Life Skills
3. Art Skills (Dry Brush, Handicrafts)
4. Growth in Reading/Writing/Narration Skills
5. Poetry/Music
6. Service
7. Culture Study
8. Family Exercise
9. Spelling/Keyboarding
10. Including Dad

WINTER

The priority list is then used to guide my school schedule for the year. You will have an opportunity to do the same in the "Fall" section. For now, continue with your letter.

3. <u>Encouragement</u>: For days when you are struggling to maintain your homeschool life, create a reminder list of ways to find encouragement. Perhaps it's spending time with a friend, restful time, or time for self-care.

4. <u>Picture:</u> Picture your family no longer homeschooling. What would you miss? What would be hard? If you have been in a school system, remember why you left an institutional setting. Consider the positive changes since you began homeschooling. In our family, it took about a year before we started seeing multiple benefits. With time, you will be amazed!

5. <u>Prayer</u>: Write a prayer or look over your letter and pray about each section. Pray for yourself, your husband, and your children, by name, and for the homeschool year.

How often should you read this letter? At first, I encourage you to read it every month, especially on difficult days. Everyone has moments where they lack enthusiasm about homeschooling. Read it whenever you have those feelings.

Put reminders in your calendar after you write the letter, as it will be easy to forget about it. Reading the letter often will strengthen your resolve and pull you back to center when you didn't realize you had moved off course.

Re-write the letter once a year. When you get to the end of a year and things are going well, it's easy to think you don't need to write such a letter. I have felt that way myself. In fact, I have skipped a year. However, no matter how "well" I think we're doing, I've never regretted the time praying, pondering, and writing this letter. I think you will find the same value in yours.

CHAPTER 7
Image

Our goal should be for our children to express
the goodness of God from their very beings.

In the remainder of this section, we will consider some of the misconceptions surrounding homeschooling, which come from both inward and outward sources.

Inwardly we struggle with feelings about educating our children. Outwardly we are bombarded with ideas from the homeschooling culture and the American culture at-large. Indeed, ideas about the proper education and development of children has become a huge commodity in our society; it can also become a huge stress. The world is a big place with big opinions. It is important to be aware of the sources of these misconceptions. In this way, we better learn what to dismiss and where to pay attention.

What are some of the ways our hearts can mislead us? Generally, these are perceptions that tell us we are not "good enough" to homeschool well. We think we are not smart enough, talented enough, creative enough, or patient enough to oversee our children's education. We might be right, but God is bigger than our inadequacies. He is more than able to help us homeschool well.

WINTER

Another factor is feeling we don't fit the typical "homeschool" image. When I grew up in the 1980s and 90s, I didn't know many homeschoolers. The ones I knew were different from the average American family. Many dressed differently and had strict rules about cultural influences. Even today, it is common for homeschool families to have more children and different rules than the average American family. We don't have to fit in a box to homeschool.

Another misconception is that our children must fit a certain mold to be homeschooled. There is an image that homeschooled children are better behaved or extremely brilliant. But if we have a child struggling with behavioral problems or other challenges, we should not feel as though they are not "worthy" of homeschooling. In fact, many have found homeschooling to be a great partner in improving their children's challenges.

Our goal should not be for our children to simply "look good" in front of others. We want them to express the goodness of God from their very beings. "So that it comes to this - given, a mother with liberal views on the subject of education, and she simply cannot help working her own views into her children's habits; given, on the other hand, a mother whose final question is, 'What will people say? what will people think? how will it look?' and the children grow up with habits of seeming, and not of being; they are content to appear well-dressed, well-mannered, and well-intentioned to outsiders, with very little effort after beauty, order, and goodness at home, and in each other's eyes."[4] Though it has lessened over time, I still care what people think of my children. What I should be focused on is who my children are on the inside.

In homeschooling, we must keep our eyes on the proper goals.

There are wonderful benefits to homeschooling that can greatly assist us as we work to grow a good heart for our children. Although homeschool families may share many values, they have different dynamics. The "image" does not need to look the same. A family with all boys will certainly have a different energy than a family of all girls. Families of varying sizes will function uniquely - whether there's one child, two or three, or enough to start a basketball team. Homeschooling is not just for the privileged few. I homeschool and you see how we started out!

Sacrifices and Atmosphere

Another common misconception is thinking the right curriculum, or the right routine, makes everything go well. But a beautifully written history lesson told in a rushed way does not make for a good experience with the material. Indeed 20 math problems completed with irritation may not be as good as 10 done without argument. I have found that great curriculum is ruined by bad family atmosphere. This was a huge change in my philosophy in our second year of homeschooling.

Two sources, one modern and one classic, changed my perspective on homeschooling. The first more modern book was Sarah Mackenzie's, *Teaching from Rest*. The second readings were the unequaled *Volumes* of Charlotte Mason. I began to put into practice a renewed image of who children are and what teaching at home should look like. Charlotte Mason's *Volumes* are so rich, I often read a page or two and stopped to process the words carefully. These volumes have taken me awhile to work through. In fact, I'm still working through them. A few years later, I found two other books extremely clarifying. One was Karen Glasses' book, *Consider This,* and Susan Shaeffer Macauley's, *For the Children's Sake*. Both books are also from a Charlotte Mason perspective.

Reader reviews of some modern homeschooling books feel messages in these books are redundant. But many moms say they need to hear the same message again and again because it's easy to stray from the foundational principles for which their schooling must be carried out. As Charlotte Mason so aptly describes, "education is an atmosphere, a discipline, a life."[4]

After interviewing other families, I discovered those who continue homeschooling over the long haul have an ability to ebb and flow with the changes of life, changes in children, and changes in themselves. They have also discovered their own rhythm and the best materials and activities to fit their flow. Those homeschoolers who seem to be at the most peace have found a way to give control to God.

To homeschool well there are some necessary sacrifices. Homeschooling can work and be beautiful. It is not always easy, and it doesn't happen quickly. Have faith. If God has called you to this path, if you believe it is right for your family, God can make changes within you to make it happen.

Characteristics of a Homeschool Mom

The "real" work of homeschooling might surprise you. Yes, it takes work to pick materials and energy to teach your children. But the real work is a change within you! There will be a change of the image you have of yourself, your children, and your purpose in life. It does take epic patience to be a mother-teacher. You will constantly balance teaching subject matters while at the same time teaching life-skills, disciplining, and getting the dishes done.

It takes diligence. You will diligently need to seek God for the patience and wisdom to know when your child needs grace and when they need a firm response. You will need loads of forgiveness for yourself and from your children as you learn this new life path. You will need to learn to be still and quiet at times when you want to shout. You will need to lay yourself upon the altar. And this is the way God designed it or we would think all we need is ourselves. "Trust in the Lord with all of your heart; do not depend on your own understanding. Seek his will in all you do, and he will show you which path to take" (Proverbs 3:5).

Be careful not to hold an image that somehow homeschool moms are perfect. They are not. However, when you make a daily habit of "losing it," as I have at times, it is a sign something is out of balance. What could be out of balance? It may be your curriculum load is too vigorous. Perhaps you have lost focus on enjoying your children. Have you placed time for the things you enjoy in your schedule? Have you forgotten to spend time focused on the Lord? These are questions to lay before the Lord on a continual basis and let Him decide what kind of homeschool family you will be. Embrace the fact you do not need to look like any other family.

Don't be too harsh on yourself or your children.
Do not overload your schedule.

Be especially gracious to yourself and your children in your first year of homeschooling. There are special considerations those first years. The first year is about exploring homeschooling. It's an opportunity to gather your family, get to know each other, and discover what materials and routine you might want. As the years go on, the right philosophy and schedule will come into view. Create a routine that is not too difficult while you get your feet wet. You don't know what you don't know. You'll learn with time.

Hit the main topics in an unburdened way and enjoy being together. Most of all, be aware of saddling yourself with misconceptions of who you or your children must be to homeschool.

CHAPTER 8

Socialization

Keep your eyes above, walk the path God has for your family, and never look too far ahead or focus too much on the past. One day at a time!

What are some of the outward misconceptions about homeschooling families? I am surprised when people still ask questions about homeschoolers and socialization. Since it is such a foundational question asked by so many, let's lay some of these questions to rest.

I want to qualify with the fact that our family is in a unique position in some ways when it comes to socialization. We live in a suburban neighborhood filled with children. We also live in a pro-homeschooling area. Our home has always been full of friends, partly due to these two factors. But this has nothing to do with our goal of "socialization." It has to do with the fact that we are Christians before we are homeschoolers, and we want to cultivate relationships, "Do not neglect to show hospitality to strangers, for by so doing some people have entertained angels without knowing it" (Hebrews 13:2 ESV).

Play is still valuable. We allow time for free play and friendship because it is good for us. Well-known author Richard Louv has written extensively on the matter of children, nature, and play. "The physical exercise and emotional stretching that children enjoy in unorganized play is more varied and less time-bound than is found in organized sports. Playtime, especially unstructured, imaginative, exploratory play, is increasingly recognized as an essential component of wholesome child development."[13]

The question of socialization often makes me ask, "When did we decide as a society that it was of utmost importance for children to spend the majority of their time with other children?" I don't think anyone would deny the importance of friendship. But the assumption is that children who are not surrounded by other children all day long will somehow be weird or lack social skills. What about the children who cooperate and learn with their siblings all day long? What about those who learn by volunteering or working with adult populations, or who simply spend more time conversing with their parents? Let's not entertain the notion that time with peers equals "socialization."

"Numerous studies, employing various psychological constructs and measures, show the home-educated are developing at least as well, and often better than, those who attend institutional schools ...no research contravenes this evidence. For example, regarding the aspect of self-concept in the psychological development of children, several studies have revealed that the self-concept of homeschooled students is significantly higher than that of public-school students. As another example, Shyers and colleagues found the only significant childhood social interaction difference between the institutionally-schooled and homeschoolers was that the institutionally-schooled had higher problem behavior scores."[14] It's an interesting thought as we consider topics our children should learn from us instead of their peers.

Developmental Psychologist Gordon Neufeld states, "Today, for most kids in the United States and Canada, kids' primary attachment is to other kids. For the first time in history, young people are turning for instruction, modeling, and guidance not to mothers, fathers, teachers, and other responsible adults but to people whom nature never intended to place in a parenting role - their own peers."[15]

Organic Benefits to Homeschooling

It is popular to let the culture dictate to our children in foundational areas which guide general behavior, attitudes, and belief systems.

An organic benefit to the homeschool life is the increased opportunity to talk about important life issues with our children. But even when we say nothing, we are their model, "In 1992, Prof. Larry Shyers assessed whether or not home-schooled children suffer from delayed social development. His research observed children in free play and group interaction activities. Shyers found that public school children had significantly more problem behaviors than did the home schooled. Possibly this is because the primary models of behavior for the homeschooled are their parents, rather than their peers."[16]

We are in an extremely fortunate position to have so much time with our kids. Let's not waste it on totally one-sided lectures. Let's put as much energy and finesse into conversations of character as we do academics. We are the bearers, not of fear, but of Good News! We are the guides of truth. We are to prayerfully consider how and when we discuss important life issues throughout our homeschool journey. We are to pray that God would open doors for conversations that will help our children navigate this confusing world. If they don't hear our voice, there are millions of other voices to fill the void. Though at times it is cringe-worthy, we are to embrace these conversations so our children are not afraid to talk to us.

If a fear of our children not being social enough because they are homeschooled causes worry, this fear is unfounded.

WINTER

Will the child be different from public schooled kids? "Yes," but that is only because their experience is different. If we compare a child growing up in urban New York to a child growing up on the farmland in Kansas, there will be great differences. Simply accept that in homeschooling, the child, their life, and perspective will be different than others. But by no means does it suggest they cannot socialize or relate to the world in a "normal" way.

It is our responsibility to make sure they are involved in outside interactions so they don't become self-centered and unable to function outside the home. With guidance from the Lord, our job is to prepare them for the "real world." Because of our influence, it is hopeful our children will be steadier and less swayed by peer influence because they were homeschooled.

Rooting for Odd

In some circles it is thought that homeschooled children are a bit "odd" and different from average kids. As our children become adults, we want them to be able to function in the work and college environments. But it is good to celebrate the uniqueness in them because they are homeschooled - that beautiful lack of assimilation spurred on by more time with family and literature, exploration into personal interests, and volunteer work.

As I've grown in my homeschool journey, I've often told my husband, "We're rooting for odd." It's a quote I pulled from the movie "Spanglish" in a scene where two characters are discussing whether it's better for children to assimilate or be different than their peers.[17] Is what we really want "sameness"? One reason we chose to homeschool is that we don't want our children to be "the same" as other children. We don't want them to be "socialized" by their peers. Nor do we want to isolate our children.

Create a home atmosphere that brings out the best in who God wants your children to be. You want them to go into the world that needs them. Appreciate your children being different than the "average child." They are individuals created by God. Let them bloom in the beautiful, various ways He has intended.

CHAPTER 9

"The matter was that never before had she known what she was doing in school. She had always thought she was there to pass from one grade to another, and she was ever so startled to get a glimpse of the fact that she was there to learn how to read and write and cipher and generally use her mind, so she could take care of herself when she came to be grown up."[18]

~ *Understood Betsy*, Dorothy Canfield Fisher ~

If you allow, God will show you that learning and teaching your children can be so completely different than you ever thought or imagined. In fact, with time, I have discovered that even the word "teacher" is often inadequate. I've learned that "guide and provider of great literature, materials, and experiences" is probably a better term for our role. It takes us out of the driver's seat, it takes our finger off the control button, and it gives God His rightful place as the One in charge of our child's path and all knowledge.

A friend reminds me often that school is our way of life, not just the work of math and reading and writing. The work of "school" is the chores, the helping siblings, the empathy, the other activities like piano and art and time at church. All these things are "school." We can easily see anything outside of the workbooks as not being "school." But this world is God's. The day is His. So, all of it really is "school."

One Day at a Time

A while back, we had a rough year due to illness. At one point we had been sick off and on for two months. In fact, during the month of March, we did not have one full "school" week. Instead of breaking down about this, I had to learn to be grateful and take it one day at a time. We still had our routine and the books and papers were waiting, and we added them back in as we could. But at that time, my job was to be a caretaker and not look too far ahead. You, too, will have seasons like this. Learn to live one day at a time.

One of the greatest challenges in both parenting and homeschooling is our day to day focus. It's like driving. We need to keep our eyes forward.

If we spend too much time looking into the distance or in the rearview mirror, we miss what is in front of us. This can cause many accidents.

The Pace of Learning

Some children are naturally brilliant learners. They come to academics with great ease. Homeschooling should allow those children to flourish. They may work way beyond what would be considered normal "grade-level." Do not focus too much on how far "ahead" they are because "being ahead" can easily become their identity. Then when something, anything, becomes hard, it can put a gash across that perfect glass. A child may reel because their perspective of who they are is wrapped up in being ahead of the pack.

Let these children bloom without a care as to how "far ahead" they are compared to others.

For those whose children learn at an average pace, the one sure way to make homeschooling miserable is to push them to accelerate above their making, and for what reason? We live in a time where comparisons are heightened. It takes great effort and practice to be "okay" with our present learning situation. Trust that the daily work will pay off down the road. Stay the course.

Because most of us attended public school, we are familiar with the question, "What grade are you in?" or "What grade did you make on your test?" As we bring our children home, it is important to remember that we are no longer on that racetrack. We are preparing our child for adulthood, which may include college or employment, and there are certain skills to be obtained for that to happen. The way we get there, however, will be different than if our children were in traditional school. Therefore, a child may not read or write well until an older age. But when they are 17, will this matter? Will they be better writers and readers because we did not rush the process? Is it worth fighting with a 5- or 6-year-old who is not ready to read? Are we making them miserable by doing so, and is this the memory we want them to have of homelife simply to keep up with cultural standards?

In his book, *Boys Adrift*, Leonard Sax reveals research stating that although children today are reading earlier than they did in the 1980s and 90s, teenagers are reading less.[19] This may have to do with competing technology and activities. Could it also come from being pushed to read so early that it becomes a chore, therefore, the joy is lost?

As we bring children home, we are wise to give prayerful thought as to what level of academics fit them without worrying if they are behind. They may catch up. They may not. Focus on teaching them to enjoy learning. Teach them perseverance. Learning takes repetition and diligence. Sometimes learning happens suddenly and big gaps are closed. Continue to endure with gladness in the daily homeschool routine. Each child will learn at varying rates, and we can't ask them to understand what their brain is not ready to undertake.

No Child Left Behind

For the first two years of homeschooling, the feeling of being "behind" caused me dread. Until I realized, "Behind who? And what? Why am I taking development guidance from a world that doesn't even believe there is a God?" There are obviously developmental goals and general standards. Yet our current school system expects too much, too fast in some areas while at the same time stunting our children's growth in other areas. It is our responsibility to teach and raise our children. We are to prayerfully consider the pace we take with them in a variety of subjects.

Homeschooling should allow us the ability to step back and let our child learn at their own pace, but to step back and slow down takes courage. We cannot compare one child with what their siblings or the neighborhood kids can do. Author of *Boys Adrift* Leonard Sax shares, "The joke I hear in many affluent suburbs is that every child in town is either gifted, or learning-disabled, or both. Some parents just don't want to hear that the reason their child is getting B's and a few C's is because he's just not that smart. They would rather hear that their child has ADHD and needs medication than that their child is merely average, or God forbid, below average."[19]

We must keep our minds on the long game while living in the here and now. Focus on the learning experience, not the academics. Continue to expose them to good study habits and great material. Your child's value is innate,

God given, no one can take that away. Make sure they know that's how you feel.

Calendars and Schedules

Homeschool life does not stick to a "school calendar."

If we plan to expose our child to a liberal arts education, there are many subjects to cover. We may discover we can't work through the math workbook as fast as we would like because we also have language and nature and history. That is fine. There is only so much time in a day. We'll discuss more in the final chapter about how to stay true to our learning philosophy.

We want to keep a keen eye on our priorities for the current season. For older children who are just beginning their homeschool journey, we may step back and re-teach some subjects to make sure they've grasped missed concepts. We can take our time with this process. Most learning does not happen overnight, but involves exposure to a subject in small bits, repeatedly, in age appropriate amounts. Over years, interaction with these subjects' layer upon each other and become deeper knowledge.

You and your child may arrive at a subject for which you deem you need and even should receive outside help. Be ever so careful. Don't jump the gun and look for a "diagnosis" because the child is learning at a slower pace than the average child. At one point my son had been tested so many times by so many people, it's no wonder he believed something must be extremely wrong with him. They need you to believe in them more than anyone else.

God has a purpose for each child and He gives them different learning styles.

WINTER

Encouragement for You

Be prayerful about how and when you choose "intervention." Continue to teach your child about family priorities and philosophy while getting the assistance you need. Be patient. God has a plan. He has a purpose. Be assured, these academic and developmental differences do not mean you cannot homeschool. It may be a hard road. It has taken us many years to get to a peaceful place with forward momentum. Children often do much better at home. But they may still struggle to learn, and you can feel overwhelmed and unsure about whether you are doing the right thing.

I must give credit to the outside help we received as a family. But we must always keep our eyes on the bigger picture. We must view our children as whole people. As a homeschool friend said, "They are not academic beings only." My son's joy, his sense of humor, his character, comes from the mighty hand of God working in our home. I am thankful I was able to walk beside him through anxiety to a place of joy. I gratefully "own" those good bits in him that only our God, working in our home, could have created.

Your child is no different. There is wonderful outside help. But God has given you these children, and there are certain things only your homelife will bring forth in them, to prepare them to share His love with this lost world.

CHAPTER 10

A slowing of the rotation gives the ability to focus on people and moments rather than accomplishments for some future we cannot see.

I recently learned that the planet Venus has a longer day than year. A Venusian day lasts 243 days while its year is 224 days.[20] Therefore, it rotates slower than it orbits.

What if we could stretch our days instead of worrying so much about our years? After all, we only have our days and our moments; we don't know how many years we have on this earth. How can we spend our time differently? Can we grab time back? Each of us wakes up and chooses everyday what we will spend our time doing. If we're bold enough, we can shave off the unnecessary.

So how do we discover what is necessary and what is unnecessary? The Bible has much to say about what is most important. The Great Commission calls us to cultivate relationships so others might know the truth of the gospel. We are to live together as brothers and sisters. "And let us not neglect our meeting together, as some people do, but encourage one another, especially now that the day of his return is drawing near" (Hebrews 10:25).

But how can that be carried out when there is "no time"? The problem is that we are technologically aware of more people than ever before, yet we know so few. How do we change that? We pray. We pray that God would show us in our endeavors where to spend our time. And when it comes to technology, we need to be wise as to when to put it away or put it down or never buy it. We connect with real people where we live and spend time. We meet for coffee with a friend or neighbor down the street rather than follow celebrities on Instagram.

We find a way to honor life-long relationships while at the same time living in the here and now. Do we need to see the random high school friends' pictures of his kids first day of school? Are we supposed to know so much about so many people? Surely, we were not created for so much! Calling a friend or having a family over for dinner used to be part of a normal life. But today, we must make a diligent effort to take our time back.

Family Bonding and Unity

One of the beautiful aspects of homeschooling is the time we have together as a family. I'm often caught off guard by how often we don't embrace this freedom. If we want to study outside, we do. If we want to spend every Friday volunteering, we do. We can spend an entire morning sketching or building. We can spend two weeks doing our Christmas baking, reading poetry, and enjoying the season. If we want to pray for one family and dedicate time and energy and love to them because that is what God calls, then we do. This is a great joy as we hold onto our thoughts about our Sovereign God who directs our days. This day belongs to Him.

> *When we learn to live in this present day that He alone controls, the fast-paced frazzled existence pulls the emergency break. The sunroof opens and we decide this one day is enough.*

Avoid Overscheduling

The freedom in deciding how we will "do school" may be challenged by a world that says, in order to be successful we must do and be connected to everything. If our point in homeschooling is to take life at a slower pace and enjoy learning together, yet we are away from home piling into every activity available to homeschoolers, we may defeat the purpose of why we came home in the first place.

Often, I've witnessed a bit of fickle activity or overactivity in homeschoolers. We often underestimate how much time one activity adds to our schedule. We make choices out of fear of what the kids might miss or what skill we're not developing. Instead, we should focus on the person they're becoming. So, on top of our schoolwork, we add in multiple activities. Then we get overwhelmed and start discarding activities like bailing water out of a sinking ship. After some time, we once again find ourselves bored at home, we pick up more activities, and the cycle starts again. Extra groups, lessons, and activities are a wonderful part of homeschooling and help our children become well-rounded. Too many, however, can stress our work and effort at home. How can we have time for read alouds and conversations and meals together? How can we remain enthusiastic towards our children and learning when we are rushed? There is a limit to how far time and energies can be stretched. It's good to have nothing to do sometimes if it is in proper moderation to the work the Lord has provided.

Reasonable free time and rest without screens should be a part of every day. It's a good lesson for us to dedicate and persevere to one or two small and manageable activities and reevaluate each year.

Whatever we do with our days, the greatest thief of time is an ungrateful heart, "And whatever you do whether in word or deed, do everything in

WINTER

the name of the Lord Jesus, giving thanks to God the Father through him" (Colossians 3:17 ESV).

Some days it's hard to follow through with the schoolwork, the prep time, the getting in the car to head to a lesson. The answer is not always dropping the activity but attempting it with gratitude and peace, which allows a slowing of time.

CHAPTER 11

Change

"Yet God makes all things beautiful for its own time."
~ Ecclesiastes 3:11 ~

I hear the deep and ominous "clank" of a jail cell door shutting. Is it closing me in? My fate to be confined in fear and condemnation? I grip the cold gray bars because in them is control. More of the same. More of me losing it, worrying, throwing papers and feeling no good thing sticks. Fearing everything relies on my abilities and meticulous planning. One misstep or misunderstood concept and their future comes tumbling down. But, could it be the sound is behind me? The slamming door a sign of freedom? Have I served my sentence? The old hostilities and expectations tamed. Am I reformed? Can I persevere and not just survive until the next dilemma?

You might be under the impression that "people don't change." Through the vehicle of homeschooling, God changed me. He also changed my children. He did it through a change in philosophy about children and education. But it's been more than that. It was an embracing of freedom and a wholehearted belief that God is in control. It was a determined choice that the fear and idols of the culture would not rule our home.

WINTER

Since then, I have run with my arms spread wide. With prison clothes still clinging, I ran out of the prison yard, boots making marks in the snow that I'll never see. I never looked back. I am not Lot's wife (Genesis 19:26). I am tempted, but never abandoned. My eyes stay on the One who is true and speaks truth over me and my family.

> May you find permanent release from whatever prisons have held you as God guides you in this homeschooling journey. Though the winter persists, yet would He bring you a new day! Happy New Year!

B.C., age 11

CHAPTER 12

Living Stories

Did you always know you would homeschool?

A large percentage (81%) of women I interviewed said they did not plan to homeschool. Some were completely against it; some were sure they would "not" homeschool. Others thought women who homeschooled were special, but they themselves did not fit the homeschooling mold. Most of the women (19%) who stated they always planned to homeschool were homeschooled themselves or felt early on it was something they would strongly consider.

What brought you to homeschooling?

With so many women not planning to homeschool, what changed their minds? Most said it was a perspective they came to in relation to their children, God, and their family. One said, "I realized I would never see my children and I wanted to be with them." Another said, "We wanted to spend time together and not live so busily." Also, "I wanted to be involved in the process and the joy of learning with them." Additionally, within this group was the strong theme of allowing their children to grow as the individuals God created them to be rather than a person "manufactured by the culture."

WINTER

Four of the women mentioned their children's learning style as being a major factor in choosing homeschooling. Some children were not being challenged enough in school. But most of these women brought their children home due to learning challenges or attention/spectrum issues that could not be cared for as well in a public-school setting.

Three women stated friends and their church environment were reasons they decided to homeschool. They were not forced to do so. Rather, they were in an environment where they saw the benefits of others who homeschooled.

Two women stated their children specifically asked to be homeschooled and missed not being with the family. Interestingly, four women specifically stated their positive interactions with teenage homeschoolers was a huge factor in their consideration. They noticed these teens had "conversational abilities, were bright, helpful and at-ease with adults." The main idea was, "I want my children to grow up and be like these young men and women." It wasn't because these kids could do advanced calculus or knew the capitals of all fifty states (not that they didn't). It was the general sense that these teens had character.

It has often been said that homeschooling is focused on the long game. Children may struggle with writing or math, but it's important to have hope of who your children will become as they reach adulthood. The point is, raising children well takes time and there are many phases of life to walk through. Often, we need to be more patient and prayerful with the process so we don't lose this focus.

In addition, if we raise our children to find their worth in Christ alone, then as they grow to be adults who are content no matter their circumstances, they won't find their wholeness in what others think, how many friends they have, how much they own, or their job title. This is counterculture. So, a content and less-rushed lifestyle could appear as laziness or lack of focus to their counterparts. But these qualities are to be embraced if they are housed within the life the Lord has given them.

Let's consider the Biblical example of Mary and Martha. While Martha was frantically busy with so many (good) things, Jesus said to her "Martha, Mary has found the better way." And what was the better way? Sitting at the feet of her Lord.

How has your homeschooling routine changed from when you started to the present?

Reviewing these answers put a smile on my face. Once a mom has been homeschooling for a while, she looks back and giggles at how she started. As time goes on, she finds her rhythm, becomes more at ease, and her feet are more firmly set. However, this is a constantly changing routine.

Seven moms answered this question by saying, over time, they had a change in philosophy. The most common word used was "flexibility." The idea was that homeschooling had to fit in as part of life and "life happens." Family members get ill, people move, jobs change, kids grow older and get jobs, and homeschooling must work with and around these realities.

One mom stated the beginning of each year is a time for her to evaluate where each kid is in their life and in learning, and the routines alter a bit. Alongside this same mindset, two moms said they learned to relax. They learned to loosen up and were okay if they had to skip a few things. They learned to accept that some days everything was not going to be done, so focus should be set on the priorities. They learned when to "call it a day" and trusted God to help fill in the gaps because there will always be gaps.

Four mothers said they came to accept that each of their children learn differently. Knowing when to do things as a family and when to give one child one set of materials and another child something different took time to figure out. As children got older, they learned to give more independence as was age appropriate. It was important to give teenagers more responsibility with their schooling.

Seven women stated the biggest change from when they started homeschooling was realizing homeschooling was not a "re-creation" of public school. It took time to let go of a traditional school structure and let the Lord guide the expectations and routine for their home.

What is the greatest challenge to homeschool families in the current culture?

A couple of the most interesting conversations were with women who had grown children. In fact, two were grandmothers. They gave an amazing viewpoint on the early days of homeschooling. They took me back to when homeschooling was barely heard of and, in many places, officially illegal.

According to the Home School Legal Defense Association (HSLDA), homeschooling was not legal in all 50 states until 1993.[21] HSLDA also mentions a man named Dr. Richard Moore who, with his book, *Better Late than Early*, was a pioneer in the movement of homeschooling. When Dr. Moore was interviewed by Dr. James Dobson on *Focus on the Family*, the interest and consideration of homeschooling by a larger population of conservative evangelical families grew rapidly. In fact, one of the moms I interviewed specifically remembers listening to that radio broadcast and its impact upon her decision to homeschool. "It was eye-opening, especially in understanding that children were getting damaged, especially in the early years of learning in institutional settings, specifically boys."

Another mother agreed and said new ideas on educational philosophies were being discussed, "The benefits of the old schoolhouse model of children of different ages being taught together, helping each other, children learning at home, with siblings, in nature, in developmentally appropriate ways was on the rise."

In addition, public and private schools were beginning to change rapidly both in social/political as well as academic teaching styles. Dr. Moore began the discussion of children being pushed too fast in a developmentally inappropriate way which was harmful. Unfortunately, any of us with children in the public-school system in the 2000s can state it has gotten worse. The increase in testing and expectations of children younger and younger has made school much more stressful for both children and parents.

These discussions and changes which began in the early 1980s laid the foundation for the advent of the growth of homeschooling. These moms also mentioned that, in the early years of homeschooling, families looked very similar. Generally, homeschooling families were conservative Christian families who wore conservative clothing and steered away from secular entertainment. One could see a homeschool family coming a mile away, "denim skirts, long hair, conservative clothes, more isolated."

One mom mentioned it was a bit challenging because some of these families almost made homeschooling feel cultish. But more and more families saw the benefits of homeschooling, the movement was less defined by our clothing or social norms, and more defined by educational philosophies, upholding truths of the Christian faith and freedoms. It is hopeful more people will discover the benefits of homeschooling while holding firm to its roots. It should feel like a community.

Because homeschooling is becoming more common, the public has begun to understand its benefits in a new way. Organizations like museums, music/art groups, and athletic facilities offer programs to homeschoolers. Homeschooling families are taking their place in the fabric of American society.

God bless these moms, these early pioneers of homeschooling. Often, they did what they did in isolation. Not that they did not love the work and the time spent learning with their children. But we should be grateful for their perseverance, diligence, and perspective for which the current growth, support and acceptance of homeschooling has been built.

Additional challenges between homeschooling and current culture:

The top answer is best summarized in Jesus' prayer in John 17:15, "I'm not asking you to take them out of the world, but to keep them safe from the evil one. They do not belong to this world any more than I do."

Many moms stated they felt the biggest challenge for homeschooling was figuring out how to allow children to function in the culture while standing apart from it. Some comments included a child's internal perspective. "Helping your kids understand that it's okay to be different and they will have a different life story than public school kids." Also, "Grasping that they have a different belief system from the world and that they need to know why they believe what they believe."

There was a strong sense that children must be rooted firmly in faith and know what the culture believes and how to respond to it wisely. From a parental perspective, the challenge was, "When to know what topics to expose them to, at what age, and how to prepare them for difficult subject matters and environments." There was a consensus that it was not healthy to isolate kids. They need to be prepared to not only "be in" the culture but also to know how to boldly reach people with the love of Christ. However, parents feel drowned by so many cultural influences. It's tough to discern when to give an absolute "NO" and when legalism has stepped in. It feels gray and unclear to many moms. It can be difficult to know when and how to hand the reigns to children growing into young adults.

The second most popular answer was the challenge of technology in the current culture. I asked moms more detailed questions about technology in the "Spring" section where we will try to unpack this a bit more.

The final group of moms spoke towards the public's perspective on homeschooling and pressure within the homeschool community itself. Moms mentioned there is a continual battle to affirm we can educate our own children who are well-adjusted socially. There are still preconceived notions about homeschooling.

We need to find the courage to find our own path, "You must know your own family and that your homeschooling is enough. Other moms will always seem to have it together better than you but find your own family's path to homeschooling and don't compare it with others."

When Jesus spoke in John 17, the theme was unity. Let us not forget that we, as Christians and homeschool moms, should support each other, help each other, and serve as a unifying support to families working through the challenges of our current culture. In this way, we can be a light rather than a stumbling block.

WINTER

~ PONDERING WINTER ~

Considerations for deeper reflection

Before answering these questions,
please take time to pray so you can thoughtfully walk through this process.

<u>Your Story:</u>

1. Are there parenting mistakes or struggles for which you feel guilty?

    Are you getting better in those areas or finding it difficult to change?

    Take a moment to pray about these difficult areas. Seek God for forgiveness. Ask others for forgiveness if needed. Embrace the freedom He offers.

2. What current parenting difficulties are you dealing with?

3. How can your homeschooling routine assist you with these difficulties?

<u>Foundations:</u>

1. What does your current time seeking God look like?

2. List ways you can seek and enjoy Him more.

<u>Home:</u>

1. How can you make your home a house of prayer?

2. What changes can you make in your current home space so it better represents you?

Reasons:

1. List the top reasons you have chosen to homeschool. If you find this list mostly includes what you are hoping to keep your child "from" instead of what you hope to provide "for" your child, you might want to have some prayerful re-evaluation.

The Letter:

1. Go back over the section called "The Letter." Write your own letter. Develop your priority list for this school year, but hold off creating your school schedule. There will be a place to do this in the "Fall" section.

Image:

1. What inadequacies do you see in yourself that make you think you cannot homeschool well?

2. Pray about each of these inadequacies and ask the Lord to help you change your perspective and fill in any gaps.

View:

1. How do you view each of your children as compared to their peers (academically, spiritually, emotionally)?

    Ask God to help you see the good in each child and His great plan for their lives. Ask Him to help you view them as He does. Pray for their areas of weakness. Ask Him to help you put the correct school and life plans together for them.

WINTER

Time:

Cutting back can be difficult. It is hard to choose between good activities and opportunities, but we must make these hard choices if we're going to live with peace. This is how we live less frantically. This is how we enjoy the few things for which we've chosen to dedicate ourselves to with excellence. Think about what to add into your life by cutting something loose. You don't want that extra free afternoon simply filled with TV instead of driving the kids to another activity. You want that time filled with something that brings peace and purpose into the home without over-extending everyone. An example might be letting go of one extra-curricular night and cooking as a family.

1. Where do you need to cutback so you can slow down?

2. What is your plan for filling that time with something more fulfilling?

SECTION II

Spring

~ To Deven: for small feet in large spaces. ~
"For behold, the winter is past; the rain is over and gone. The flowers appear on the earth, the time of singing has come, and the voice of the turtledove is heard in our land"
~ Song of Solomon 2:11-12 ESV ~

Spring brings visions of new life. Purple henbit and yellow dandelion peek their heads over the dead grasses of winter. Nests are swept and readied for eggs. We remember a stone that was moved. Yet, there are other shiny attractions in this world. Many objects in life catch our attention and our affections. Can we let go of what the world's eyes adore and look through God's microscope to find what is of value?

Please Lord, bloom within our hearts a love that flows fragrant to a dark and noisy world. As a seed pulls both down and up simultaneously through the soil, may we reach deep into what You value, while our hands, like shoots, reach high in praise to You.

SPRING

It is hard to pull ourselves away from workbooks and schedules, but spring bubbles up most beautifully in the intentionality we give to God's great gifts. Let's venture outdoors, engage in unhurried conversation, read meaningful literature, and develop an empathy and a love for God and His people.

B.A., age 10

CHAPTER 1

Attention

"All I have seen teaches me to trust the Creator for all I have not seen."[1]
~ Ralph Waldo Emerson ~

Deepening our children's attention is a vital part of teaching them any number of important concepts. This idea is as old as the parent-child relationship. "Johnny, are you paying attention?" If a child cannot focus on a subject matter for a specific amount of time, it will be difficult for them to grasp and hold onto it. Knowledge and understanding float like a halo on top of his head, never quite sinking into his innermost thought life.

More importantly, attention is necessary so they might hear wisdom. Through our words and in the materials we present, we pass along ideas we believe are of the most value. In this way, our hope is to encourage the growth of not only an intelligent child, but a thoughtful child of virtue.

For hundreds of years we took paying attention for granted. We live in a time where there is an assault on our attention. These assaults come from many directions: technology, educational standards and practices, consumerism, and cultural norms and values. We have a great opportunity to take back and own what is God given: the parental responsibility of training our children to focus their attention on the things that are true.

SPRING

I have shared in many conversations with friends whose children have been diagnosed with attention disorders. We live in a particularly diagnosis-heavy culture. In *Boys Adrift*, Dr. Leonard Sax highlights four main cultural and environmental changes that have added to attention and motivation problems, especially in boys. These include "video games, teaching methods, prescription drugs, and devaluation of masculinity."[2]

Additionally, Robert Melillo, in *Disconnected Kids* states, "I believe- and there is plenty of supporting evidence to prove- that the rise in neurobehavioral and neuroacademics disorders is being caused by negative influences in the environment- namely, many of the practices that make up the typical American lifestyle. Things such as negative health practices of parents, later marriages that result in older parents giving birth, health of mothers during pregnancy; traumatic pregnancies, including the traumatic rise of C-sections; the number of toxins in our atmosphere; kids who spend too much time being sedentary in front of computers and television; and the very touchy subject of absentee parenting."[3]

Some of these issues we can impact while others are more difficult. We cannot go back and change a traumatic delivery or make ourselves younger at pregnancy. Some children end up with a trifecta of pre-birth and post-birth environmental situations that have made them more susceptible to challenges. These challenges affect the whole family. If we take a child with these predispositions and then pressurize them under a culture of fear and overstimulation, we have even greater problems.

The choices we make in our daily routines can make a big impact.

The good news is, there is much we can do as homeschooling parents to help our children grow in their ability to focus their attention. But, let's be clear, this is a progressive type of learning that takes time. This house is built brick by brick as we add intentionally healthier activities, habits, and choices into our family life. We choose less of what everyone else in the culture is participating in so we can embrace the best.

As we discuss more about this topic, we find that many of these healthier lifestyles were simply a natural part of life in years past. Now, we must make a concerted effort to choose them. Many families new to homeschooling are bringing children home with a variety of differences. Their children may have been diagnosed with autism, ADHD, dyslexia, OCD, sensory processing, or other disorders. In addition, others may be homeschooling children with mental and emotional health challenges such as anxiety and depression. A big question for these families is how to proceed in order to improve the lives of their children and give them the best shot at a fulfilling and redeemed life.

This is something all parents must manage, but those of us raising kids with unique needs experience the tension at heightened levels. As Sally Clarkson, homeschool mother and author shares, "We also learned, through the same trial and error and grace, to hold fast to what our hearts insisted (at least in quiet moments). That our boy was not a diagnosis. Not a problem to be solved or a disorder to be fixed. He was a child to be guided and trained and gloried in."[4]

We fight between believing our children have problems not easily solved with the feeling of giving too much attention and introspection. The answer probably lies somewhere in the middle. Before children were given the diagnosis of "dyslexia" they were left to label themselves as "stupid." The right label brought clarity and freedom, helping them to understand that their brain simply sees things differently. However, a child with excess energy can be mis-classified as ADHD.

Because each child is unique, and each family dynamic is unique, each path is also unique. This is why the journey at times can seem lonely. Please be gracious, loving, and prayerful with friends and family dealing with such challenges. Less criticism, more prayer!

The requirements of one who teaches a child with special needs is to become cleverer and more skillful; to believe for that which no one else sees; a woman of great faith.

What can we do to help our children experience the most life giving homeschool atmosphere in which to grow, no matter the challenges?

Attention and Focus Begin with Mom

It took me years to realize my children would struggle with attention if I could not be gentle and simple in my approach. So, why could I not be that kind of mother? When my attention was focused on what other kids could do that my child couldn't, it revealed itself as anger and frustration against him. When my focus was on getting a break or feeding my need for comfort, I could not be an enthusiastic teacher. When I let the day become chaotic instead of keeping a healthy routine or habits, we never seemed to build on the learning from the day before. But when I directed my attention to Christ and found reasonable material that supported our family's priorities, things turned. When I found a philosophy and teachers who helped me see the changes I needed to make in my parenting and educational style, freedom came. I began to accept and celebrate the differences we had been given. We began liking each other more. When I learned that a checklist was not my master, we had more peace. And when I learned to bring down the noisy world, attention heightened; in all of us!

One of the best lessons regarding attention came from Sarah Mackenzie's book, *Teaching from Rest*, as she discussed the importance of not multi-tasking.[5] One of the reasons I lived so stressed was because I tried to do too much at once while finishing little. One of my first changes was to complete one task at a time. Practically, I may have to work on multiple lessons with children at the same time, but I stopped including the chores of laundry and dishes during that same period. On the other hand, if the kids are doing independent work then the laundry and dishes have a place. I also stopped looking at my phone until the bulk of schoolwork was complete, usually around noon.

Learning to put my responsibilities to external organizations in their proper place was another important component. I started giving allotted times and days to those organizations rather than trying to keep up with them every day. For example, I have a leadership role in two organizations which meet on Mondays and Fridays. I focus on my tasks for the Monday night group on Sunday, Monday, and Tuesday. On Wednesday, I put the first organization aside and focus on planning and communication for the second one the rest of the week. In this way, I am not constantly thinking about all my responsibilities, releasing me to pay attention to each task separately. I stopped trying to text, email, or call people all week. The groups were given a certain amount of attention and then I moved to the next task. When the work was put in its proper place, I experienced less burnout. Some may naturally be able to handle more. But I had a better attitude and better work when I put multi-tasking aside.

The refocusing of attention is a family affair. It's the only way it will work. We need to create a routine that is an advocate for our family's attention. How do we do that?

In the following sections I discuss some of the various aspects of our culture and homelife that can impact attention. Like so many parts of homeschooling,

SPRING

this starts with us moms. Our children need a model of good attention. If we don't have the self-control to put down our smartphones and look them in the eye, how can we expect it of them? When we're running around stressed and overburdened in our schedule, it's no wonder they feel it too.

CHAPTER 2
Nature

> *"Let the real boys and girls have their picnic.*
> *They will not see us, for very few boys and girls know how*
> *to use their eyes when they go to the woods."*[6]
> ~ *Uncle Wiggily's Storybook,* Howard Garis ~

Connecting with Creation

It's deep into March. The wind is blowing hard; I thought I'd left West Texas. The afternoon spring sun is shining down, and the children are playing at our neighborhood commons area. I'm taking a walk, always with eyes open these days. Suddenly, that color that you can't quite explain, but most like fuchsia, pops out of the gray branches of the redbuds. I must get a close-up look.

The words of Psalm 24 come to me because we've been memorizing it. God has a way of showing His Word in Scripture coming to life. "The earth is the Lord's and the fullness thereof, the world and all who dwell therein, for he has founded it upon the seas and established it upon the rivers." It hits me. I have always understood God created the world, but the very idea of water, land, animals, and people were all His. None of it would be without Him, not even the idea of it. Maybe we'd be a spinning ball of gas like Jupiter or an uninhabitable dusty Mars. He decided to place us on a planet teeming with life.

Connecting with and appreciating the many creations of God draws us to Him.

Like a small child peeking around her father's workshop door, we are in awe of the Master Workman. He created these things to be enjoyed and in relationship with Him. Maybe when we ignore creation, we ignore Him. When we notice the hummingbirds hovering and the honeybees working, we suddenly appreciate life. Maybe we see God's order and uniqueness. Could we transfer this "awe" to how we see people? We look into the eyes of our family and friends. We notice a stranger. The busyness is set aside to check on a friend. We suddenly slow down, and life's value is recalibrated.

When we stay disconnected from nature and teach our children the same, do we devalue life? I was unaware as a child what a gift it was when my grandfather would walk with me to the boat dock to look through his tackle box for fishing lures. He was unhurried, he seemed to have nowhere else to go, thoughtfully picking up a golden lure and then a silver one with various hooks, pondering which one would work best for his purposes. Afterwards we'd fill the bird feeders. That evening as the pink sun dipped behind the river, we'd eat dinner and watch the animals come to feed. I did not yet understand why these things were so peaceful and fulfilling. Listening to him call the osprey and watching him pick up Spanish moss as we leisurely walked up the back steps showed me the value of slowing down, the value of a simple moment.

More Time Outdoors

We, too, can indulge our children in the simple moments of nature, like checking on the hummingbird feeder or observing how the new zinnias are growing. It only takes a few moments. God understands and even designed the experience of a fulfilling and healthy life that includes connecting with nature. Maybe that's why Adam and Eve lived in a garden, not a city.

Spending time outdoors, enjoying God's creation in its many forms, is an important part of being a "whole" person, adult and child alike. Nature grounds us, causes us to breathe and makes us slow down, among other rewards. Yet in today's culture, time in nature is seen as an activity with no tangible product and, therefore, purposeless. If we are outdoors, there must be a goal such as training for a marathon, getting our steps in, losing weight, or participating in a soccer game. At best, time in nature is seen as something we do on vacation. Over time, we have passed this idea to our children. We don't say this with our words, but we model this in the lack of outdoor time in our weekly routines. To be outdoors with no agenda? With all the competing priorities to raise a successful child, is it really that important to give our children time in nature?

I would hypothesize that it is probably one of the most important priorities we can make in our child's life, especially with the fine-tuned attention-obsessive machines which inundate our current culture. The beauty of homeschooling is that we can schedule time outdoors. But it does take courage and planning. It is not going to happen organically. Thankfully, we have wonderful resources and wise pioneers as our garden guides.

"There is a great deal to be accomplished in this large fraction of the children's day. They must be kept in a joyous temper all the time, or they will miss some of the strengthening and refreshing held in charge for them by the blessed air. They must be let alone, left to themselves a great deal,

SPRING

to take in what they can of the beauty of earth and heavens; for of the evils of modern education few are worse than this—that the perpetual cackle of his elders leaves the poor child not a moment of time, nor an inch of space, wherein to wonder—and grow. At the same time, here is the mother's opportunity to train the seeing eye, the hearing ear, and to drop seeds of truth into the open soul of the child, which shall germinate, blossom, and bear fruit, without further help or knowledge of hers. Then, there is much to be got by perching in a tree or nestling in heather, but muscular development comes of more active ways, and an hour or two should be spent in vigorous play; and last, and truly least, a lesson or two must be got in."[7]

Surely, you might say people who lived in the 1900s would be able to encourage children to be outside. It was safer then and they were not as busy and had fewer distractions. But voices who speak on the topic of attention today often point to the same solution. "The end result of a childhood with more time spent in front of computer screens than outdoors" is what Richard Louv, in his book, *Last Child in the Woods,* calls "cultural autism."

The symptoms include tunneled senses, feelings of isolation and containment, and a wired, know-it-all state of mind."[8]

Outdoor Explorations

More time outdoors causes us to look up, to see the wide world, inhale a deep breath and take it all in. As Kim John Payne, author of *Simplicity Parenting,* suggests, "In its complexity and sensuality, nature invites exploration, direct contact, and experience. But it also inspires a sense of awe, a glimpse of what is still "un-Googleable" . . . life's mystery and magnitude."[9]

The goal of much of the technology in culture is to suck our time away. The goal of time in nature is to slow time. We are no longer in Eden, but when a child holds their breath to walk closer to a butterfly, or their eyes widen as they catch a glimpse of a delicate spider-web, something inside them yearns for the garden.

We don't all have the benefit of living in the country or near grand state parks. Many of us must ponder a good bit about how to add more nature into our lives. We can take advantage of what we have. We can buy or make a simple bird feeder and place it in our yard. The birds will come, and suddenly each morning the kids race to the window to see which ones return for a visit.

More time in nature is a great place to start as you look at increasing peace and attention in your home.

Give each child a small pot or section of the front yard to plant their seeds each season. Not only is this a great lesson in nature, but they also learn about taking care of nature by being responsible for watering or changing out seeds.

For longer trips outdoors, generally a 20 to 30-minute car ride might get you closer than you think. Time in nature includes simply taking schoolwork outdoors and adding a specific nature study. Both are extremely beneficial. Consider sitting in your backyard. Lay on a blanket and look at the clouds. Read outdoors. Give the kids allotted time to enjoy the sunshine and fresh air while they work through a tough math problem. For older kids who have cultivated a foundation of being outdoors at a young age, the hope is they will enjoy taking a walk, reading, sketching or drawing. Plan an afternoon picnic. As children work on their school lessons more independently, move the studies outdoors!

As children get older, many voices will call them. Now is the time to give them some independence. Older children can ride their bikes to a park and take work with them. Siblings can walk or ride to the park together. This encourages not only time outdoors, but enhances skills of problem solving, leadership, and relationship building. There is a call for nature study to be included in the curriculum the same as reading, writing, and arithmetic.

Awakening the Senses

A longer day outside awakens the senses God has given us and allows for independent exploration. These "nature days" scheduled once a week or once a month are not for the usual daily schoolwork.

We are thankful friends included us in their nature group during our second year of homeschooling. Every Friday we met at a park with nature trails. In that first year, we read from *The Jungle Book*, discussed art prints, and tried our hand at nature journaling using watercolors. Mostly, it was an opportunity for kids to be kids. They ran through the creek and made makeshift treehouses. My oldest child began showing wonderful signs of being freed from anxiety by these weekly experiences. It was quite different than just playing at a playground. The other kids were so free and unafraid. This was quite refreshing and was our first barefoot steps into the possibilities of what God could teach us in nature.

Three years later, we had seven families in our nature group with children ranging from ages 4-16. We deepened our studies of artists and composers; we enjoyed poetry teatime and focused on special areas of nature to study. All the while, we kept the spirit of exploration alive. I give great credit to my friend, Deven, for starting this group, and credit also goes to the wonderful resources which have guided us, including "Simply Charlotte Mason"[10] and "Sabbath Mood Science."[11] However, simply giving the kids outdoor time alone is sufficient. It will be enough for some parents to practice the skill of letting children out of their sight and not attempting to teach at every turn.

A large part of the enjoyment of nature is undirected time. "Let us suppose mother and children arrived at some breezy open wherein it seemeth always afternoon. In the first place, it is not her business to entertain the little people: there should be no storybooks, no telling of tales, as little talk as possible, and that to some purpose. Who thinks to amuse children with tale or talk at a circus or pantomime? And here, is there not infinitely more displayed for their delectation? Our wise mother arrived, first sends the children to let off their spirits in a wild scamper, with cry, hallo, and hullaballoo, and any extravagance that comes into their young heads. There is no distinction between big and little; the latter love to follow in the wake of their elders, and, in lessons or play, to pick up and do according to their little might. As for the baby, he is in bliss: divested of his garments, he kicks and crawls, and clutches the grass, laughs soft baby laughter, and takes in his little knowledge of shapes and properties in his own wonderful fashion––clothed in a woolen gown, long and loose."[7]

Time in nature can be one of the best times for siblings to develop their relationship with one another. What memories they make together! Nature time also seems to lessen some of the effects of screen time so common in our culture. "Time spent in nature is one of the most cost-effective and powerful ways to counteract the burnout and sort of depression we feel from sitting in front of a computer all day."[9]

We are working to improve skills of perseverance, observation, and joy. "All the time, too, the children are storing up memories of a happy childhood. Fifty years hence they will see the shadows of the boughs making patterns on the white tablecloth, and sunshine, children's laughter, hum of bees, and scent of flowers are being bottled up for after refreshment."[7]

SPRING

Nature Study

The experience and relationship with nature is expanded tremendously when we begin to grow in our knowledge of it. This happens with a more focused and specialized nature study. Nature becomes a friend instead of an acquaintance. A child begins by saying, "Mom, see that bird?" Then, we place a bird feeder in the yard, and they run to say, "Those male and female house finches are back." Finally, they begin noticing, at different seasons, which birds return, and they are well acquainted with a variety of bird types, songs, and calls.

We give our self and our children eyes to see and appreciate God's handiwork which helps children be awed with the seemingly small. We might eventually choose an artist study, a special nature story, or read a great piece of literature. Take it one step at a time. Others may want this time to exclusively be focused on finding a piece of nature and capturing it in art form. There are many wonderful ways to create a nature study group. As children get older, nature study can be more advanced.

Gardening

I personally thank God for naturally bringing His creation to our front doorstep in suburban Texas. We began by taking a butterfly gardening class. I planted a few sprouts I received in class. We prayed over our little garden in the hopes something would survive. In the spring, black swallowtail butterflies left tiny yellow eggs on our fennel. We had about 6 butterflies go to chrysalis and fly off into the world. The second spring we added a bird feeder. House finches, doves, and red-winged black birds came to eat at our feeder. The mourning doves decided to nest in our front yard in the late spring. Two baby doves emerged after what seemed like a lifetime of waiting.

The next year we planted lettuce in pots. Once a week we had enough lettuce for each of us to have one to two leaves to dip in Italian dressing at the dinner table. Our garden grows in small steps and God has been extremely gracious. It's not all roses of course. Last summer our fennel grew so large wasps from across the country came to feast, taking most of our caterpillars with them. Along with our regular visitors to the bird feeder, grackles constantly bullied the rest. Even a little garden needs constant tending. But, oh what life and conversation it gives!

Nature Journaling

When we first started nature journaling, I had no idea what it was. We had friends who journaled for years. I observed them and their children and thought it was amazing, but I had no idea how to do it. In addition, we are not a family of artists. I received guidance through the help of seasoned homeschoolers and great literature, but I also found one trusts the process and does not give up. It's not about creating perfect sketches or diagrams. Instead, it's our eyes and mind being opened to the busy little world of nature all around.

Journaling is simply a collection of what we notice and the details we see. The knowledge of nature builds over time as we seek it. A child's journal may start with a small watercolor depiction of a wildflower, and we jot down their observations. As they age, the children write their own observations of their piece of nature. We might use other resources to learn more about the object, such as field guides and nature books. We might provide them with a variety of mediums to use and nature journaling guides to deepen their experience.

The most important part is to keep our own nature journal alongside them. This is the aspect moms so easily forget. Having our own journal will keep

SPRING

us from over-analyzing what they are doing and allows us to join in on this beautiful activity.

Try to keep from comparing one child's journal to the next. One of my children struggles with painting and writing, but he loves nature. So, I teach the discipline of doing his best representation in his journal without turning it into an exercise in creating a perfect journal. This can be a difficult balance.

Who knows exactly how God will use it? It won't be wasted or regretted time. Nature journaling is a lovely addition to homeschool life missed by many families. Make a little corner of unrushed hours in the schedule once a week for it. There are wonderful resources and materials to guide us in nature journaling. Many of these materials are listed in "Resources for Spring" at the end of this section.

Balancing Activities

We might confidently say then, that being outdoors is an important part of a well-balanced homeschool life. Could we even say a "safer" life? "An indoor (or backseat) childhood does reduce some dangers to children; but other risks are heightened, including risks to physical and psychological health, risks to children's concept and perception of community, risks to self-confidence, and the ability to discern true danger."[8]

Unfortunately, we may find as our children get older and as we balance competing activities, time in nature is one of the first things taken out of the routine. Why? Because it is easy to forget the benefits of time outdoors as compared to a finely delivered piano recital or an eloquently delivered debate speech. Pairing nature study with the study of science can be a great way to continue the exploration in God's world as children mature. However, carving out time for nature will always be a must, and in different seasons, this means choosing it above other activities.

Carving out time for nature takes bravery, Little Buttercup, but it will give you an immense sweetness for your journey.

A supportive group of friends is a big motivator in continuing with nature study. Friends make time outdoors more motivating and fun for us and our children. If we have partners in our journey, we will more likely continue with nature study.

Suburbia Embraced

Many homeschooling mothers realize they did not grow up with much time in nature themselves. They, too, were stuck in desks and passed through the revolving door of the American education system. They feel a sense of freedom to offer a completely different experience for their children, and they should. "Wild and Free" is one organization that has worked to connect homeschool families who want to preserve the joy of childhood with time outdoors as a big part of their mission.[13]

When I first embraced more time for nature in my homeschooling, I made the mistake of thinking that, to reject America's societal standards, I needed to move to a ranch, raise sheep, and teach my kids to till the land. It doesn't take much searching to find a variety of beautiful photos of families walking hand in hand across a wheat field and wonder if that is the answer. The little cabin among the pine trees, the treehouse with a beautiful bookshelf covered in ivy. (We all know those books being left outside would get ruined, right?) We become restless thinking nature must hold all the cards of joy and freedom. We confuse thinking critically about the American lifestyle means we must repel everything in it. If we don't offer our children a "farm life"

SPRING

they will be held in the vice of technology; stuck in the same old cultural patterns.

I thought I needed to go off the grid! I felt the only way to receive the benefits of nature was to completely turn away from my suburban life. Over time, God graciously revealed this is not the answer. For us, the answer is to make time for nature nearby, read classic nature materials, and find a place for nature in the home where we live. In this way, we can connect with our church, our community, and find a healthy balance.

Many homeschoolers live in a suburban neighborhood. It is not practical financially or otherwise for most of us to move to acres of land. Please don't think that, because it is not a possibility for you, it means you cannot seek out and enjoy nature. You will waste precious time searching for a perfect oasis. And, I never complain that Chick-fil-a is at the entrance of my neighborhood!

Let's not forget that our true freedom is in Christ alone. Neither nature, nor relaxed homeschooling, nor a world without standardized testing will give the freedom that is His privilege to give. Otherwise, what hope is to be given to the martyr stuck in a jail cell, the poor refugee, or the middle-aged man who must go to a job every day? Nature is a gift, it has its place, but it is not our savior.

Animals, Nature, and People

I have often heard people say they are an "animal person" or "a nature lover." It appears these people have been placed in a category which is to say they prefer animals and nature over humans. I understand this because animals and nature do not place the same demands on us as humans. But it is my hypothesis, and I hope it to be true, that if we can connect to nature more in this frantic culture, we can slow down enough to care for people, too.

The truth is, no matter where we live, God calls us to people.

No matter how much nature study we do, the end goal should be to love the Creator and His people even more. If our child has watched a line of ants carry a leaf to their hill or the grasshopper, legs and wings spread wide, leap from one brown blade of grass to another, then maybe, just maybe, they can perceive a friend in need.

A.M., age 6

SPRING

"Deep in the Quiet Wood"[14]
James Weldon Johnson, 1871 - 1938

Are you bowed down in heart?
Do you but hear the clashing discords and the din of life?
Then come away, come to the peaceful wood,
Here bathe your soul in silence. Listen! Now,
From out the palpitating solitude
Do you not catch, yet faint, elusive strains?
They are above, around, within you, everywhere.
Silently listen! Clear, and still more clear, they come.
They bubble up in rippling notes and swell in singing tones.
Now let your soul run the whole gamut of the wondrous scale
Until, responsive to the tonic chord,
It touches the diapason of God's grand cathedral organ,
Filling earth for you with heavenly peace
And holy harmonies.

CHAPTER 3
Nothing

"Unrestrained busyness leads to anxiety."[6]
~ Pastor Chuck Swindoll ~

Moments of Solitude

Increasing our attention also includes adding beautiful moments of solitude. It is easy to feel the need to jump in or give our children some form of entertainment when there is a lull in the day. It is important to create various points in the day when a child has nothing scheduled or planned and no screens available. In these moments, children must decide for themselves how to fill their time. "Too many scheduled activities may limit a child's ability to motivate and direct themselves."[10]

Having a structure of school, chores, extracurricular lessons and family time helps the day move along and builds a variety of skills. In the same way, some moments of nothingness can build a child's ability to problem solve, and strengthens muscles of creativity, patience, and endurance.

We must slow down and live in the present.

SPRING

To enjoy nature, art, building, cooking, or conversation, we must have the ability to stay in the present. Moments of quietness help us become comfortable with managing ourselves when the schedule is not laid out. These moments slow us and remind us of our value even when we're not producing. "Therefore, do not be anxious about tomorrow, for tomorrow will be anxious for itself. Sufficient for the day is its own trouble" (Matthew 6:34 ESV).

So, how do we slow down? We teach our children to live in the present when we first practice the mental task of disciplining ourselves to keep our thoughts on the task of today. As a parent, I do the opposite of this when I'm hurrying the children from one lesson to the next, and I'm often "trying to get through." It is quite a discipline to learn to live in the moment. What you are doing right now matters. So often, we live from one day to the next, like a bad episode of "Groundhog Day." But, what's at the end of that day? Live for this day!

A practical way to do this is to purposefully stop a few times during the day, simply breathe, pray, and ask the Lord for help to live in the moment. Stop in between tasks, take a moment to breathe and look around before moving to the next activity. Set a 5 or 10-minute timer and walk outside or sit still with eyes closed.

In a recent podcast, computer scientist Dr. Cal Newport discussed his book, *Digital Minimalism,* and his thoughts on how we recapture solitude. He reminds us that we used to have moments of solitude built into our everyday lives, whether it was sitting at the doctor's office or standing in line at the bank. We simply had to sit with our thoughts. He suggests that there are probably unknown benefits to our brain in these moments.[15]

Now, we must choose moments of solitude by intentionally setting our phones aside or picking multiple opportunities to avoid screens. When we find a slight lull in our day, we can be a great example to our children by filling it with beauty instead of screen time. This may include sitting down in the afternoon to read, draw, stitch, or do nothing at all. It's amazing what happens to children when they watch their parents capture free time and do "nothing" of value.

Devotions and Prayer

Another good example for our children is to complete morning prayer and devotions when everything pulls strong and taut and says that we must "get going."

My mother is an amazing example of this holy habit. When she visits in the summer, she turns our little guest room into a prayer haven. Early in the morning, her grandchildren get up and go into her room and, there she is with her bed made and her notebook out, her glasses laid across an open Bible and worship music playing. The children sit on the bed with her, watch her, and have a relaxed conversation. Children are drawn to adults who carry this peace and take time for beautiful and godly moments. I don't think they would have been as drawn to her if she was consumed with cleaning or distracted by the computer. We teach our children the value and beauty of the average moments of each day. Devotions and prayer can do wonders for redirecting our mind and calming our home.

Keep in mind that it is a treasure to simply enjoy being in God's presence with our children. Our relationship is not just about crossing off the academic or behavioral "to do" list. We can be with our children for the pure enjoyment of our relationship. Imagine if we treated our friends the way we do our children at times? What if our friends felt like every time we communicated with them, we were trying to improve them, correct them, or give them a job to do? No! We sit with our friends, sip coffee and catch up on life and let them know that we simply enjoy being with them. Obviously, we have a different authority over and obligation to our children. However, there is nothing wrong with enjoying their presence in the here and now. Not always looking for a correction to be made. Not bringing up their past failures or projecting all the things they've yet to learn. Expecting nothing from them and simply enjoying their company might make us both more receptive when a difficult situation arises.

Balance

We must also be okay with "missing out." We might miss a text, a skill, an extra-curricular activity, because we need to slow our schedule in order to increase attention. Pastor Chuck Swindoll said, "Unrestrained busyness leads to anxiety."[16] Unrestrained is a great description for how we live. We sometimes act as though we have no other choice.

At one time I thought if my son was not on a soccer team at age 4, his future athletic ambitions would be dashed. Now, that's crazy talk. But it took me awhile to get there. I have had conversations with friends who see many good opportunities and don't want their child to miss out. Yet, they feel overwhelmed with their full schedules. We can't do everything, nor should we. The joyful reading time at the family table or the math that needs extra care is often completed with irritation and hurry because of the over-full competing activities on the schedule. There is no time for the extra book we'd like to share or the family walk because our schedule is so packed. Little room is left for a last-minute change.

If we have chosen deep and meaningful homeschooling material, including time for great literature and nature, it will take a good portion of our day and energy. If we try to maintain those materials on top of too many other activities, we may drop some schooling or simply feel burned out.

On the other hand, if the academic portion of our schooling is so weighty that we can never leave our home and our children are not getting outside experiences, this is also unhealthy. A balance must be found.

> *When our schedule is balanced, we feel a sense of peace and forward momentum.*

For example, we might feel there's too much down time because our child's only outside activity is violin lessons. But that open time allows for schoolwork to be finished under less pressure and allows the child to have time for chores, playing with his siblings, or free reading. It's in this extra space there is time to make a new friend in the neighborhood or bake a cake together.

If we go back to the child who is only involved in violin lessons, he continues with violin for years because it is not weighing anyone down. But if that violin is paired with a sport, volunteer work and a co-op, our time suddenly begins to shrink, and nothing is experienced well. If we have excess time, see that as a good thing, and fill it with other family priorities such as being outdoors, cooking together, or learning some life skills.

If mom is feeling exhausted and overwhelmed, whether it's from too many play dates or too many classes, it's probably time for a reset of the routine. On the other hand, if mom is feeling isolated and needs community, a different set of choices must be made. This busyness factor is another area where you prayerfully focus on our family. We will see plenty of families running from one activity to the next. We will wonder if we are missing out. Some will certainly choose a busier schedule. However, if we want room for beauty and relationships, we'll have to live differently. This does not mean never leaving home, it means being intentional when we do.

CHAPTER 4
Habits

If we can successfully train our children to love the beauty of a well-balanced life, they will be much more content as adults.

A common problem is trying to put younger children in too many activities. Many of us do this when we only have one child or with our firstborn. Young children need plenty of rest and outdoor time. In addition, Charlotte Mason suggests this is an important time for instilling good habits.

What are these habits? Sonya Shafer of "Simply Charlotte Mason" suggests habits, according to Charlotte Mason, can be categorized generally into habits of attention, obedience, and truthfulness.[17] These habits are created by what we consistently expect from ourselves and our children. They permeate our homeschool atmosphere.

We don't talk very much about the importance of good habits, nor how much effort it might take a mom to teach these good habits to her children. As we work this out in the home, it means there must be time to teach a child how to perform habits of daily living and what it means to be a part of a family. Yet not only the how, but the spirit and character that support these habits.

SPRING

We think a child should just "know" how to fold their clothes. If we shout loud enough, perhaps the dishes will get done. Or, regardless of how much screen time we give them, they will be able to pay attention.

Some habits children will pick up easily, others need to be taught slowly before they will be performed well on their own. But each child is capable. Learning that we are part of a family and will always have obligations to other people is extremely valuable. Selflessness cannot be taught in one moment with a sibling. It's taught in reading books about empathetic people, taking food to the nursing home, and playing with the child no one else likes. The trouble is, often we pick academics and activities over good habits.

Bad habits come easily; good habits take time.

If we see value in the habits, we must give them time in the schedule. We must daily show the six-year-old how to make the bed until they are ready to take it over well. There must be time in the evenings to converse over the family dinner, so the children have time to develop listening skills. The children must be given many chances to try a recipe before they have the confidence to do it with ease. Chores and other habits of daily living are important to integrate along with the academic schedule. If these habits are important, reshuffling other activities to make room might be necessary.

Other parts of habit training have to do with the interaction we have with our children throughout the day. Teaching good attention and honesty happens in the atmosphere of the home. We must slow our thoughts and our daily speed, so we are aware of the Holy Spirit. The small conversations and opportunities we have throughout the day encourage good character. If we're running at the speed of the world, these moments will pass us by. These are not moments we can always plan in our schedule. But we need to make space so God can bring them in where He sees fit.

Though it's best to instill these habits when our children are young, please know there is still hope if this did not happen. It might be harder, but God can redeem more than we think He can. I started instilling good habits much later with my children, and over time, I have seen good fruit.

CHAPTER 5
Technology

> *"It is a rock, approximately two feet across. It is roughly textured, gray in color, but a portion of it is flat and smooth as glass. From this surface comes a glowing light that is quite beautiful and pleasing to look at."*[18]
> ~ The Wretched Stone, Chris Van Allsburg ~

We are fortunate that technology has provided us with access to wonderful materials and networks of support. New technologies help with academic studies as well as creative endeavors. We can visit the Amazon Rainforest on the National Geographic Channel, find ideas for art projects or science experiments on YouTube, and even get help with our child's learning struggles through specialized programs.

In addition, we have homeschooling history and support at our fingertips. If we want to find out what other moms find effective, there are a variety of blogs and podcasts. We can research every curriculum or homeschooling philosophy too. We also have access to a variety of online classes and support groups. However, a main concern that homeschooling mothers have is related to technology. Technology is a broad subject.

In this book, we look at technology through the lens of how it affects our everyday lives as parents, educators, and friends. Our private lives with our small screens cover everything from leisure, education, and connection. There are serious problems associated with our devices including gaming addiction, family disconnection, privacy, socialization issues, and even sexual temptation. I'm generally using the word "technology" to mean personal devices.

The decision we have before us is how much and what kind of technology will be allowed into our homes. As much as we may wish, we cannot hope that technology will simply be "dis-invented" or that our kids will never see a website they shouldn't. We must converse with our kids, set up appropriate protections, and have re-evaluations of what kind of technology is okay in our homes.

As more technology becomes rooted into our culture, an abundance of research has revealed the negative effects of these devices. At the root of the issue is a decision we must make. Will we allow the culture to dictate what we deem appropriate? This does not necessarily mean we do not watch TV or own an iPad, but it does mean we will not simply comply with what culture says is normal. We must think about what our family priorities are and decide technology and this culture will not be our Masters. It's a beautiful freedom that we are allowed to a greater degree because we have chosen to homeschool. We can make technology work for our family, not the other way around.

Are there areas of our lives where we are a slave to technology? The first step is the realization that most forms of personal technology were created to tap into our consumer driven nature. So, we ask ourselves these questions: Do I use technology mainly as a form of escape, boredom, or loneliness? Do I seek it at the end of the day as a replacement for relationships or time in the Bible?

As Steve Almond's article in the *New York Times Magazine* states, "Because aren't we just kidding ourselves? When we whip out our smartphones in line at the bank, 9 times out of 10 it's because we're jonesing for a microhit of stimulation, or that feeling of power that comes with holding a tiny universe in our fist. The reason people turn to screens hasn't changed much over the years. They remain mirrors that reflect a species in retreat from the burdens of modern consciousness, from boredom and isolation and helplessness."

He goes on to say that we pass these habits to our children, "It's natural for children to seek out a powerful tool to banish these feelings. But the only reliable antidote to such burdens, based on my own experience, is not immersion in brighter and mightier screens but the capacity to slow our minds and pay sustained attention to the world around us. This is how all of us - whether artists or scientists or kindergartners - find beauty and meaning in the unceasing rush of experience. It's how we develop empathy for other people, and the humility to accept our failures and keep struggling."[19]

One of the reasons we may find ourselves and our children on a constant search for comfort is we have so little ability to struggle, even a tiny bit. We find, as a society, a lack of resilience paired with a heightened stress-response in the face of very little external stress. This is because we find even a few minutes of boredom unbearable. We must now choose a bit of uncomfortable, because slowing down is what allows us to be still before a Holy God.

Balancing Personal Technology

The reason technology is often hard to balance is because it IS such a delicate balance of some good and lots of bad, and we're quite naïve to its impact upon our psyches. It takes strength and self-discipline to decide where technology fits into our lives. Be confident. This is an important task to undertake in our homes, and it is not something we can close our eyes and cross our fingers and hope will somehow work out.

SPRING

Proper versus improper use of technology in our day can make a huge impact on our home atmosphere. It is easy to get swept away by the newest technology before taking account of how much time and effort this new technology will absorb. Will it be just one more thing to manage? Is it necessary just because everyone we know has it? It's quite freeing to realize we can take charge. The truth is, it is much easier to not have the technology than to manage it. We must first decide if there are any forms of technology we need to get rid of. What is left, we must learn to manage in a healthy way.

An example of how the same technologies can be used for good or bad in our homeschool day might look like the following scenario.

During a school day we use an app to work on math drills, we watch a science video about zebra mussels. During writing or math, we use Spotify to listen to music, and after all the schoolwork is done the family streams a show together after dinner. This scenario is different than letting the children start the day with an hour of TV or iPad games before school, hurrying through the school day so that everyone can get away from each other and onto their personal devices, doing all of our schoolwork on the computer, or allowing unending hours of video games and access to technology which causes laziness, irritability, and a disconnection with one another.

In choosing to homeschool, we choose to be together.

A tell-tale sign to know if our family is in this situation is, if the thing we most look forward to in our day is our screens. Are we consumed with social media or the next episode of a show? Sometimes we do want time alone, but finding healthier ways to do this brings peace and less irritability at the end of the day. It may be that we have not realized what a wonderful job we have undertaken. We get to direct our children's daily schedule and we have many amazing tools and activities to make the most of our time with them. The diligence to choose the hard work over the easy technology will pay off in the long run.

As we work through these issues regarding technology, it's always important to keep this overarching idea in mind. At some point in our child's journey, he is going to have to manage technology independent of us. We may have put every control in place, but there will be a moment when the child's own convictions must stop him from watching something or posting something. In little bits, we will slowly let go and give more freedoms, but this may be done at a much older age than the culture around us will prescribe. We will discuss this further in the coming section. Your main job as a homeschool parent is to point our children to Christ and seek His wisdom. Be an example and guide your children in their daily decisions. Take hold of the fact that we are modeling for them appropriate uses of technology.

This is not something we communicate with fear and a tight fist. It's something we discuss openly and with firm instruction. But they will have to own it when they come of age. They must have a "heart of flesh" not of "stone" that is willing to be pliable in the Lord's hands (Ezekiel 36:26 ESV). And that is built day-to-day in our home as we share Christ with them and pray for them as they grow in their faith and knowledge of Jesus Christ. We give them such a lovely, enjoyable, full homeschool life that technology will simply become a side item that is more of a necessity of life and leisure at the end of a long, hard week. Develop these habits now and our hope is they will be kept long after the children leave home.

As parents, we spend a lot of time trying to figure out a correct balance of the "when" and "how much" of technology to allow in our kids' lives. We constantly reevaluate these standards as our children age and content evolves.

SPRING

The Following Chapters in this Section

When I first began writing this book, I could not find adequate information and advice regarding technology and the homeschool life. Therefore, I have spent a good portion of time reading and working to layout some thoughts regarding these basic questions.

The following detailed sections discuss research and thoughts regarding screen time, videogames, smartphones, and social media. My hope is not to bore you with too much research, but to equip you with important information as you make these decisions.

CHAPTER 6
How Much?

Thank the Lord!
He can give us wisdom when we're not sure what to do.

My husband and I were those parents who said our children would not watch television until the age of 2, and we stuck to that for 17 months. One spring day, my perfectly well-controlled routine got rocked by a stomach virus and my husband was out of town. With a heart of guilt, I put on *Curious George* for my son to watch. My third child was watching movies from the time he came out of the womb so I could get some rest!

Balancing technology has always been hard for me. It's hard for many of us. Growing up in the 1980s and 90s, our parents simply had to make decisions about what TV shows and movies were okay and that's about it. Once the news or a show was over, the TV went off. There was nothing left to watch. Now we have many new technologies to manage, and the range of what parents feel about them can go from "no technology at all" to "my kid has a smartphone and an iPad and a screen in the minivan." So, my goal is to simply share commonsense ideas on technology in the homeschool life.

My personal experience has been that too much screen time, whether TV or devices, causes a lot of irritability and attention problems for children. This may be your experience too. The negative effects of too much technology on our psychological health is common knowledge and backed by research.

According to the American Academy of Pediatrics (AAP), the average child spends seven hours a day looking at a screen. What? Seven hours. That does not seem possible! But even two hours a day shows psychological difficulties in children.[20]

I have gone to different extremes. There is the day-to-day reality and, like other moms who have busy days, I get tired and just want to throw on a movie and take a nap. Does it really do that much harm? The answer lies somewhere in the middle. Every family must figure out the appropriate amount of screen time. Most research today says one to two hours a day is a good goal.

In recent years, the AAP has focused less on there being a "perfect" amount of screen time. They suggest instead a balanced approach with a great deal of parent interaction and discussion with their kids.[21] Much of this is based on the huge discrepancies in quality of content. For example, the family watching a National Geographic show or Historical Documentary is different from a child watching an hour of random YouTube videos alone at bedtime.

The more time we spend on any screen means less time on other activities such as exploring the outdoors, reading, prayer, or chores.

But time is time. We may find we can make adjustments based on the reasons our children are using the screen. "The Common Sense Census: Media Use by Tween and Teens" identified four main categories of screen time: Passive consumption (watching TV, reading, and listening to music), interactive consumption (playing games and browsing the internet), communication (video-chatting and using social media), and content creation (using devices to make digital art or music).[21] So, we have a choice about how screens are used in our home.

Rules, Guidelines and Restrictions

We probably are not going to make one set of rules our family will follow forever. However, if we find we have arguments with our children every day about how much screen time is allowed, this is wasted energy. We may find a child working on a project for which we deem it okay to allot a bit more screen time than usual. That is our privilege as a parent. We must look at our child's age and what he is using technology for and then choose a balanced approach. But whatever technology we allow, the idea is "less is better."

I have never come to the end of the day and said, "You know, what we really needed today was more screen time." But how many times do we think we could have done with less screens? The key is setting boundaries for the school week and planning special times where we might allow more technology after work of some kind has been completed.

The best thing we can do is to create standards, make them clear to everyone, and stick with them. We don't want a constant stream of discussion about how and if children can get more screen time.

Set a System

Don't forget that technology can be good for learning and some appropriate leisure is not bad. Set a good system for the family and, over a period reevaluate if needed.

Remember to allow a break when there is illness or an unusual situation. Some extra technology here and there is not going to ruin our children. But, endless hours of screen time will affect their attention, attitudes, and motivation. In so doing, it will affect the atmosphere in the home. Often the break we are seeking is short-lived, and we may simply be creating bad attitudes in our children we will have to deal with later.

One recent study looking at 4,500 US children ages 8 to 11, with the highest levels of cognitive functioning including memory, processing, attention, and language, had less than two hours of screen time per day. They also received adequate sleep and at least 60 minutes of physical activity.[22] A small amount of screen time balanced with other healthy habits allows for the best brain health.

Use technology to bring the family together rather than encouraging private, closed-door pursuits.

It is easy to make technology either something we let ride freely and don't realize the consequences it is causing, or we make it an idol and decide as long as we get the quota right, we will have peace. Neither is correct. The living stories section at the end of this chapter give ideas about how other parents are grappling with the amount of technology to allow.

CHAPTER 7
What Kind?

The Bible tells us the "days are evil", so we are commanded to "redeem the time."
Let's do that today by teaching our young sons and
daughters to use godly discernment.

Video Games

In conversations with moms of pre-teen or teenage boys, at some point, a discussion about video games will likely occur. What games are appropriate for the children? Is it something the family plays together? Many boys can play a couple of hours of video games and then pass a test with flying colors. There are fathers and sons who enjoy playing sports video games together after a long day. They laugh together and enjoy a little competition.

In our home, we've decided generally to rule out video games. Why? I have a child who can't sleep at night after watching Superbowl commercials due to overstimulation, so video games are out of the question. I worry about the effects of video games on attention and irritability. I also don't like the way it changes our home atmosphere. It's just too much noise and stimulation for my brain. But, am I imagining this?

What are the effects of video games on the average boy? "The destructive effects of video games are not on boys' cognitive abilities or their reaction times, but on their motivation and their connectedness with the real world."[2] Our greatest concern here is the disconnection with reality and the violence of first-person shooter games. A special concern for boys, who tend to use video games more than girls, is the effect on motivation. Our youth seem to be slow to take on adult responsibilities more than any previous generation. According to the Pew Research Center, for the first time in more than 130 years, Americans ages 18-34 are more likely to live with their parents than in any other living situation."[23]

Now, if your children are living with you and going to school and working towards a goal, this is different than the child that refuses to grow up. Economist Erik Hurst and colleagues found that between 2004 and 2015, young men's leisure time grew by 2.3 hours and 60% of that time was spent playing video games. The study also showed that men in 2015 ages 21-30 were working 203 fewer hours a year than their same age counterparts in 2000.[24]

The researchers asked the question, "Why don't young men want to work?" One of the answers has to do with the social aspect of video games. Today's gaming "online community" can spend days participating in some battle that never ends. Basically, game creators are making a better, more addictive product. This situation creates long hours of play which makes it difficult to stop. In fact, the problem is so pervasive, the World Health Organization has now listed "gaming addiction" as a mental health condition for the first time.

What about the impact of video games on other areas of mental health such as violence and depression? One study published by two Montreal researchers in the academic journal of Molecular Psychiatry in 2017 appear to be the first to show conclusive evidence of grey matter loss in the hippocampus, a part of the brain that is crucial for orientation and memory, as a result of direct interaction with video games.

In the study, participants played popular first-person shooter games: *Call of Duty*, *Medal of Honor*, and *Borderland 2*. The more depleted the hippocampus becomes, the more a person is at risk of developing brain illnesses and diseases including depression, schizophrenia, PTSD and Alzheimer's disease.[25] With the rise in school shootings, it's wise to look at what has changed in our culture that might be impacting these problems. The majority of people who play first person shooter games will not go out and shoot someone. But, for those predisposed to mental health issues, these games can be especially negative.

I was curious to look at research regarding the impact of video games and violence. I was surprised to find little evidence showing a causal relationship between video games and violence. So, maybe videogames do not cause violence. But, does watching violent images repetitively, especially when you're the perpetrator, have some effect on our brain? Researchers say "yes," but it mainly has to do with aggression, attention, and possibly empathy.

In 2018, an analysis of 24 studies involving 17,000 youth from countries including the U.S., Canada, Germany, and Japan, and published in the Proceedings of the National Academy of Sciences, found those who played violent games such as *Grand Theft Auto*, *Call of Duty* and *Manhunt* were more likely to exhibit behavior such as being sent to the principal's office for fighting or hitting a non-family member.[26] That sounds like violent behavior to me!

So, as researchers explain, we know there is an association between violence and video games, there's just not enough evidence to prove video games cause violence. Violent video games seem to be one more added factor that has a negative influence over those that are already struggling with mental health problems, but to what degree is still unknown.

Many video games are not violent, so how might they affect us? And what about attention? Although some studies suggest that playing video games enhances a child's concentration, other studies, such as a 2012 paper published in *Psychology of Popular Media Culture*, found that games can hurt and help children's attention issues - improving the ability to concentrate in short bursts but damaging long-term concentration.

Writing in the *Annals of General Psychiatry*, Dr Philip A Chan and Professor Terry Rabinowitz concluded that, "Adolescents who play more than one hour of console or Internet video games may have more intense symptoms of ADHD or inattention than those who do not."[26]

Being Wise Guardians

So, what are the positive aspects of video games? Many studies show that video games help with fine motor skills, problem solving, strategizing, mapping, quick thinking, and pattern recognition.[26] As I was going back and forth about the pros and cons, something became very clear. Most of the positive aspects of gaming are self-focused, whereas many of the negative ones revolve around a person's interaction with others. So, Jimmy might be quick, able to focus on something he is interested in, and even do well on a math pop quiz. But he may not have the attention to listen to a family discussion at the dinner table, or the self-control to handle a fight with his sister without aggression.

Regardless of what the research says or what our neighbors do, if we dislike video games or if we see negative changes in our child because they play them, then it's our responsibility to say "No." Making our own experiment at home is the best way to discover what's happening in our family. Maybe we consider taking video games away for a couple of weeks and observe whether it changes the atmosphere and attitudes in the home. This gives a clearer view of what's going on and gives us the facts to support making changes in the home. In the end, we may choose to reduce videogame consumption to one or two days a week as family or friend time.

We should prepare our children for the reality that many people play video games in their spare time, especially young men. This is where common sense needs to rule the day regarding any technology we bring into our homes.

As our son has reached his teen years, some of his friends want to play video games. We had to find a balance for when he visits a friends' house as well as developing rules in our home. I have no doubt we would have a completely different atmosphere if we let video games have a regular place in our home.

> *As a family we discuss the negative effects of gaming and, in many ways, we are working to help our children be their own advocates to their generation.*

Are we fighting a losing battle? Maybe. But I'd hate to have my children be the kind that sit back and accept what the culture is doing as normal simply because it's uncomfortable to stand out. How else will they be tough enough to own their time and their responsibilities? We want them to grow up and be independent. We want to raise boys who will be men with a focus on taking care of their families. It's no wonder many boys at 18 don't want to work when they've never been asked to do chores or allowed to go anywhere alone. When they've been allowed to think that it's a reasonable use of their time to stare at a screen with fake characters fighting fake battles when there

SPRING

are real battles to be fought, we're giving them the easy way out. This will hurt them and their loved ones in the long run.

God made this world and all its creatures to be seen and touched and experienced with all the senses that He has given us. We strip that sensitivity away when we replace it with a cheap, fast paced substitute. Then, we wonder why we have raised a generation of lazy, disconnected, and hyperactive kids. Not good! We can do better by being wise guardians over the games our children play and using this gaming technology for true educational or family-focused purposes, if at all.

CHAPTER 8

Smartphones and Social Media

Be thoughtful and capture beauty.
Go after it and teach your children to do the same.

Smartphones

I don't suppose there would be much conversation around phones if they provided our children with voice calling capabilities only. We would be in the world our parents lived in. We wouldn't have much to say other than, "Sam talks to his friends for hours," or "Sarah spends too much time texting."

This tiny device we place into the palm of our child's hand is not a phone at all. It's phone-like capabilities are only a small portion of what this device is capable of, it's the least of our worries. This device is access to the internet, texting, pictures, and video options which hold a host of disagreeable possibilities.

The problem occurs when we have young people with smartphones and unfiltered internet access. In the tween or teenager's life, this mainly involves opening their phones to spend time on social media apps. The other added access to manage is their use of texting. This can bring a fast shift in responsibility upon parent and child, a quick change, especially in the ways the child might socialize.

Will we allow our child to have a smartphone and at what age? On average, children get their first smartphones around age 10, according to research firm Influence Central.[27] The average age children received a smartphone in 2012 was 12. Therefore, we are seeing a dramatic reduction in the age of what is seen as culturally appropriate to begin self-management of a smartphone. So, what is the right age? Internet safety experts say the later, the better. Some experts say 12 is the ideal age, others say to wait until they are 14. Later is safer because smartphones can be addictive distractions that detract from schoolwork and may expose children to online bullies, child predators, and sexting. "60% of families who give their children smartphones, do so between the ages of 10 and 11 (20% give their children phones between the ages of 8 and 9). This is in fact the same age that the average child in our nation is exposed both voluntarily and involuntarily to explicit material."[28]

Jesse Weinberger, who wrote the smartphone and internet safety book, *The Boogeyman Exists: And He's in Your Child's Back Pocket,* surveyed 70,000 children and found that on average, sexting began in the fifth grade, pornography consumption began when children turned eight and pornography addiction began around age eleven.[29]

Some parents turn to the old flip phone as a first phone to completely bypass the dangers of smartphones. Close to one-third of teens don't have smartphones. One survey found that 30% of teens have a basic cellphone that does not access the internet. While this group tends to come from lower-income families, one interesting anomaly was that there was a high percentage of teens whose parents graduated from college who have only basic cellphones. The researchers found this result surprising and said that some parents who could easily afford smartphones are choosing flip phones for their kids for economic responsibility and personal reasons.[30]

Many smartphone companies offer parental restrictions which can help. But this can be difficult to manage; many kids learn to work around these unless you simply shut-down internet access altogether. But then why get a smartphone at all?

In addition, companies such as GABB Wireless are creating phones that allow kids many of the benefits of a smartphone.[31] They have the look of a smartphone including a screen and easy texting. A camera is included but pictures cannot be sent to contacts and there is no internet access. Overall, we seem to have a perfect storm between the beginning of puberty and handing over smartphones and social media to our growing children.

So, if parents can spread these choices over time, we might save our child from a lot of pain. For example, a child gets a flip phone at 13. He or she shows maturity and is allowed a smartphone at 16 (paid for at least partly through his/her own income). It may be that in those last years of homeschooling we teach our children to wisely manage a social media account. Otherwise, they leave home without the opportunity to converse with us as they make choices regarding their time and usage. The main idea is to be thoughtful and prayerful as we make decisions regarding smartphones. Do not get caught up in what our children, their friends, or the culture says is a necessity regarding these technologies. We are the parents, and there is ample research to suggest we should wait.

Social Media

As I began writing this section of the book, Facebook came under fire for its data sharing procedures. It goes without saying that the more information we put on social media, the more likely our opinions and preferences will be shared with consumer-driven companies.

Let's take a step back and look at why people use social media. There are positive uses for social media. Many people find that Facebook streamlines communication for their organization or business. People can spread prayer needs and receive support that would otherwise be more difficult to achieve. However, if we take out the percentage of the positive that social media provides, what are we left with? Are we choosing social media support over church interaction and the support of close friends? And is the percent of good found in social media equal to the percent of time that is wasted or worse, having a negative effect?

A recent article from Fast Company magazine states that a 2013 study found the more people used Facebook, the worse they felt. Instagram, Snapchat, and Twitter also correspond to low self-esteem among adults. The article goes on to state we use social media as distractions. No big deal, but is it? "Yet the ability apps have to distract us so completely that we don't notice the passage of time, also serves to eat up the most precious commodity any of us will ever have."[32]

The point is, we mindlessly allow ourselves and our children to add these apps into our lives. But each app must be managed, which takes up more of our time, and for what benefit? In addition, these technologies correlate with depression, for which teenagers are particularly vulnerable. Though we cannot say depression is caused by social media, a recent article in Psychology Today suggests it may be that depressed kids seek out more social media sites.[33]

We can see a relationship wherein, especially the focus on pictures and beauty, can harm a young girl's sense of self-worth. In fact, current young teens are the first generation whose entire form of socialization has been defined and changed by their phones and social media. As psychologist Jean Twenge, who studies generational patterns, concludes, "Even when a seismic event—a war, a technological leap, a free concert in the mud - plays an outsized role in shaping a group of young people, no single factor ever defines a generation. Parenting styles continue to change, as do school curricula and culture, and these things matter. But the twin rise of the smartphone and social media has caused an earthquake of a magnitude we've not seen in a very long time, if ever. There is compelling evidence that the devices we've placed in young people's hands are having profound effects on their lives - and making them seriously unhappy"[34]

At what age should a child be allowed access to social media? According to Influence Central's 2016 Digital Trends study, 50% of kids age 12 and older have a social media account. The top platforms being Facebook, Twitter, and Instagram.[27]

A 17-year-old friend recently told me that much of her day at public school revolves around managing her different social media accounts. She was aware of how unhealthy this was for her generation, and she limited herself to one or two accounts. But most of the people she knows "have" to manage their social life with these apps, as though there is no other option. They feel there isn't.

Social Media and Peer Pressure

It is hard to remember what it was like to be a teenager. But think back for a moment. In the past, peer pressure meant friends had a certain pair of jeans or listened to a certain type of music and, if we didn't, we felt left out of the loop. Now compound that many times for what teenagers today deal with in regard to the energy they must put towards being included in their virtual community.

Not being able to afford a pair of Guess or Girbauds jeans was a bummer, but it did not really impact our mental health. But, getting real time opinions regarding our personal photos and innermost thoughts can have a profound impact on a child's mental health. Imagine if your teenage diary was placed online? Kids today are just as naïve and immature as we were, but their clothing choices and inner struggles are available for the cyber world to respond with likes and comments.

> *The easiest and most clear-cut way to deal with social media is to not allow it into a teenagers' life.*

Teens' hormones and bodies are changing rapidly, and they are highly vulnerable and still maturing. It is not a good time to hand over such social platforms to them.

Studies have suggested that young people who spend more than two hours a day on social networking sites are more likely to report psychological distress. "Seeing friends constantly on holiday or enjoying nights out can make young people feel like they are missing out while others enjoy life," reports the #*StatusofMind*. "These feelings can promote a 'compare and despair' attitude."[35]

Social Media and Validation

People are beginning to wake up to the realities of the negative impact of social media. In recent days, we hear of executives that once worked for social media companies leaving as they face a moral dilemma about the work they've participated in and its impact on society. As Sean Parker, former Facebook president states, "The thought process that went into building these applications, Facebook being the first of them, was all about 'How do we consume as much of your time and conscious attentions as possible?"

The company achieved this by adding a "like" button and by letting people comment on posts or pictures with Parker calling these "a social-validation feedback loop, exactly the kind of thing that a hacker like myself would come up with because you're exploiting a vulnerability in human psychology."[36]

"Likes" and "Comments" are now vehicles for validation and shaming. Validation is seeking someone to tell us we are good enough and worth something. But Someone already did. "No amount of self-love can fill the God-shaped hole in someone's heart. We are created and called to love each other, and no self-absorbed spa treatment or Instagram post can supplant our innate yearning for love from God."[37]

With the overwhelming amount of evidence against social media, is it wrong to wonder if spending our time on any of these sites is healthy? Should we consider banning social media altogether within our family? Since some organizations only use Facebook or social media sights for communication, at some point our child may have to use a social media website. But I recommend avoiding it as long as possible.

In addition, instead of simply handing the smartphone or social media app over, help children set clear rules and boundaries about when and for how long they are allowed to use this form of communication. This doesn't have to be done in a negative, degrading manner. It's much more productive to speak to them about the realities of what's going on in the culture, and practice responsible use of these outlets. Before we do that, we may need to have our own personal evaluation of how much we currently utilize social media.

SPRING

What if I want to leave Social Media?

"But the wisdom from above is first pure, then peaceable, gentle, open to reason, full of mercy and good fruits, impartial and sincere" (James 3:17).

Juxtaposed to these characteristics is most of what we find on social media. My husband and I chose to stop using social media four years ago. Initially our reason was because we felt like we were wasting time. Though we often planned to look at it for a few minutes, before we knew it, an hour had gone by. I also felt there was a sudden shift in social media.

When we first started on Facebook in 2007, it was because we ran into a group of old college friends at an alumnus gathering who told us it was a great way to stay in touch. I do think it was great, for a while. It was fun seeing photos of friends' homes and children. After a couple of years, we noticed we were caught up on what was going on in the lives of our old friends. Then we started seeing pictures of what people were eating for dinner, and everyone wanted to share their political views and fighting. I remember one incident specifically where a group of parents were talking about a teacher negatively and people were taking sides. Suddenly I thought, "I don't need to have this all going on in my head." I concluded that I did not need to share my opinion on every little thing going on in other people's lives. Even less, I didn't need to be thinking about it. I could not possibly keep straight my daily responsibilities while I was pondering the 10 articles or posts I read on my feed.

And there is that awful word, "feed." Tell me your imagination doesn't go straight to the image of a bunch of cows mindlessly eating what's placed in front of them. And then it hit me! Social media had become a weird social experiment. It's like a soap opera in our pocket. Avoiding real-world responsibilities keeps us scrolling, and a desire to constantly capture ourselves in the "best light" keeps us posting.

And what happens when we don't get as many "likes" as we hoped? We feel like the rat in the psychology experiment who keeps pressing the button, but no cheese is coming out of the door. We will just keep pressing that button. We'll post again until we get that cheese! But we won't be satisfied for long, the hunger will return. Now, you might be thinking, "That is awfully cynical." I don't think you realize the power of who is behind social media.

Social Media and Polarization

Social media is being used to polarize us on many fronts. It supports extreme views and pushes us toward purchases and politics under the guise of some algorithm created by people with the ethics and the social skills of a thimble. But they are extremely intelligent and know how to tap into the human psyche.

I'm not trying to start a revolution. When people find out I'm not on social media, I get a glimpse into what pastors feel like. People are always confessing to me why they, too, would like to get off social media but just can't for one reason or another. Many of the reasons are valid. It is the norm and I am the weird one. I just don't think everyone has taken the time to consider the deep costs.

Certainly not everyone is affected equally by involvement on social media. Consider an experiment of taking a break from social media for two weeks and keeping a journal about your feelings. After you review your journal, decide what you think about putting social media back into your life. You may not want or be ready to get rid of social media, but most of us realize we need to make sure it only takes up a specific amount of time in our lives.

Minimalist Joshua Becker lists some great ways to reduce time on social media. Specifically, on Facebook, this includes choosing friends wisely, skipping applications and games, removing email notifications, hiding unnecessary notifications from the newsfeed, not using Facebook chat, and syncing your social networking sites. The best advice is limiting yourself to logging in once a day and drastically limiting your time.[38]

Obviously, protecting your privacy has become another major problem with social media. A few new social media outlets have organized themselves as an alternative, for example Cocoon.[39] These might give you a better option of sharing your life with truly close family and friends without having your data shared. Time will tell if these businesses will succeed. One study cited on the Today show states that "82% of people mistrust Facebook" but 2.8 billion people use it at least once a day.[40] Again, we struggle to make our beliefs impact our behavior.

Overall, it's simply important to pray and evaluate what role social media has in our lives and take control of what God asks of us. This is an intentional pursuit. No one is going to do this for us. We should plan time in our schedule to read our Bibles and good books, listen to great podcasts, talk to our parents, be a part of a church community. It is surprising how beautifully packaged technology groups can make "life on social media" or any media for that matter look. Like most things on the internet, social media can be used for good or evil. Use wisdom. Proceed with caution.

What about all the organizations that I connect with on Facebook?

Many people say it's unreasonable to stop the use of social media. I have friends who tell me they want to get off Facebook, but all their children's activities or their organizations communicate through Facebook. It is true that some of you may need to stay in touch with organizations through Facebook. There is a way you can do this without accepting the constant

Facebook friend feed. My husband was the first one to show me how to do this. I'll list the steps below:

First, delete your old account.

Next, create a new account and do not accept any friends. Under Privacy Settings and Tools where it states, "Who can send you friend requests?" you will select "Friends of friends." In this way, because you have "no friends" on Facebook, no one can send you a request.

Now, select only the organizations you want to stay in contact with on Facebook. You can also remove yourself from search engines that Facebook allows to connect to your profile under Privacy Settings and Tools. You will get a feed and notifications of the activities and organizations that you choose. Let Facebook work for you, instead of the other way around.

A final note. Plenty of other apps and programs have taken their cues from social media and, without realizing it, we can get sucked into their black hole as well.

At the end of a long day, we want to relax and laugh or check what's going on in the world. The difference with a nightly news program on TV (or a podcast or a blog) is they have an ending to the story. Can we find an end to a social media or news feed? It's like the pot of gold at the end of a rainbow; people keep looking but it eludes them.

When we find ourselves on any platform using an unending scroll of information, it can become mind numbing. That's usually when we can't stop. Because there might be one more story we don't want to miss. A trick I've learned is to set a timer and take back control. This all may sound like a lot of time management strategies in combating hyper-information, but it's something this new tech world has brought. So, whether we want to or not, we do have to manage it, or it will manage us.

If we want to have time for beauty, technology is probably the number one thief. I feel like Professor William Waterman Sherman in *21 Balloons* when he said, "It seems strange to me that mechanical progress always seems to leave the slower demands of elegance far behind."[41] Or as one college student aptly put it after his professor collected his cell phone for a nine-day experiment, "It is almost like the earth stood still and I actually looked around…"[42]

CHAPTER 9
What Message?

"He created them male and female, and he blessed them and called them human."
~ Genesis 5:2 ~

How did a concept so simple become so complicated? I sit on my bed looking outside my window on this cloudy spring afternoon. I watch the red-winged blackbird with his dark black coat and a sudden burst of yellow and red peeking out from under his wings. Then, I see the female, she is not particularly striking. If you look close enough, you can see a small hint of yellow on her wings, but otherwise, she is a simple brown all over.

We often see this same story played out with many other bird species. The male wears the beautiful clothes while the female is camouflaged. But we see in these differences, a great purpose. The male birds attract the females with their beautiful colors while the female bird must blend in to protect her eggs from predators. This is one of the many beautiful ways God says, "equal in value, but different in function."

SPRING

Gender

It is desperately sad that we live in a culture that is embracing the blurring of gender distinctions. We must hold firm to the truth of God's Word in our homes and teach our children about God's design for gender. Much of what our children will be exposed to through today's media is a slow and purposeful message of gender neutrality, pro-homosexuality, and sexual "freedom."

Albert Mohler's book, *We Cannot Be Silent,* speaks to the idea that we must first have an evangelical theology of the human body. "Scripture clearly refutes any theory that promotes gender as only a social construction or that human beings are free to define themselves in a way different than the way God defined them in the act of creation."[43]

We graciously want to understand the stories of those who struggle with gender identification. The church must become more educated and better prepared for how to embrace and minister to these individuals in the coming years. They will become a growing population in need of compassion and help. But it starts with clarity about authority and purpose to gender. Mohler continues, "That biological assignment is not a naturalistic accident, but a sign of God's purpose for that individual human being to display His glory and aim for flourishing and obedience to that creative purpose."[43]

Of course, there is room for differences within the genders. We are still individual people. There is room for sports stars and artists, adventurers and bookworms among all genders. God's plan for them is to promote His glory. We don't get to choose. It's one of those essentials.

We encourage our children early, without fear-tactics, that God made them a male or a female for a reason; we speak to the beauty of this plan.

Women can uniquely bare children. This is a great gift. Married men are to love their wives. Together, as husband and wife they are to pro-create. Together, they protect and provide for their children. As our children get older, we will need to speak to them plainly about how Satan has distorted God's good plan. We do not live in a Christian culture. So those that are struggling with gender and sexual identification are simply embracing what the culture teaches. It is our job to stand for God's order. We must help our kids do the same.

Sex Education

You will be faced with speaking to your children about God's design for marriage and sex far earlier than you may have planned. When you think of the topics that matter most to you in homeschooling, sex is probably not at the top of the list. But I hypothesize that one of the most important subjects to cover and have an open dialogue about is sex education.

In a way, our culture has given us both an awful and a wonderful opportunity. Many of our parents might have gotten away with not discussing sex. But parents today simply cannot. There is so much confusion regarding marriage and gender that we are hurting our children if we don't talk often about God's design for their bodies and sexuality.

Pornography

We must address the topic of pornography. It is smart and wise to set up protections on computers at home. Create passwords and controls that will eliminate children from wandering onto inappropriate sites. But truly, there is no fail-safe system. Also, there are times when our children will be away from our protections and smartphones are everywhere. It is important to talk with them about pornography and how to respond when they are exposed to it.

Past statistics on pornography said the age of a child's first exposure to pornography is 11. However, *Bitdefender* reports that children under the age of ten account for 22% of the online porn consumption, which includes the porn mega site *Pornhub*. In addition, they found a tenth of the 12 to 13-year-olds reported they may be addicted to pornography. Many experts believe this is due to mobile accessibility and desensitization at an earlier age.[44]

We need to understand that exposure to pornography affects us neurologically. Suddenly, a young man thinks every girl is a sexual object and sex becomes an unrealistic and twisted fantasy. Like any other drug, as one's tolerance grows, the need for greater stimulation grows. For boys, this can greatly affect their connection to what a real wife's body will look like and their expectations of sex.

It's a scary thing to consider that for many boys and girls, their first exposure to sex will be pornography. It is confusing and can trap them in a cycle of guilt. Conversations should happen early, and children must have a clear plan for what to do when exposed to these materials because they have a profoundly negative impact. We must have protections on the internet at home and we must teach our kids what to do when faced with unprotected internet outside of the home.

Please view the resource list at the end of this section for materials on discussing sex and pornography with your children. In the end, there is no computer protection that will teach your children what only you can teach them. Only you can teach them God's design for gender and sex and help them be prepared to respond when faced with pornographic images. If you don't teach them, someone else will. We used to think pornography was only an issue for young men, this is no longer the case. Because of this unfettered access, many young women are also becoming addicted. So please, communicate with all your children.

Body Image

In addition, girls are often bombarded by images of their attractiveness. One summer, I taught a 4th grade Sunday school class. I recall that we were presented with a great object lesson which showed each child how much God loves them. The gist of the activity was that we read a verse out of the Bible which listed characteristics of who we are in Christ with words such as forgiven, righteous, faithful, made holy. Each child took a marker and wrote one of these words onto a full-length mirror. At the end, the entire mirror was covered with these encouraging words. Then one at a time, each child was asked to stand in front of the mirror. Then we'd read aloud the words written on the mirror. In this way, they would see their own image reflected in the mirror and hear the words that God says about them. It was very moving; it caught me off guard for a Sunday School lesson for that age level. But, do you know what caught my eye? Suddenly, I could predict how girls versus boys would react to the exercise.

Now, keep in mind, these are not teenagers, they are 9 and 10-year-old girls and boys. Every boy stood in front of the mirror, listened to the encouraging words, then sat down. But almost every girl looked in the mirror and the first thing she did was say, "ugh," or fix her hair, or check how she looked. It was like a million childhood memories swept over me as I remembered how often I felt good enough or not good enough based on my appearance.

Do we not still do that as women when we wake up and look at ourselves in the mirror? I wanted to shout to these girls, "The way the Lord sees you is literally written on this mirror!" But girls so quickly learn not to see it! Why? Because like it or not, we are wired to hold a very high value on our appearance, and the culture we live in does as well. It is a free woman indeed who can take care of herself yet is content and does not give too much attention to her appearances. She is a woman who truly accepts what God says about her.

Can we somehow teach this message to our daughters? What does the culture tell them exactly that feeds into these ideals? Though we can appreciate some companies have moved towards embracing different body types, the image of a "perfect" body still looms over us. On the one hand there are more appropriate swimsuits to choose from and pictures of average-sized models at the makeup aisle of your neighborhood grocery store. On the other hand, turn on the TV and see most female performers half naked yet touting a message of "Female Power."

It's all confusing. When I was growing up everyone wanted to be Kelly Kapowski from the show *Saved by the Bell*. The most important thing was to be pretty, popular, and a cheerleader. Today, even though the theme is certainly supposed to be a stronger, smarter, and more independent woman, there are few examples of women of God who love their husbands and show strength by taking care of their families. Women who are smart, wise, and capable without being required to put men down. Social media only exacerbates girls' insecurities.

A recent study of 1500 European teenagers and young adults (age 14-24) found that *Instagram,* where personal photos take center stage, received the worst scores for body image and anxiety. As one survey respondent wrote, *Instagram* makes girls and women feel as if their bodies aren't good enough as they often add filters and edit their pictures for them to look "perfect."[45]

If our daughter is spending too much time on social media or watching shows that purport these images, she will be told to assimilate. This is why girls need strong female role models in their lives to drown out the voice of the culture. They need to read books about strong women who have served and loved the Lord and their families. Women who have invented, taught, and lead in a variety of vocations. They need to spend time in groups where compassionate, hard-working women with normal shapes and sizes show joyful leadership. We need to make sure our daughters have much stronger positive voices speaking into them than the negatives ones in the messages the world provides.

Technology and Theology

Many of these technologies we have looked at are going to be a part of any person's life today. To completely remove them could even be harmful as we prepare our children for modern life. As David Murray states in his article "Digital Theology," "The longer I've wrestled with this problem in my own family, the more convinced I've become that the ultimate answer is not "no technology" or "more technology" but "more theology." If we want deep, lasting, and spiritual solutions, we need to learn and teach deep, lasting, and spiritual truths. Sound digital theology is the answer to digital technology; the oldest truths are the best rebuttal to the newest challenges. More Trinity is more effective than more technology."[46]

Each family must decide what the role of "screens" will play in their home. However, it is important to remember that research has shown negative effects of too much and specific types of these technologies and that must not be ignored.

A real blessing is when my family is enjoying technology together. When we are laughing together or learning together using technology, it's at its best use. Just as we carefully choose materials and activities for our homeschool days, we want to plan what role technology plays in learning and in leisure for our home. Too much of it will steal the beauty and stillness of the day.

SPRING

I know there is a lot of information in this section on technology. It's my hope that you will be inspired to take some time in the "Pondering Spring" at the end to review your technology usage. The goal is not for you to feel overwhelmed or under legalism. The changes made should empower us to manage our technology and feel a sense of freedom.

CHAPTER 10

Beautiful Words

How wonderful to lift your voice with the sounds of God's promises.

Throughout the "Living Stories" of this book, we explore the answers that homeschooling moms gave to a variety of questions. But there is one question I asked that deserves special recognition, "What is your favorite part of your homeschooling day?" Almost every mom said, "reading together." No other question had such uniformity of answers.

There is nothing that brings such connectedness to the family like shared stories. It is almost palpable. Whether laughing about the overflowing donut machine with Homer Price, holding our breath as Frodo slips on the ring of power, or gasping as we imagine the journey of missionary Gladys Aylward through the hills of China with a hundred orphans in tow during WWII. We feel all the emotions together as we read great stories. It's a shared experience. Nothing we do together in homeschooling will quite compare to the memories we build as we read great stories.

When we read to our children, we feel something innate. It's in our DNA. These stories impart character, wisdom, empathy and all the things we want to say to our children when we can't quite find the words. As Sarah Mackenzie puts it in her book, *Read Aloud Family*, "There is simply no substitute for a

SPRING

story...A story meets the child where he is. It sparks an authentic desire within him to do better, try harder, and love more."[47]

In addition, reading together is quite easy. Yes, at times attentions may wane, but generally it's much easier for us to complete than a difficult math problem or science experiment. When we read to our children, the material should be age appropriate and cheerful, leaving them wanting more. A good 15-20 minutes is plenty at a couple of points in the day. They can narrate back what they heard and an inspired question here or there is fine. We let the organic conversations flow. Sometimes these conversations happen long after a book is read. Ponder the story for a moment. Later, in the car or at dinner, we might bring up how the situation made us feel and see what the children think.

I remember one instance when we were studying the conflicts between the settlers and the Native Americans in the late 1800s. I asked the children if they thought one side was right and the other one wrong. They concluded that the two sides should have found a way to peaceably share the land. Later that day, I asked my daughter this question, "What if citizens from another country decided they would like to live in Texas now and they came in and just started living on land in parts of Texas where we live . . . what do you think?" She said, "Well, that would not be fair, this is our land." We suddenly saw there was good and bad on both sides, which opened the way for a conversation about how human trouble begins in the sinful human heart. Some conflict is inevitable in life.

And so, the world becomes a bit bigger, the children put themselves in someone else's shoes and see there are many sides to one story. They discover God is sovereign over both suffering and joy and life is certainly not fair. They see the value in doing what they don't feel like doing because it's what's right. When they become adults, they can accept the unknown of why a young mom dies of cancer or understand why someone might be homeless.

They might decide a friend is being rude for some unknown reason and realize that we all sin and need God's forgiveness. They have seen it lived out repeatedly in stories. All these realizations occur together as we read and share, which go hand in hand.

Reading is Connecting

In our family, we read every time we eat, the two coincide. Reading at bedtime or another time during the school day while the kids rest or have free time can be best. You will find your own family's rhythm. As children get older, they read more on their own, which is wonderful; but continue with the together read aloud time. It's more than just reading, it's connecting. It may be the older sibling reads to the younger or the family reads one story at bedtime or on Sunday afternoon together, but never let it go completely. Listening to someone else's story makes us forget our own for a while and participate in the family chorus of an adventure, a part of history, or something extremely lighthearted and funny. When we've discussed a book together, sometimes conversations open about our own struggles. We connect past historical moments with current ones. Overall, when our guard comes down, we tend to talk and share with each other more.

Friends recently encouraged me to make special reading times during the holidays. Thanksgiving and Christmas are especially wonderful times to put aside the usual routine and read some sweet holiday stories together. There is a whole host of great literature, poetry, and music that lifts the spirits during these special seasons. So, if we find we are not in a joyful place in our homeschooling, we can evaluate what our reading time looks like. Are we reading books together or have we taken them out for what we feel is more important academic or individual pursuits?

If we place good literature in a prominent place, even a few times per week, we might find a little lift in our wings.

Beyond read alouds, other beautiful materials to add to our school week are found in poetry, hymns, creeds, Bible verses, and artist studies. We must be reminded that these materials are inspiring and moving and are so lovely for us and our children. We can find helpful curriculum online to guide us. However, we do not have to over complicate these pleasant works. We can choose a book of poetry and read it together once a week. Maybe our children can memorize one. We can pick a favorite hymn or praise song and sing it at the start of our school day or at dinner time. Creeds and Bible verse memory are meaningful because children are repeating truths of what we believe.

How wonderful to lift our voice with the sounds of God's promises. These children will be going out into a world that will proclaim the exact opposite. Not only memorize these pieces but discuss them and think about them deeply. There are many wonderful and simple ways to place some delightful additions into our home and it will be well worth it! There are wonderful helps available. I've listed some of these in "Resources for Spring" at the end of this section.

CHAPTER 11
Fairest Lord Jesus

*"The longer we live, and the more we know,
the more we shall be made aware of how little we do
know, and how vast this Christ is."*[48]

~ T. Austin-Sparks ~

The loveliest of all there ever was and ever will be is Jesus Himself. "Hear O Israel: The LORD our God, the LORD is one. You shall love the LORD your God with all your heart and with all your souls and with all your might. And these words that I command you today shall be on your heart. You shall teach them diligently to your children, and you shall talk of them when you sit in your house, and when you walk by the way, and when you lie down, and when you rise. You shall bind them as a sign on your hand and they shall be as frontlets between your eyes. You shall write them on the doorposts of your house and on your gates" (Deuteronomy 6:4-9 ESV).

Of all the things you will want your child to know, it is the good news of Jesus Christ. How you start the day, how you carry out your day, how you handle conflict, how you teach life lessons, in what you promote the most, the greatest goal for your child is to know and love Jesus.

This concept is quite beautiful because it requires no striving, no perfection. But it does require a diligence and a choice to put Christ first every day. One of the worst things we can do to our children is push a legalistic faith upon them. It is easy to do this when we are fearful that our children might turn away from the Lord. We must clearly help our children understand that nothing in life matters more than Christ and their relationship with Him. Our vulnerability and our honest seeking of Him each day will be our best testimony. We don't do this by constant lecturing or drilling questions of faith. We don't do this by taking non-essentials and making them the pinnacle of a faithful life.

> *We are one of the first witnesses of Christ to our children. Our personal testimony plays out every day. This is where the rubber meets the road.*

As one of my favorite Bible teachers, Hank Hanegraff, says, "We should not make the mistake of making the Bible shout where it is silent or be silent where it shouts."[49] Don't mix preferences with Biblical truths. We let God's Word speak for itself. And when we don't understand, we turn to pastors and teachers who know more than we do.

Our prayer for our children is that they will not create a false God but worship the true God of the Bible. We pray for our children and let God do what only He can do in their hearts. Our children must know that the Lord deserves the utmost of their attention and affection. He is deserving of all praise. He is the first love. They must know He enjoys communing with them and their worth is in Him. "So now we can rejoice in our wonderful new relationship with God because our Lord Jesus Christ has made us friends of God" (Romans 5:11). He wants to guide them, and they need to be taught they are dependent upon Him, every day. And when they truly know how loved they are, they will be able to use whatever other knowledge they have to serve Him. "If I speak in the tongues of men or of angels, but do not have love, I am only a resounding gong or a clanging cymbal. If I have the gift of prophecy and can fathom all mysteries and all knowledge, and if I have a faith that can move mountains, but do not have love, I am nothing. If I give all I possess to the poor and give over my body to hardship that I may boast, but do not have love, I gain nothing" (I Corinthians 13:1-3 NIV).

Train Your Child

Knowing Him, there is nothing lovelier in this whole world. As early as possible, we can begin training our children towards personal Bible reading, spiritual studies, prayer, and service, as these are disciplines that can help them to develop their personal dependency on Christ. We can have open communication with them and help them find answers to some of their tough questions. Please don't allow other subject matters to wash out the time they need to commune with their God. There is absolutely nothing else that will fill their lives with joy, peace, and beauty besides Him.

Do you know the old song "*Spring Up, Oh Well?*" Life, and strength for our bones comes from the river flowing from the Spirit of God, "I've got a river of life flowing out of me…spring up, o well, and give to me that life abundantly."

> May the season of spring be for us more than
> beautiful flowers and green grass.
> May spring be like a well or a fountain in our homes bringing
> overflowing, abundant life, flowing out from our relationship
> with Christ Himself and all the lovely living He offers.

SPRING

M.D., age 12

CHAPTER 12

Living Stories

Do you have any children with special learning or behavioral needs? If so, what has helped the most?

I was surprised to find there was an even split between families who said they had children with specific learning, attention, or emotional needs (10) and those who did not (11). As the mothers shared these challenges, the learning differences collapsed into three categories. There were children with dyslexia (4), children with Attention Deficit Hyperactivity Disorder (ADHD), Obsessive Compulsive Disorder (OCD) or both (3), and even though I did not specifically ask about emotional concerns, a third group had children struggling with anxiety and/or depression (3).

For families with children who had dyslexia, the moms found helpful solutions. Even though traditional schoolwork was more challenging for these learners, they focused on non-traditional methods of learning. The timeline of what age they could expect their children to perform academic pursuits such as reading or writing needed to be delayed. Often, these children were great at athletics, mechanical or artistic skills. Finding time for them to explore and put effort towards areas where they have both an affinity and confidence is extremely important.

SPRING

The key to teaching these children well is patience and letting God's timing unfold. These children may not grasp concepts the first time or even the fifteenth time. Let go of comparing these children to siblings or other children their age and trust God's greater plan which is of paramount importance! Although there are special curriculum and help for dyslexics, moms found that giving them more time with great encouragement and hope was the best plan.

Interestingly, it is the same for moms with children who are diagnosed with ADHD or OCD. The beauty of homeschooling is that these children can learn at their own pace and environment. These children did not have to be tied down to a desk or a particular curriculum. Moms learned to step back and reevaluate their expectations so the day was positive. This may include ending formal instruction by noon, using timers for shortened lessons when attentions were waning. These faithful women trusted in the sovereignty of God and loved and accepted their children within their strengths and limitations. Mom's had to keep an awareness of when there were particularly difficult days and allow for last minute alterations.

Some families used medication for a short period of time, but most stopped because they found it was not helpful or necessary. Some stated they were simply no longer comfortable with their children taking medication. As for moms with children struggling with anxiety and depression, they found home education reduced the stress on their children and allowed them to work through emotional difficulties. There was more time in the day to fit in professional help if needed. Moms were able to help their children manage eating habits and the daily schedule. Working with these children on a balanced life was important and easier to do at home.

For all these families, patience, endurance, and trust were key factors in their peace. Most of these moms felt some guilt at different points in their journey. They felt guilty about, and sometimes blamed themselves, for the problems their children experienced. They felt guilty about losing patience with their children.

Although professionals had been helpful, they didn't have all the answers. At times, the challenge was accepting there were no answers, except to pray and trust. These moms felt deep wounds and pain which caused them to feel a deep need to cling to Christ.

These mothers have been given a special path. I can't help but believe God has blessed these moms, like beauty for ashes, with a deeper appreciation for living one day at a time and trusting in Christ alone for their children's future. It is a daily journey.

What is your philosophy on technology for education and leisure? How much technology do you allow?

Not one mom said technology was "easy" and "not an issue." Although we may not manage technology the same way, we are all working toward using technology in healthy ways. Technology includes TV, computer games, smartphones, and movies.

Three moms specifically stated that managing technology seemed like a constant battle. Other moms used descriptive words like "highly addictive" and "disconnects" and "robber of time." Many felt we need to be watchful of the amount of technology in our children's lives. Five moms stated we also need to be careful about over-controlling, staying in tune with our children, and training them to listen to the Holy Spirit so they can judge for themselves when technology is not appropriate.

Needless to say, the way we think about and manage technology is not always easy or clear. Most families have a specific time limit on technology use in the home. From the group I interviewed, most families have a limit of ½ hour to 1 hour of technology a day that is not school related during the school week and more lenient rules on weekends. Some families have absolutely no technology during the week and give some time on weekends, or they have a family movie time. A couple of families allowed up to 2 hours per day of leisure time using electronics. All these amounts are far less than the national average.

It was mentioned by more than one mom that they hate videogames, but they have found limiting the time is a good balance. Parents who had older children kept them from social media for as long as possible. Those with grown children mentioned they feel their children are on technology more than they would prefer. Finding a way to make technology family time, whether it be a movie or a favorite show or playing a videogame together, opened the door for connection versus isolation.

Also, electronic leisure happened at the end of the day after all other schoolwork and chores were completed. Children may do some of their schoolwork on computers, but these parents stated that using computers for all education was not a good idea and it disconnected the student from the family atmosphere.

How do you think your relationship with your kids would be different if you did not homeschool?

The first response was, "I would not know them" (9). When unpacked a bit more by other moms (4), they agreed there would be less time for conversation and closeness. Moms felt they would be more of a chauffeur and manager and less of a teacher and confidant. Relationship was built together at home over years and when the child is older, he or she has lived life so closely to his or her siblings and parents, it is no great leap to lean on them when life gets hard and questions get harder. Two mothers pointed out that public school would have caused a conflict due to competing authorities in their children's lives and differing worldviews leading to a disrespect for parental authority.

I loved the way one mom put it. "Homeschool boys still love their moms." Two other mothers brought up the thought that if they had not homeschooled, they would not have truly understood their child's learning styles and they would have unrealistic expectations. Because of homeschooling, they found the hidden talents inside their children. Beautiful!

What books have inspired you?

Books are such a central part of schooling. I asked the moms to list what they would place on their list of most inspiring, encouraging or enjoyable books. What were some of these mom's favorites? What were the first ones to come to mind? I have listed their favorites below under various headings. I have not read every book mentioned in this list.

It is possible that some of these books do not align with your theology or philosophy, so be thoughtful and prayerful as you read this list or use it for your own purposes. It goes without saying that Christian mothers rely on the Bible as their foundational book. I do not mention curriculum in this section, though some women did tell me about their favorite materials. Those will be listed in the "Fall" section of the book.

One final note. These moms would have probably mentioned more books had they been able to take me to their home libraries and be reminded of some of the great books they've read over the years. This is probably just the tip of the iceberg.

Homeschooling Books

The number one most mentioned book was Sarah Mackenzie's, *Teaching from Rest*. It is a must for all homeschooling families, in my opinion. Second to this was Susan Schaefer Macaulay's book on education from a Charlotte Mason perspective, *For the Children's Sake*.

Almost a year after completing these interviews, I read *For the Children's Sake,* and I share these women's responses as they said, "When I was stressed about how or if I could do this homeschooling journey, I read this book and felt a peace and freedom wash over me." This book taught them about this different educational philosophy and how God created children and the learning process. The ideas were unique in that learning takes place in a particular atmosphere.

For the Children's Sake, and many books like it, stem from the teachings of Charlotte Mason. Her six volumes were also listed as inspirational in changing many moms' philosophies regarding education. Other books the moms found to be helpful included various books by homeschooling mom, author and conference speaker, Sally Clarkson including *Mission of Motherhood* and *Mom Walk*. For those with children who struggle with differences, her book *Different* will be touching. Other books included *Better Late than Early* by Raymond and Dorothy Moore, and *The Well-Trained Mind: A Guide to Classical Education at Home* by Susan Wise Bauer and Jessie Wise.

Fiction/Children's Literature

The most popular children's fiction book was *Understood Betsy* by Dorothy Canfield Fisher. It is one of my favorites. It has a particularly timely message regarding our culture of helicopter parenting. Other books mentioned were C.S. Lewis' *Chronicles of Narnia* series, *The Wingfeather Saga* by Andrew

Peterson, *The Little House* book series by Laura Ingalls Wilder, and *The Secret Garden* by Frances Hodgson Burnett.

Non-Fiction

Non-fiction books included: *One Thousand Gifts* by Ann Voskamp, *Boundaries* by Henry Cloud and John Townsend, *Crazymakers* by Paul Meier and Robert Wise, *The Hiding Place* by Corrie Ten Boom, *Bringing up Girls* and *Bringing up Boys* by James Dobson, *Kisses from Katie* by Katie Davis Majors, *Shepherding a Child's Heart* by Ted Tripp, *Man's Search for Meaning* by Victor Frankl, *Mere Christianity* by C.S. Lewis, *That's Why They Call Him the Savior* by Max Lucado, *Born to Fly* by Tom Black, *Parenting* by Paul David Tripp, and *Grace Based Parenting: Set Your Family Free* by Tim Kimmel, and and *Stepping Heavenward*, following a young Christian woman's journey through her personal journal in the 19th century, by Elizabeth Prentiss.

When your children leave home what is the one thing you want for them?

It's easy to get bogged down in the routine and the amount of materials or topics we need to cover when discussing homeschooling. As mom's, it's common to worry about our children's future academic successes. But when I asked these women what they want for their children before they leave home, the answers were all about Jesus.

These moms wanted their children to have "a solid, strong walk and relationship with the Lord" (8), "to walk in an honest, happy Christian life with community and their own spouse and children" (3), and "to function as an adult, contribute to society, take care of their family, and live with character" (4). The main idea was not how much money these children would

SPRING

make or how successful they would be in the eyes of the world, but that they wanted their children to love the Lord and others and to be able to take care of themselves and their families. Their hope was that their children would grow up to be kind and care about other people.

As I write this, my mind goes to the two commandments given us by Jesus. "You must love the Lord your God with all your heart, all your soul, and all your mind...a second is equally important: love your neighbor as yourself" (Matthew 22:36-40). It is good to pause and consider; what should our daily homeschooling look like and how should we focus our time to obey these two great commandments? Not that I am suggesting a legalistic over-spiritualization of our routine. We are not to study the Bible alone. To the contrary, we want to study a wealth of topics. But, if our most precious long-term goal for our children is their relationship with the Lord, and secondarily their role in their future family, then it should show in how we teach and what we teach.

~ PONDERING SPRING ~
Consideration for deeper reflection

Before answering these questions,
please take time to pray so you can thoughtfully walk through this process.

<u>Attention:</u>

1. On an average day, what are you most focused on?

   Is your focus good or does it need to be altered? If it needs to be altered, how can you implement a change in focus?

2. How is your child's attention?

   If you find it takes your children a long time to finish their schoolwork, there are some things you can do. Charlotte Mason discusses the Habit of Attention in Vol 1 of her writings. Short lessons with more variety will help. As their attention improves, lesson times can be lengthened. Keep in mind that some children struggle with attention difficulties more than others. It is worthwhile to step back and do less with greater excellence.

3. What changes can you make to help your child improve his/her attention?

<u>Nature:</u>

1. Do you see value in spending time in nature?

2. How could you add more nature into your week? What might that look like?

3. What barriers do you see to spending time in nature? How can you add nature study given your current schedule?

4. Could you ask another family to join you in nature?

<u>Technology:</u>

1. What devices do you own? What platforms do you use daily?

2. How much time do you spend on your personal device and/or television? How much time do your children spend on their personal devices and/or television?

3. Would you like to reduce devices and/or spend less time on various platforms? If so, please think through the following statements:

    a. Decide if it's more important to reduce time spent on your devices or to remove certain devices/platforms altogether. You will want to set up a plan for yourself as well as for each of your children. Do you just want to reduce your screen time? Do you want to remove social media or videogames?

    b. List below how much time you will allow for screen time:

    c. List what platforms you would like to continue using and list what platforms you would like your child to continue using:

    d. List what platforms you would like to stop using and what platforms you would like your child to stop using:

    e. Decide on a plan for how you will implement these changes:

4. As you reduce technology, what are some of the activities you would like to add back into your daily life:

Books:

1. List three books you would like your family to read together this year:

   Homeschooling author Sarah Mackenzie's website, www.readaloudrevival.com, is a great source to help you get started.

RESOURCES FOR SPRING

Nature Journaling:
The Laws Guide to Nature Drawing and Journaling by John Muir Laws
Pocket Full of Pinecones by Karen Andreola
The Naturalist's Notebook by Nathaniel T. Wheelwright and Bernd Heinrich
Keeping a Nature Journal by Clare Walker Leslie and Charles E. Roth
Nature Journal: A Kid's Nature Journal by Alice M. Cantrell
*Please keep in mind these are extra resources which may enhance your nature journaling experience. A child only needs a small book of plain white paper, pencils, and paints to observe and capture nature.

Nature Handbook:
The Handbook of Nature Study by Anna Botsford Comstock

Nature Authors:
Jim Arnosky, Gail Gibbons, Arabella Buckley, Jean Craighead George, Jean Henri Fabre, Robert M. McClung, Thornton Burgess, Wilfred Bronson, and Millicent Selsam.
*These are simply a few suggestions. For a full list of authors who write living books about nature, for a variety of ages, visit Sabbath Mood Science: www. sabbathmoodhomeschool.com

Read alouds:
The Read-Aloud Family: Making Meaningful Connections with your Kids by Sarah Mackenzie
The Read-Aloud Handbook by Jim Trelease
Honey for a Child's Heart by Gladys Hunt
*I also like the Sonlight curriculum's readers and read aloud selections, www.sonlight.org

Poetry/Hymns:

Ambleside Online, www.amblesideonline.org

Simply Charlotte Mason, www.simplycharlottemason.org

Puberty and Sex Education:

The Story of Me (Book Series) by Stan and Brenna Jones

Launch into the Teen Years by Focus on the Family

Good Pictures, Bad Pictures by Kristen A. Jenson

Technology:

Digital Minimalism: Choosing a Focused Life in a Noisy World by Cal Newport

iGen: Why Today's Super-Connected Kids Are Growing Up Less Rebellious, More Tolerant, Less Happy--and Completely Unprepared for Adulthood--and What That Means for the Rest of Us by Jean M Twenge, Ph.D.

Content Education and Control: The NOVUS project: www.thenovusproject.org; Netnanny: netnanny.com; Circle: www.meetcircle.com; Protect Young Minds: www.protectyoungminds.org; Protect Young Eyes: www.protectyoungeyes.com

SECTION III

Summer

>To Lori: for laughter that permeates every atmosphere,
>for the root of compassion that graces your steps.

The older I get, the more I realize I can't hide in a bathing suit. There's only so much fabric that can cover bare skin from the scorching sun or from onlookers. When I embrace my age and my figure, I lay back in the lawn chair and enjoy. I close my eyes and the sound of children jumping in the water fades to the back of my ears. I can feel a slow, single drop of sweat that starts from the top of my forehead and travels down my face.

Suddenly, a thousand memories of summer flood my mind: sparklers, Pappy's lake, warm sand in my toes, performing skits with cousins, birthdays (too many to count). Yes, I'm growing older. I'm not so concerned with what others think about me. I don't need so much approval. God has made me freer than a firecracker on the Fourth of July, through this homeschooling journey. He has laid me as bare as I was on the day I was born. It has taken 40 years of stripping me down, accepting all that is sinful and embarrassing, and all that is beautiful. All these memories are wrapped in a warm beach towel as I celebrate this one life God has graciously given me.

SUMMER

A.D., age 11

CHAPTER 1

Who Am I?

Sheila: (in labor) "So many songs seem to belong to the woman I was before."
Sister Julianne, "And you still are all of those people.
Every woman alive is a sum of all she's felt, and lived, and done."[1]
~ Call the Midwives ~

I am the granddaughter of storytellers and lake-lovers, people whose mouths and flip-flops didn't slow down much. I'm the daughter of strong teachers, encouragers, prayer warriors, of chefs whose secret recipes I'll never know. I'm the sister of missionaries and actors, of soft-hearted humorous geniuses. I am the wife of an honest, genuinely good man. I am the beneficiary of a godly, generous bunch that I've never felt quite worthy to be included. I too, am from a broken home, a latch-key kid, people-pleaser, pretty, but not pretty enough, shameful, unintelligent, guilty, insecure, and impatient. I have had sorrow and pain that I never expected, and I have had freedom and joy that the younger me would never recognize. For the first time in my life, with open arms, I can accept all of it and thank God for it, and know that it all makes me who I am. Can you?

SUMMER

Who are you?

One of the things that will make you a great homeschooler is accepting yourself. You can only truly be genuine when you accept all that has happened in your life. It's not that you must scrape over the washboard and rehash every good and bad detail of your past. But you must graciously and honestly accept them. In this way, you can look at all of it with open eyes and be honest about who you are and about your past. You are not alone. You have faced unmet expectations in your life, of your loved ones, and of yourself. Though you may not realize it, you are not living on an island of isolated pain. It is true. Your story is your own and no one has experienced exactly your set of sufferings. However, others have dealt with abuse, shame, grief, and loneliness. And each one of us, no matter the journey, must embrace what was while also embracing that we are now free in Christ!

Our identity is in who God says we are.

A sure way to tell if you have dealt with your past and have accepted how your life has unfolded is if you can acknowledge those events, without an overwhelming hold on you. If your past freezes you in your tracks and your insides curl up with shame or anger or anxiety, it may be that you still need to work through these issues with a counselor or a trusted mentor.

I don't believe any of us can be great at homeschooling until we accept ourselves. If you're not firm in your identity in Christ, you will live trying to cover up the past and who you really are. It will be hard to stand on those two feet. You will easily get swept away by every wave of new curriculum or extra-biblical subjects that make the rounds within homeschooling circles. You will look at other homeschoolers, not as mentors, but as models of perfection that you must assimilate to and idolize. Homeschooling will not be what God intends it to be for your family. More importantly, you will never feel truly accepted for who you are.

If you feel this is you, prayerfully consider talking to someone who can help you let God's healing light shine in you. Don't put it off for another time or a calmer season, talk with someone and give God space to do some deep healing.

There are seasons of my life I can't get back because I chose to push situations down or chose to grin and bear it. I even acted as if everything was fine. There are some things in life that will heal with time, but not all things. I encourage you to take some time to think back on your life and lay out in words, through journaling, some of the difficulties you have gone through. This can be done as a prayer to the Lord. Seek acceptance of your circumstances and ask God to enable you to move into whatever season is next.

CHAPTER 2
Your Advisers

"Peter did not feel very brave; indeed, he felt he was going to be sick. But that made no difference to what he had to do. He rushed straight up to the monster and aimed a slash of his sword at its side."[2]
~ The Chronicles of Narnia: The Lion, the Witch, and the Wardrobe, C.S. Lewis ~

Being a parent takes great bravery. Often, we are called to do that which we feel completely ill-equipped to do. It is good to realize we are unable. We were created to walk forward in faith, trusting that God is able. We are to seek out and listen to His voice. Complete dependence on the Lord every day is paramount. Though, in our current time, it is easy for His voice to be silenced by many contradicting ideas. The voices we choose to listen to will either strengthen us or weaken us; push us towards the Lord's voice or distract us from it.

Voices often come in the package of opinions, and we have access to opinions like never before, coming at us from all directions. We have a library of parenting books, health care providers, educational systems, social media, and news outlets. All have various thoughts about what is most important in our parenting journey. We also have a community of people around us through our co-ops, activities, and Bible studies for which we share intimate details of our struggles. So, we are constantly surrounded by a host of possible opinions on a variety of subjects.

> *We want to be incredibly careful about who and where we seek advice.*

Some of these voices are wisdom. We should always work towards keeping a humble and teachable heart. However, some voices keep us in a place of condemnation and confusion, they make complicated what God has made simple. We end up heaping laws upon ourselves that God never intended. In his book, *Essentialism,* Greg McKeown states, "While much has been said and written about how hyperconnected we now are and how distracting this information overload can be, the larger issue is how our connectedness has increased the strength of social pressure. Today, technology has lowered the barrier for others to share their opinion about what we should be focusing on. It is not just information overload; it is opinion overload."[3]

How do we know which voices we should heed and which voices to remove from our inner dialogue? "Finally, brothers, whatever is true, whatever is honorable, whatever is just, whatever is pure, whatever is lovely, whatever is commendable, if there is any excellence, if there is anything worthy of praise, think about these things" (Philippians 4:8 ESV).

Our tendency is to think that, as long as we are not watching inappropriate material, (though that is a broad term), then what we're putting in our minds is okay, or at least neutral. But almost nothing we spend our time reading or watching is neutral. We live in a consumer driven culture, and the strongest voice we may need to fight is that of simple discontent.

After watching one of those home improvement shows, do you ever look around and wonder why your house never looks that clean or organized? Do you feel a sudden urge to buy something new? Have you ever been perusing blogs or homeschool magazines and felt like you needed to change all your curriculum, or that your children must be missing out? Ever dream of a life in the country? (Me too!)

Trading in Discontentment

For the first time, maybe ever in America, we have so much free time, so much money, and so much comfort, that we spend a lot of time over self-analyzing and literally seeking out discontent, "What is not quite right here and how should I fix it?" Discontent is sold to us in a package of TV programs, entertainment news, and even Hallmark movies. We must learn that, though some voices we listen to may not be immoral, they are unhealthy for our personal contentment. We are almost always being sold something: a political view, a beauty regimen, a better life. Be smart and evaluate everything you put your eyes and ears to and ask, "How do I feel when I'm finished watching, reading, spending time on this particular platform?" We may need to evaluate how we feel after spending time in conversation with certain friends. We heap upon ourselves wasted hours considering options and ideas that are completely unnecessary. We already have a full life that needs our best focus and attention.

Taking an account of the voices we listen to daily is an important step. If we don't make a conscious decision to pick good voices, there is an ample supply of bad ones that will take up the holes in our day. We focus on what God has put in our lap and we seek His perspective and guidance. We also seek wisdom from close friends and wise elders who've lived through these phases of life to give us an appropriate view.

So, what counts as a "good" voice? The Bible, of course, primarily. Then, those voices that uphold Biblical truths in music and podcasts, books and

SUMMER

sermons. But even choosing to read a good classic book versus spending time binge watching a show would be included in positive voices. The goal is putting our mind on information that has a maturing effect on our intellect as well as our spiritual and emotional health.

Where does the news fit into this scenario? You need to be aware of current events, but you don't need to watch the news all day. There is a lot of propaganda our there, so pray and seek wisdom in your news choices.

In addition, we might find we need to seek more silence. It's hard for the Lord to have a chance to speak when there is never a silent moment for contemplation. I was moved when I read how, when Martin Luther King, Jr. was a boy, he would, at times, turn away invitations to play with friends because he simply wanted time to daydream and think.[4]

Remember, we don't always need to be producing or learning new information. We don't need to know everything that's going on in the world. We may not need to listen to a sermon every day. Much goodness can come from moments of processing the information we've encountered on an average week. We move from information to information so quickly, when do we process it? Think deeply and pray about the opinions heard, then decide which ones to follow.

Gratitude Changes Things

Even without cultural sources, all we need is our own inner voice to destroy our peace. After I read Ann Voskamp's book, *One Thousand Gifts*, I put into practice changing my negative words into grateful ones to God. I had no idea how engrained it was to wake up with a bad attitude that carried into my day. Gratitude is the key to contentment.[5]

In the first scenario, I wake up and walk to the mirror and notice the increasing number of wrinkles under my eyes or scars on my face. Then, as I'm getting dressed, I might notice my expanding waistline or that I'm wearing two-day old shorts because, once again, I didn't get the laundry completed. Simply ten minutes after waking, I've torn down my looks, my eating and exercise habits, and my inability to take care of my household. As one can imagine, then faced with someone else in need, I handle it with great irritation.

The new practice is to wake up and thank the Lord for warm water to wash my face, for clothes to put on my back, for a husband and children! Suddenly, that tight grip on my attitude is set free. I stop hunting for comfort and start embracing my work. I can breathe and my heart is open, not closed in and self-centered. I'm okay that I don't look like that cute college girl anymore. You know why? She had to leave to make room for a kinder, wiser version of me.

Take time to think through a normal week. What voices are you listening to on a regular basis? Challenge yourself to praise God for good things from the moment you wake up, no matter how hard you want to focus on what is not perfect. Start with your own voice. Many things are hard, some unbearable. But dwelling on all that is negative as a habit can create a life that is unbearably unhappy for you and for those that live with you. As is often the case, the simplest answer is usually the right one. It sounds simple but start your day with a voice lifted in praise. Secondly, you cannot wait on the outside world to change to make you feel good about your life circumstances. Silence those negative voices and put everything between you and the Lord.

We want to lean into those honest and encouraging voices and lean less into distracting and debilitating ones.

SUMMER

You don't know which voices you're listening to? Start with taking note of what you listen to most. If you spend a lot of time getting advice from technological resources, are these godly or mostly cultural? If you're seeking your parenting, homeschooling and daily living guidance from the vast array of random information in podcasts, blogs, and the general consensus on Facebook, you might find it leaves you feeling more confused and anxious. You might need to step back from outside voices and open the Bible and devotionals, wonderful godly discipling voices and prayer.

If the first thing you do each morning is check your phone, work on putting that aside for a while. Read the Bible and pray first. Reduce your platforms to those that are most beneficial, whether it be social media, blogs, or podcasts. You may have to drop out of some groups on Facebook or stop subscribing to every homeschool group who extends an invitation. You may need to reduce how much you share with your larger group of friends. Why? When you share your story with a group of people, you will get a thousand different suggestions. When you need to talk about something difficult, think about a close friend or family member and have a face-to-face or phone conversation.

When I was young and struggling in my parenting, I thought if I could just talk out the issue long enough with enough people, I could find an answer. Sometimes we simply must accept that no person has an answer for us. We wait. There are times when we must stop talking and shopping for opinions because they only make the issue bigger.

We are told to seek Christ. Spend your energy seeking Him and eventually the answers will come, or a change will happen. Overall, you must decide it is okay to disagree with other people and for them to disagree with you. If all your friends are gluten free or only follow a certain curriculum or watch specific programming, it does not mean you have to do the same thing.

Hold yourself back from constantly researching online for an "answer" to all of your kids' quirks. Pray instead. God is big enough. Stand on the things you believe to be true. Listen to the Lord's voice. Be kind and stay true to Him and to yourself. You don't have to swing on the pendulum of everyone else's opinions. You will find you live in much greater peace when you quit worrying about what other people think about you and your kids. Spend more time asking God His opinion about your family.

In addition, you don't always need to share your opinion. Be selective about when and how you share your thoughts. When strange and rapid changes happen in our culture, spend time educating yourself so your focus is on becoming a wiser person. Your goal is to share good resources and what you've learned with the people you can influence, not to change the world's opinion by one random uneducated statement on social media. At times, there will be a call to stand for truth. Be discerning. Be thoughtful with your words.

CHAPTER 3
Your Need to Know

> *"We live with our hands clenched tight."*[5]
> ~ Ann Voskamp ~

The first couple of years of being home, there were moments when homeschooling gave me heart palpitations. Waves of anxiety washed over me as the pressure of my children's future would hang like a shadow, a dark finger pointing accusations at me. The accusations fell most of the time under the category of, "You are not doing enough."

That finger still returns now and again. I've learned to recognize it as worry and fear, and give it to the Lord quickly in prayer, instead of picking at it like an old wound until it bleeds again, leaving me frazzled. It was especially hard on days when, no matter how creative or prepared I was, nothing clicked. I would do my best to calm and self-talk myself off the ledge. But some days, it's just hard. I can feel an overwhelming sense that I'm not doing enough for my children's education and their future.

The truth is, if I feel a sense that others approve, I breathe a sigh of relief. But what if the opposite is true? What if many around me raise an eyebrow about what I'm doing or "how" I'm doing it, but it's exactly what my children need for the future God has planned?

SUMMER

It takes work to learn contentment. Not just contentment, but trust. I can be happy for the seemingly endless ways other people's children breeze through schooling, and still trust God has a plan with whatever mixed bag of joys and failures I, and my children, face each day. I renew my mind each day knowing I am doing the best I can before God, and I don't need anyone else's approval or praise. When it comes to homeschooling - endurance, hope, faith, and joy are the names to be spoken with honor and notoriety, not perfection.

Deep down, with much prayer and time, I have discovered most of our anxious feelings are about our future. Will this effort pay off? But what does "pay-off" look like or mean? Is it about getting into the right college, being gifted, getting a scholarship? We want our children to become healthy adults. But what if the "pay-off" is right now, right here, this moment? What if I could grasp, could soak myself in, be drenched in the understanding that the "pay-off" is the discussion at the end of a read aloud, the laughter as everyone clears the table, or the happy smiles of my children? The prayers, the friendships, basking in the light of God's creation together, and even the fights that teach us something and help us grow? Can we live like that instead? Can we live in gratitude instead of fear? I know the world says, if we live like that our head is in the clouds and our children will not be prepared. But what if living free from fear is exactly what will best prepare them for the future? When we listen to fear and the hard days come, that insecure voice says it was just as we suspected, and it was what everyone else whispered under bated breath. How did we possibly think we could do this well? How could we possibly be preparing our children for the real world?

God's Good Plan

The truth is, the Lord has a good plan, and our effort alone is not what brings it about. We seek God each day to know where our time and energies should be spent. We may want a "perfect homeschool day," and we get mad at everyone when it doesn't happen. But what was the Lord's plan for that day?

> *Some days will have suffering. Some days we need to choose right over comfort, patience over self, relationship over routine, discipline over laziness, trust over knowing. Let's be content with His teaching methods.*

As homeschooling mothers, we get this one moment. So, live each day and let it be. Let us stop wishing our moments away to a future that only has a new set of concerns. One day, we will miss this special time with our children at this particular age.

Sometimes I come into my homeschool mornings with my hands and my jaw clenched tight. I think if we hurry through, I can dash for the finish line and pat myself on the back that we got through all the material. I didn't even know it at first. It's just that I've been paying attention lately. It's not out of anger. It's out of the need to control and the need to know. It's my need to prove that I'm doing it right and that I can do this! But to who? I must accept that the day belongs to the Lord. I must open my hands, breathe deeply, and He will help me work through the ups and downs of teaching real children.

On the days when our mind begs to know everything is going to work out and be okay, we can trust in the One who knows it all, and we can lay it all

SUMMER

down. We can pick up our cross and take on His yoke, "Take my yoke upon you and learn from me, for I am gentle and humble in heart, and you will find rest for your souls" (Matthew 11:29 ESV).

That's all that's required. Keep coming to Him, keep praying for your children. Pray for the day, for the material, and rest and trust in the Great God who can do far more than anyone knows.

CHAPTER 4
Your Value

> *"..but what of the schoolboy who has little left after a year's work but his place in a class list?"*[6]
> ~ Charlotte Mason ~

In one of my first college psychology classes, the professor was a middle-aged man with a jolly smile, not unlike St. Nicholas. He was the first family counselor I encountered. He was a Christian and an inspirational teacher. The first week of class, he introduced us to a book by Max Lucado about these little wooden people called "The Wemmicks." Along with this, the message he repeated in class was, "We are called human beings, not human doings." I know he did not come up with the slogan, but it fits perfectly with the message of this book.

Our value comes simply because we exist, not in what we do. So, why DO we feel the need to do so much? Because maybe in our titles and in our busyness, we think we matter. Ah, the desire to be great! We live in a society that values life from a hierarchy. As pastor Skye Jethani states in his book, *With*, "Horrors like slavery, sex-trafficking, abortion, euthanasia, and genocide are only possible when people are seen as commodities – measured by usefulness and not by their inherent worth."[7]

SUMMER

If you have enough boxes checked off, if you're pretty, wealthy, smart or athletic, you are of value. When you lose your job or status or become an inconvenience, down the pecking board you go. It feels great to be at the top and lousy to be at the bottom. But what if you lived so close to Christ in your identity that your place on the list did not phase you?

We are not unlike these Wemmicks, who, all day long, are given (and give) yellow stars for talents or gray dots for embarrassments.

One day, the main character meets a wooden person to whom neither dots nor stars stick. How does she do this? Every day she meets with the Woodcarver and He tells her of her worth. She learns she has value because He made her and no one else's opinion counts.[8] It is okay to admit there are some areas where a child is not going to excel. It is okay to admit there are areas where we have failed as a parent and to admit we do not have the perfect family.

One of the problems I saw when my child was in public school was a push for all students to be great at every subject. This was happening at a very young age. This is what causes many parents so much anxiety. Sadly, it has caused some over-medicating. Children spend hours on homework, even very young children, just to "keep up." Because of the testing, there is no other way. No wonder parents and children burn out after years of this schedule. Very few can keep this pace. Add in the many activities we feel we must pursue. Where is there time to teach our children how to be "whole" people? So, "Johnny" at age 9, goes in early for tutoring, stays after school for tutoring, and does one hour of homework. Where does he go from here? I suppose the idea is that, targeted early enough, he will not always need this extra help. Maybe this would be fine if he were an academic being only.

"At the same time the custom of giving homework, at any rate, to children under 14, is greatly to be deprecated. The gain of a combination of home and school life is lost to the children; and a very full scheme of schoolwork may be carried through in the morning hours."[6] Sadly, many have decided, for many years now, that the most important possession for children is academic in nature with athletics a close second. (If you live in Texas like I do, the first two may be switched!)

Academics, of course, are immensely important, but when we treat children as academic beings only, are we truly preparing them for life? Is this all they need? "If a human being were a machine, education could do more for him than to set him in action in prescribed ways, and the work of the educator would be simply to adopt a good working system or set of systems. But the educator has to deal with a self-acting, self-developing being, and his business is to guide, and assist in, the production of the latent good in that being, the dissipation of the latent evil, the preparation of the child to take his place in the world at his best, with every capacity for good that is in him developed into a power."[6]

And what is this good power we are trying to strengthen and bring forth? Is it academic only? With the dawn of constant testing and homework at earlier ages, on top of extra-curricular activities, a 24-hour day filled with so much "school" leaves little time for a young mind to journey to a place of discovery or helping around the house. Teaching my child to be joyful as they do the dishes is probably just as important to their lives as learning a school subject. We must be ever so careful that our academic standards are not so high that we forget we are raising a person. God may have given us extremely bright children and we want to honor that. Yet, it is still only one aspect of who they are. The truth is, we have no idea what God has in store for them.

It's hard to say what God's idea of "success" will look like for our child. When I choose to treat my children as a commodity, they feel it and they sense my disappointment. I have told them they have value, but I have shown them otherwise in sideways glances and sighs when one more math problem is missed. We are to encourage them to do their best, we are to ask them to do the hard work, but we are never to attach their value as a human being to their skills! This is a hard but freeing task. We should stop seeing their entire future through bad handwriting or mis-read words. At the same time, we must not see a completely smooth future because academics come easily.

When I was in school, I was an average to below average student. I discovered very early that I was a slow learner and I decided if I could not be smart, then I would be special by being busy. What saved me in high school was that I was athletic and had some moderate talent in band. So I found places to fit in. That's the thing about most institutional schools. If we don't find our place to fit, like a peg on a board, it is hard to survive. The immense amount of time kids spend in the microculture of middle and high school, particularly, presses into them a message about who they are. These definitions may carry through the rest of their lives when, in reality, those seven years of life are only a very small portion of the entire picture.

How many of us feel like we're still trying to escape our high school shadow, while some may just wish they could go back. Why is this? Because our culture puts emphasis on the teenage years through music, television, movies, and social media. All these medias speak right into our kids about what they should wear, say, and watch in order to be accepted. Then, we pack all these insecure and vulnerable kids into a building to attempt to survive well and learn. The picture of the Wemmicks comes back to mind: the giving of dots and stars for looks, academics, and athletics.

The beauty of homeschooling is that we get to limit some of that influence so our children can take time to learn who they are based on what the Bible teaches. We should all be a bit careful to balance the reality of those thoughts that help us prepare our children for "the real world" with not owning the worlds standards and pathways. The point is, especially regarding academics, to guard against pre-set notions based on what our child's academics look like today as to what their future holds. But as the story unfolds, we learn we can't judge success by its cover, for potential for success is no promise of success" [9] We have been promised something else. We've been promised that "God causes everything to work together for the good of those who love God and are called according to His purpose for them" (Romans 8:28). We've been told God looks at the heart; "But the Lord said to Samuel, 'Don't judge him by his appearance or height, for I have rejected him. The Lord does not see things the way you see them. People judge by outward appearance, but the Lord looks at the heart'" (1 Samuel 16).

This does not mean we do not put effort and energy toward our children being excellent and diligent to do the work God has placed in front of them in a variety of subjects. But if their worth and identity is about academic, artistic, or athletic success, what happens when they must hold down that boring job. Where does a child place their worth when the last concert or final game has ended? Or what happens when the mom with the Ph.D. decides she wants to stay home with her kids. What will be the most important things they learn, and what will they never use again? How can we possibly know?

Let us be mindful to seek the Lord, to pace our expectations and our academic pursuits for our children, and to pursue "wholeness" in our homeschooling routine.

If we can let go of our need to make sure our children are "successful" in the world's eyes, we might find we can sit back and enjoy our relationship with them a bit more. We let God walk out the plan He prepared in advance for us to do, "For we are God's masterpiece. He has created us anew in Christ Jesus, so we can do the good things he planned for us long ago" Ephesians 2:10.

CHAPTER 5
Your Friendships

Homeschooling can be extremely lonely without good friends.

As you navigate your homeschooling life, you will be faced with many decisions regarding friendships. Often during your homeschooling years, friendships evolve from the groups you join or the church you attend. You may be lucky enough to have neighbors that homeschool as well. Deeper friendships may form when you discover people who share common philosophies, theology, and personality, or sense of humor as you. Some connections form because you have children of similar ages who strike up a close bond.

During our first year of homeschooling, it was important we didn't get burned out by joining too many groups. I needed time to figure out what homeschooling looked like for our family. We didn't have homeschooling friends for a long time. I prayed fervently for God to bring us the friendships we needed and, in time, the right activities. A year later, in natural and sometimes miraculous ways, the Lord brought wonderful friends into our lives. When we wait on the Lord, He will guide us to the right friendships.

We are not meant to join every group or every activity or even make friends with every homeschooling mom we meet. It may be that God is protecting

SUMMER

us from unhealthy environments and saving us to enjoy other ones handpicked for our family. There are times when it seems simpler to go it alone.

Maintaining friendships will cost something. Why? Because the more we let people in, the more we let them see our weak spots. Friendships bring great joy but also must be managed. These years will be much fuller if we have friends to share the journey. Reaping the benefits of friendships may mean we give our time and energy to others, not just to our family. This is how we participate in community.

I have witnessed that those who tend to make closer friends are those who volunteer or lead in some compacity within their chosen groups. Some people find themselves in a position where they attend many activities but only have acquaintants. This is because friendships take effort. We must invite people into our home and into our life to become friends. Real friendships are built on shared time, experiences, and many conversations.

Cultivating Friendships

When you first begin seeking out homeschool friendships, be genuine about who you are, and genuinely care about the people you meet. As much as you want to share what's going on in your life, try to be a good listener and be present with the person speaking. Be prayerful before walking into any playgroup or parent meeting. In this way, your heart and mind are set on the Lord, and you can work on seeing yourself and others in the proper light. Keep in mind that everyone is in a different season of homeschooling.

Homeschooling families are so adaptable that even if your kids are not the exact same age, most are still willing to get together for a visit. It is also good to find friends with some children of similar ages as your own. When your children meet other homeschooling friends they click with, make time for those friendships. Close homeschooling friendships are not a dime a dozen. As best you can, treat those friendships as a priority, not like they are easily replaceable. An extra-curricular activity is not more important than a dear friendship.

Although most homeschooling families are your average folks, some may have <u>extreme</u> views about a variety of issues. If you find yourself amongst that type of group and you feel uncomfortable, you might decide this is not the group for you! These are simply things to be aware of as you seek healthy and close friendships. You may find it's easier to become close with those who share your educational philosophy. I am not saying you should only be friends with people who share the same educational views. However, having friends that share similar books and ideas about routines can be a huge support. God knows where you belong, and everyone belongs somewhere. Pray, and God can bring you lifelong friends.

> *Lasting friendships are cultivated, they won't just happen accidentally.*

There is a special bond between families who share in this homeschooling journey. Many times, as I struggled, I would discuss my problems with a homeschooling friend who would offer sage advice. On other days, I would share that same advice back to her. It is a circle of encouragement as we "spur one another on toward love and good deeds" (Hebrews 10:24 NIV). So, ask the Lord for these special friendships. Ask that He might show you what it means to be a good friend.

Be a cheerleader for your friends and their kids. Our natural inclination is to size people up and see how we compare. If you stay in this mindset, it does two things. One, you constantly feel "less than" others. Two, you want to be better than others, so you become hypercritical of others and their kids. The outshoot of this is expecting perfection of yourself and your

SUMMER

kids, especially in behavior or performance. It can become a dangerous standard and example for your kids about what matters. How do you change this thinking for which you can so easily become ensnared? Find out what your friend's children are interested in and how they are doing. You have a responsibility to encourage them in their walk with the Lord. Every conversation is important, and every child is important. If you learn to cheer for someone else's child, you teach your children one of the greatest lessons in humility and Christian brotherhood. How can you possibly teach your children empathy if you teach them that they or their performance is all that matters? If you teach them it's not important to support a friend by showing up to a concert, or sports game, or simply being interested in how someone else is doing, what kind of adults will you raise?

I hope you will give me some license here. What good is it to raise a brilliant jerk? If empathy is a key goal, you must show it by how you care for your friends and their children. This is simply done by having conversations that don't revolve around you. If you learn to care for and support other people's children, they stop looking like competition, and they start looking like family. Indeed, some of the things that once annoyed you about these kids becomes endearing. For example, some of your friend's kids will be wild and a little careless. Some kids will be quiet, and you may have a hard time getting them to say anything. Some won't shake hands (maybe touch is difficult for them). Others will speak their mind and be quite bold. Some of them will be so mature and thoughtful they can teach us quite a bit. The point is, they are young. Give them opportunity to mature by being a person who cares for them.

In the same way, you need to have friends who support you and your kids. If you find yourself around people that don't "get" your kids or are not willing to pray for you, cry with you, or talk you through things, these are not real friends. They don't have to agree with you on everything, but if they downplay your struggles and don't have patience with your kids, or if they give you simple steps to solve your problems, are these the people to whom you completely open your heart? Use wisdom in how much you share with these friends. You might find some are the ones you share about homeschooling curriculum while others may be the ones you share about your fears or struggles.

All friends have great value in their own way, as do you. You will probably find a few you can discuss everything with, and those friends are a great treasure. But always remember, no friend can ever fill the place of Christ.

Choose Your Words

Be careful how you speak about your friends and acquaintances. Be thoughtful that your general discussions do not turn into gossip. If gossip hasn't bitten you in your life yet, hold on, it will.

In my senior year of high school, a friend caught me speaking ill about her on the phone. The girl and I had served on a team together. The situation was so bad we were both called into the coach's office to discuss what happened. I was embarrassed and asked for forgiveness. Over the course of the year, it was like water under the bridge. But we were never the same. Not only that, but I don't think my coaches ever felt the same about me. I was young and immature, but I was a Christian and I knew better. It was a bad habit. On some days, just trying to crack a joke, or out of frustration or a desire to feel better about myself, I chose to talk about people.

The truth was, this high school friend was much more mature than me, and she did not mind standing out among the crowd. I was known for being a strong Christian, but I would never rock the boat of the popular crowd. In the end, she did me a huge favor and so did God. Every time I consider

SUMMER

saying something about someone else, I think of her and what it did to our friendship.

May you be someone who lives above the noise of gossip, comparisons, and judgment: a peacemaker and a true friend. "Those who consider themselves religious and yet do not keep a tight rein on their tongues deceive themselves, and their religion is worthless" (James 1:26 NIV). Overall, handle your friends with care. Handle your friends with forgiveness. No one is perfect. Appreciate rather than deprecate the rainbow of personalities. Before you open your mouth, think to yourself, "Is this necessary to say or share?"

A friend shared a quote from Elisabeth Elliot, wife of martyr Jim Elliot, "Never pass up an opportunity to keep your mouth shut."[10] Speak of your friends and their kids carefully or say nothing at all. Not only will it be the right thing, but you will grow less critical and more loving in your dealings. You model this to your kids. When you speak critically of others, do not be surprised when your kids do the same thing. When you speak with grace, you realize you have enough on your own plate, purity will cleanse your heart, and you will love more.

Always remember, friendships – like the seasons of the wildflower – are constantly changing.

Some friendships are budding with the excitement of new color peeking out. Some are in full bloom. Others are closing. But as the flower dies, new seeds take flight and new life and friendships are created. No matter how the friendship changes, the beauty is, as believers, we are one in Christ forever.

Hold your friends close and gently. You never know when a west wind will blow unexpectedly and carry them to a new field. Let go of petty differences, and don't hold your friends to standards that are beyond human abilities. Be gracious.

"Is it true? Is it necessary? Is it kind?"[11]
~ Mary Ann Pietzker, ~

Oh! stay, dear child, one moment stay,
Before a word you speak,
That can do harm in any way
To the poor, or to the weak;
And never say of any one
What you'd not have said of you,
Ere you ask yourself the question,
"Is the accusation true?"
And if 'tis true, for I suppose
You would not tell a lie;
Before the failings you expose
Of friend or enemy:
Yet even then be careful, very;
Pause, and your words well weigh,
And ask if it be necessary,
What you're about to say.
And should it necessary be,
At least you deem it so,
Yet speak not unadvisedly
Of friend or even foe,
Till in your secret soul you seek
For some excuse to find;
And ere the thoughtless word you speak,
Ask yourself, "Is it kind?"
When you have ask'd these questions three—
True, — Necessary, — Kind, —
Ask'd them in all sincerity,
I think that you will find,

SUMMER

> It is no hardship to obey
> The command of our Blessed Lord, —
> No ill of any man to say;
> No not a single word.

Value

A final thought on friendship; teach your children to value their friendships. It is a normal part of life that your children's friendships will grow and change. The best friends at 8 may grow apart at 14. Teach your children they have inherent value no matter how another person treats them. It hurts when a once close relationship can no longer be so. These are some of the first lessons in boundaries.

Remind them that not everyone needs to be their best friend, but they should not throw people out like a worn shoe, nor should they be thrown out. These are people, after all. Help your children be honest and forgiving with their friends. Help them understand what a true friend looks like so they will not be controlled or manipulated by others. Walk them through ways they may not be acting as a good friend. They will learn lessons that will last them through many adult relationships.

CHAPTER 6
Your Boundaries

Setting and keeping boundaries is one of the most important aspects of our relationship with our children.

It is the quiet dusk of summer, and a warm breeze gives ease from the depleting heat of the day. Ruby-throat hummingbirds zoom about, dipping in and out of the deep-red glass feeder. Juvenile mockingbirds hop on the humid grass, still needing their mother's help. They flit quickly after her as she sets to flight. Sweet-faced scissor-tails perch near the cedar trees. All is quiet and there are no signs of the busyness of wasps swarming fennel and bees collecting pollen in sticky pouches, as during midday. When we step back and observe, we notice each piece of nature seems to follow an unspoken rule of place and time. There are understood boundaries in all of nature. In this way, we sense order.

"Who is this that darkens counsel by words without knowledge? Where were you when I laid the foundation of the earth? Have you commanded the morning since your days began? Can you bind the chains of Pleiades or loose the cords of Orion? Shall a fault finder contend with the Almighty?" (Job 38-40)

SUMMER

How deeply God knows and respects the difference between Himself and His creatures. No matter how deeply He loves us, the boundary of who He is and who we are is never blurred.

Setting similar boundaries with others is an important part of maintaining a peaceful life. But more than that, if we have unhealthy bonds in our life, we must re-set them in order to live in freedom and security. *Boundaries,* by Henry Cloud and John Townsend helps us learn to set healthy boundaries with others, which keeps us functioning as the individual God designed us to be.

"Misinformation about the Bible's answers to these issues has led to much wrong teaching about boundaries. Not only that, but many clinical psychological symptoms, such as depression, anxiety disorders, eating disorders, addictions, impulsive disorders, guilt problems, shame issues, panic disorders, and marital and relational struggles, find their root in conflicts with boundaries."[12]

The basic ideas surrounding boundaries is understanding who we are and what our responsibilities are versus others in our life. When our boundaries are crossed into other people's boundaries, we take on too much and give others influence, power, or effect on areas that are ours alone. We also step over other people's boundaries and try to do the work that is their responsibility.

We can see how, as homeschool moms, this could be an easy line to cross. Learning to set boundaries can be a special tool in keeping clear what our role is as wife, mother, friend, volunteer, and home educator. We need family members and friends to support and encourage us during this journey. But let's be clear, it is our journey, and no one can do it for us. God will be our strength; we are not alone.

We cannot look to others to be what only God is supposed to be in our life. If we look for constant validation or wait for constant guidance from others, we will never get our feet grounded in our role. In other words, if God has called us to this position, we need to be strong and courageous and take hold of it. "Have I not commanded you? Be strong and courageous. Do not be frightened, and do not be dismayed, for the LORD your God is with you wherever you go" (Joshua 1:9 ESV).

Setting boundaries also protects our homeschool routine.

Often our biggest ally will be learning to use the word "no" more frequently. We want to say "no" often, so we can say "yes" to the true things God is calling for our time and efforts. Every time we are invited to something or asked for something, we can wait before giving an answer. We should think about what that "yes" will cost us in time and energy. We can pray about whether it is something we can do well.

Remember, we are not in control of other people and we cannot walk on eggshells so every person in our life is pleased. We are not in charge of another person's happiness. We should be thoughtful and honest in our dealings with all people. But we cannot control how others react.

In addition, setting and keeping boundaries is one of the most important aspects of our relationship with our children. How do we do this? We must see our children as individuals, not as extensions of ourselves. Respect that you have separate identities. Our role as a mother will need to change over time.

Boundaries revolve around many daily areas of life, including acceptable attitudes, obedience, time, responsibilities, freedoms, personal space, and respect. As children age, independence may change, but there will always be boundaries. Problems arise when we are not willing to accept how the boundaries need to change, or if we never had boundaries to begin with.

Codependency

In a recent YouTube video, Dr. Henry Cloud states simply that codependency is when we allow someone else's needs to take over our lives. He shares that the origins of the word "codependency" began when therapists saw that, after a chemically dependent patient stepped back into their homelife after successful treatment, they quickly picked up old habits. Therapists found this was partly due to other people in their lives enabling the patient to continue in these unhealthy behaviors.[13]

In the case of the homeschooling mother, codependency may look like an excessive reliance on our children for approval or a sense of identity. Another helpful definition is when we confuse caretaking and sacrifice with love and loyalty. Our worth is wrapped up in always needing our children to need us. So how does this affect our children? We enable their addiction, poor mental health, immaturity, irresponsibility, or under-achievement.[14]

These are areas of life the growing child can manage on their own, but we do not want to let go because we fear no longer being needed. We also believe if we can keep our hand in the situation, our children will make the right choices, they will be kept safe. We set forth good habits, we share the goodness of God with them in scripture and in nature, we work toward diligence to prepare them for life. But at some point, whether they make the right choices or not, the responsibility is no longer ours. "Though the emancipation of the children is gradual, they are acquiring day by day more of the art and science of self-government, yet there comes a day when the parents' right to rule is over; there is nothing left for them but to abdicate gracefully, and leave their grown-up sons and daughters free agents, even though these still live at home; and although, in the eyes of their parents, they are not fit to be trusted with the ordering of themselves; if they fail in such self-ordering, whether as regards time, occupations, money, friends, most likely their parents are to blame for not having introduced them by degrees to the full liberty which is their right as men and women. Anyway, it is too late now to keep them in training; fit or unfit, they must hold the rudder for themselves."[15]

We are reminded that we have a finite time in which to raise our children and prepare them for adulthood. We don't want to hold to a legalistic view that, as long as we don't make any missteps in our parenting, our children will live blissful lives. That would mean we are perfect parents, and there is no such thing. It would also mean we have perfect kids, and there is no such thing. Pain comes, and we are all sinful human beings. But have we done all that we could, all that God asked of us, to raise children who have the possibility of becoming resilient and capable adults? Will we set up healthy boundaries in their childhood, so they understand all choices have consequences? We pray for opportunities for growth along the way. But when it is time, we let go, because they need to understand we will not always be there to save them or to fix situations they find themselves in; this is adulthood. But they will always have our prayers and love. In the end, we should see boundaries as freeing and God ordained for a healthy relationship with our children.

Other boundary issues may be rooted in our past. Without being aware, our motivation in our parenting can be to resolve whatever went wrong in our own childhood. We think if we give them all our attention it makes up for the parent who gave us none. Then we wonder how it is we have raised a selfish child. We struggled in school, be it academically or athletically, we then push our children in ways to achieve where God may not have designed. Our children then, feel our love is tied to performance. When we look back on our choices as a young adult, we feel shame. We think if we press enough spirituality upon our child, they will make better choices. But we end up with an environment of legalism.

Parenting is truly an art, not a science.

We must wake up each morning and ask the Lord for perspective in setting the right boundaries with our children. We all struggle at different times with setting proper boundaries. If the topic of boundaries is confusing or if you struggle to set boundaries with your children, please read or view Cloud and Townsend's many books and videos regarding boundaries.

Marriage Protection

We especially want to be thoughtful toward our spouse. We need to set boundaries with our children, so they don't get *all* of us.

If you are married, your husband is your partner in this homeschooling journey. It is important to have your husband's support as you homeschool your children. There will be days when he is the only adult in whom you hold a conversation. He is the only one who truly understands you and your children. In addition, your husband has knowledge and skills to share with your children, and it is important that he be involved in the learning atmosphere. Some dads teach entire subjects or step in for mom when she has other duties.

Make sure your husband knows you appreciate and need his support and you value his ideas. Your kids need to see him! The home is not a woman's place only, but it is about the family. It's easy to feel you must do it all, but you rob from your husband's role when you don't trust him with some of the schooling decisions. He should not have to feel like an end to your means or simply a paycheck!

Do not compare your husband to others. Some husbands can teach math or economics and others teach the kids how to fish or change the oil. Encourage your husband to teach topics that bring him joy and grow his relationship with the children.

At the same time, it's important to remember that you were a wife before you became a mom. Take care that teaching your children does not obsess your attention. Make time for you and your husband to have a relationship that is not solely focused on the children or your homeschool life. This takes some planning. But it is important to the health of your marriage. What you show your children with a strong marriage will far outweigh what you teach them through a homeschool curriculum.

CHAPTER 7
Your Helicopter

"But the fussy parent, the anxious parent, the parent who explains overmuch, who commands overmuch, who excuses overmuch, who restrains overmuch, who interferes overmuch, even the parent who is with the children overmuch, does away with dignity and simplicity of that relationship which, like all the best and most delicate things in life, suffer by being asserted or defended."[15]
~ Charlotte Mason ~

Our family is a fan of air shows. From the time my oldest son was two years old, he has been captivated by them. The thing I've noticed in the different feats of flight at these shows is the difference between airplanes and helicopters. Both vehicles take great skill to control, but the feelings evoked are unique.

Airplanes can perform aerobatic stunts, maneuver and change direction quickly. These feats leave the audience in awe and inspired. One feels like a kid as the pilot peaks his head out of the cockpit to wave to the crowd as he lands and struts down the runway. Helicopters, on the other hand, have large blades. They lift straight up where they can see everything. They hover, are loud and somewhat menacing, and almost unmoving in their performance. Due to their nature, most helicopters are not able to do many tricks.

SUMMER

It is quite telling that our generation of parents is compared to the helicopter. Why is this? What does it mean? What is the damage? A helicopter parent is one who pays extremely close attention to a child's experiences and problems. Helicopter parents are so named because, like helicopters, they hover overhead, overseeing their child's life.[16] The increase in helicopter parenting coincided with two social shifts. The first was the comparatively booming economy of the 1990s, with low unemployment and higher disposable income. The second was the public perception of increased child endangerment, a perception which free-range parenting advocate Lenore Skenazy described as "rooted in paranoia."[17]

> *The helicopter parent wants to reduce any chance their child won't succeed.*

Many do not realize we are helicopter parents. But it is extremely important to free ourselves of these tendencies as we raise a child to one day leave the nest. We must grasp that our helicopter tendencies are harmful to our children's future. A recent study in the *Journal of Child and Family Studies* found that students who reported having over-controlling parents reported significantly higher levels of depression and less satisfaction with life. Furthermore, the negative effects of helicopter parenting on college students' well-being were largely explained by the perceived violation of a students' basic psychological needs for autonomy and competence.[18]

There are varying levels of helicopter parenting. Some hover due to a constant fear of danger to their child. Others hover hoping their children can avoid any type of failure or the least discomfort in life. The root seems to be a desire for our children to experience a pain-free life. In the least, we want to reduce negative emotions that may come due to being left out or mistreated. We want to keep them from making bad decisions, least of all, decisions that might embarrass us.

Free-Range Parenting

Over the years, my husband and I have become advocates and participants in "free-range" parenting, and I have seen tremendous benefit to our children's independence and confidence. I never considered myself a helicopter parent because I have never particularly been a worrier about my children's safety. Yet looking back, when my oldest was very young, I did "hover," concerned about his interactions, successes and failures. Over time and with much prayer, I stopped intervening in every facet of his life.

It is extremely difficult today to be a free-ranger. We not only live with helicopter parenting, but a helicopter culture, especially in America. We watch 24-hour news cycles and television shows that basically tell us if our child is out of site for two seconds, they will be kidnapped, murdered, or damaged by something. Kidnapping does happen. Horrible things do happen. As hard as this is to accept, we can only be a responsible adult preparing our child for the world, praying over them constantly. But we cannot physically protect them from all accidents, evil people, and bad influences that may come. And statistically speaking, if we keep a constant shadow over our children, we are far more likely to create "Peter Pans" who struggle to grow up and respond wisely to these potential situations.

As I was writing this section, a perfect example placed itself in my lap. One morning during our break, we decided to ride our bikes to the gas station. We have made this ride many times. The ride is about ten minutes from our home and runs through our neighborhood before opening to a busy intersection for a straight shot to the gas station. My older two were on bikes, while the younger was riding a scooter. As time went on, the youngest decided he was too tired to keep going on the scooter and he decided to walk the rest of the way. This left us going at a slower pace than the older two. My oldest stopped to wait for us, but my daughter kept on. I was fine with this because we have completed this ride many times and she knew where

SUMMER

we would meet. She could not have gotten more than five minutes ahead of us. But, as I turned the corner, a man in a truck stopped to ask, "Is that your daughter?" "Yes sir, she just got a little ahead of me." "Well ma'am, this is a busy street, there is some construction, I thought she was alone." "No, sir, we are coming up right behind her." The man, not satisfied with my answer said, "Well, this is not safe and I've called the police." My daughter is small for her age and I, too, would have thought it a bit unusual to see her riding by herself on a school day. However, his first reaction was to call the police.

Today, it is extremely important to prepare our children with how to speak to strangers properly and confidently. If we feel the freedom we are giving is appropriate, they will need to know what to say when asked, "Do your parents know where you are?" In this situation, my son, who desperately needed the opportunity to work on his independence, was shaken. Children genuinely need us to show them what they CAN do and to give them opportunities to live in less fear. The entire way home, my son worried if his sister got ahead at all, and he only rode a few feet ahead of me.

This has not been the only time I have had conversations with other adults about allowing my kids independence. I have spoken to worried strangers when my kids were within eyesight at parks. I have spoken to adults when police were called because a child in our co-op accidentally left a backpack in a public park. My kids have explained, a handful of times, that their parents know they are walking to a friend's house by themselves. I have looked in the eyes of my worried friends who wonder why their kids are filled with anxiety. It's hard to find the words to express that it's often the parent's anxiety which fuels the increases of worries within their own children.

These experiences begin to fade as our children age. But, if we don't start giving appropriate independence earlier, we may stunt our children's desire for normal developmental independence. No matter how relaxed a parent we are, we live in a helicoptering culture and we must accept that. But we do not have to live the same way. Do not expect the culture to agree with these views. Prepare with love and grace accordingly. Many of our friends may also differ with us, but we need to hold true to what we believe. Finding a balance between respecting rules and the general way people think nowadays is a tradeoff we make with giving our children thoughtful freedoms.

Most people are just taken aback by young children who have been given responsibilities. A great resource for how to help children safely work on independent skills is through the *Free Range Kids*[17] resources, whose movement was begun by Lenore Skenazy. This resource has been helpful and encouraging for me and provides insights. It also provides resources, such as the "Free Range Kids Cards," that our children can keep with them to show if they are stopped by an adult questioning why they are not with their parent.

Get off the Helipad

So, what can a parent do who wants to get off the helipad? Begin with prayer and discussion with your spouse. First, pray for God to reveal your areas of helicopter parenting and how it might be damaging you and your child. Ask the Lord to show you specific ways to give your children more freedom.

Some of this freedom might simply reveal itself as freedom from your voice.

A lot of hovering happens when we give constant praise and direction to a child who needs to motivate themselves. For some, this means allowing your child to play alone in the front yard or walk to a friend's house by themselves; maybe they attend a sleepover. For others, it may be allowing your child natural consequences for not completing an assignment or getting somewhere on time. Changes may include not watching every gymnastics

SUMMER

practice or discussing every detail with a coach. You might not ask your child every detail about how they feel after a retreat, performance, Sunday school class, or interaction with friends. Begin to let some things just be theirs.

There is a big difference between being an involved parent who teaches their children how to process feelings and experiences and being a helicopter parent. A way to know the difference is asking, "Is this action or conversation necessary to teach my child how to manage their own life and relationships, or is this action or conversation intervening so that I can *'save'* my child from an embarrassment or painful lesson or basic life experience, or so that I get to know every detail of their lives?" Remember, it is God who is in control of your child's experiences and future. You cannot, by yourself, keep them free from all harm, pain, embarrassment, and failure.

Our job is to point them to Christ and prepare them the best we can. We create situations where they must have perseverance to weather the difficulties of childhood so they can transition to weather the difficulties of adulthood. You cannot possibly foresee and protect them from all the experiences they must go through. Besides, it's difficult to know which experiences are God's sovereign will for their growth and refinement. Therefore, the best "hovering" we can do is hovering over our children with prayer. Every morning, every evening, throughout the day! When you are tempted to hover, ask the Holy Spirit to hover instead.

What about those children who do not want independence? Find ways to slowly require it. For some, it might be riding bikes together and slowly allowing the kids to go the route alone. It might be teaching a child to mow slowly and methodically until they take it over. Another child must choose one group activity to join where you are not a volunteer. For others, it's as simple as making them place phone calls, texts, or ordering meals on their own.

Children who are reticent to independence generally don't do well being forced into these situations or by being told, "You are ___ years old, kids much younger already do this!" Staying positive, finding small ways to help them succeed, and letting them move forward when they are ready will generally go much better. However, we can't give these kids a pass. We want to intentionally and prayerfully keep working with them. With repetition, the natural positive feelings of doing something on their own should begin to take over. Courage embraced.

As you prepare your homeschool routines each season, it's important to reassess how your kids are doing with independence and where you can make some forward movement. Overall, it's absolutely exhausting being a helicopter parent. It is well worth your time and effort to make small changes to release your children as God sees fit.

CHAPTER 8
Your Voice

There is one last aspect we must consider. No matter what curriculum you use, the tool which can be used for such good or evil is your very own voice.

I love words. Anyone who knows me knows I love to talk. But great peace has become mine as I've learned to keep a tighter leash on my volume and persistent yapping. Learning to be more succinct and knowing when to stop talking or to slow down has allowed us to enjoy a peaceful learning atmosphere in our home.

At the end of our second year of homeschooling, I got a polyp in one of my vocal chords from over-use. My voice was often strained from over-explaining, re-reading, reading too loudly, and feeling like I had to get to every bit of material, no exceptions. It's taken me a long time to realize that saying less is often more, and often saying nothing is extremely important as a child works through the process of learning.

So, why do many women struggle with saying too much? Often, in an anxious home, one of the ways we try to control others' behavior is through our voice. It is, in many ways, another version of helicopter parenting. We think if we talk enough, we can control our child's reactions and happiness, even their understanding of a school subject.

SUMMER

Passions and Affinities

When we were growing up, most of our school experiences involved listening to well-trained teachers who lectured because they were teaching twenty students. They had an organized curriculum to maintain. If we take that model home, it may look like repeating or drilling information in the hopes that our children will comprehend it all in that moment. Because we work at home, it is too easy to step in, give the answer, or over-drill "to make" the information "sink in". The truth is, our job is to provide our children with a vast opportunity to interact with God's Word and world so as they grow older, they find their "affinities," as Charlotte Mason would say, and they have perseverance to go deeper.

We tend to use the word *passion* as in "What are you passionate about?" It's not necessarily a bad question. But passion is more like a flame that might burn out at some point. The reason I like *affinity* better is because it's a focus on the loves and abilities that God has already placed within a child. It speaks deeply to the idea that God created each of us with a deep interest in certain areas of study.

There is a natural aspect to how these affinities will appear as your child ages. They don't work for a good grade or to make us proud. They begin showing their affinities as they pick out books, choose activities, and speak knowledgeably about an area we know nothing about. As Karen Glass, author of *Consider This,* states, "The important point is that this diet of ideas, like a physical diet, must be appetizing and varied. It would not be healthy for a child's physical well-being to attempt to extract nutrition from whole food and feed it to him in some sort of artificial form. It is equally unwise to reduce a child's mind-nourishment to some predigested ideas which we have selected to offer instead of original content. Like physical food for the body, ideas are absorbed best when received in their natural form. There are many ideas contained within a full novel, poem, or history book, and we are not able to discern which of those ideas will be the one that is needed to feed an individual child's mind."[19]

When it is time to teach something, we should do it creatively, enthusiastically, and cheerfully, but we should not make the mistake of thinking that teaching means we do all the talking or even most of it.

Let the material teach!

Loud Talking and Lecturing

We may make the mistake of thinking if we speak long enough, loud enough or with excitement, all needed facts will come together in those eager minds, and we have done our job. Little do we know, the young boy's mind has drifted off to fighting some battle in the icy Arctic while we're still big eyed and discussing, for the tenth time, how to conjugate a verb.

Lecturing does not guarantee it will be comprehended or move a child's memory, heart, or character. No matter how easy we think 2x2 is, nor how much we want a child to memorize 2x2, if the mind is not inspired or ready to accept and hold onto that information, our red-faced effort is in vain. It's a great art to learn how to hold our tongue and let our child interact with material and wait to see if they can figure something out on their own. Give it time, be consistent. Help with direction or confusion but do not spoon feed.

We find that learning is less like building blocks and more like icing a cake. The goal is not to hurry and get one block down so we can get the next one up. The goal is more like laying out thoughts and ideas and, as they solidify, another layer goes on and they all meld together and build a beautiful creation. Instead of making a white wedding cake, suddenly

SUMMER

blues, yellows and greens come into view and we've made a beautiful lemonade sunflower cake to share with friends over tea on a summer's day. This is one of the reasons I have found the Charlotte Mason gentle art of narration (rather than bombardment of analytical comprehension questions) a more natural and educational way to discuss information with my children.

When I ask a child, "Who was the main character of this story?" or "Who won the battle?", a child who has listened and heard these main ideas will give the correct answer. However, when I instead say, "Tell me about the story." or "What did you hear?" or even "Narrate the story," we quickly see how much was understood or not heard at all. We find out how much, from beginning to end, was ordered in the child's mind. In addition, we discover what parts stood out the most that go beyond facts and figures. We find ourselves surprised at what moved them. Even more, we learn to stop feeling good as a mom-teacher only when we hear the correct answers to our questioning. We become true educators when we inspire our children to engage with material for pure joy rather than a simple grade.

In the end, when we talk constantly, it is hard for children to hear the change of cadence and volume when we say something of value that should be heeded with greater intensity. When we learn to use our voices when it's of greatest importance, our children may very well hear with greater attention, as they have not had the drip of a leaking faucet in their ears all day long.

As Proverbs 27:15-16 states, "A quarrelsome wife is as annoying as constant dripping on a rainy day. Stopping her complaints is like trying to stop the wind or trying to hold something with greased hands."

Here are a few practical thoughts on slowing down and decreasing your speech:

Sound instead of voice:
When possible, we can use a sound on our phone or have our kids set their own timers for when activities are to start or end. The kids begin to understand when a song plays or a chime sounds, it's time to move back from a break onto the next subject matter.

Re-reading:
When we get to an important part in a book, it is easy to want to go over it again and again to make sure the kids pick it up. We need to fight the feeling that we need to repeat sections. It makes for pleasant reading to remind everyone at the beginning of a story to pay attention, but then let the story flow naturally. Only stop if a long story needs to pause for narration.

Read Quietly:
I have this loud voice I've earned from generations of teachers in my family. We can be heard from a mile away! One of the greatest pointers my speech therapist gave me is to speak slower and quieter. Often when I'm reading, it's just to my three kids, but I would read as though I were giving a graduation speech to 1,000 kids.

When we slow down and read quietly, we enjoy the reading more and it strains us less. Rather than trying to just "get through" the reading, we may need to reduce the amount of material we're trying to cover in one sitting.

Over-questioning:
Instead of asking a barrage of questions after a reading, simply ask each child what they heard and let that suffice. If natural discussion and observations by the kids have happened all along, then no narration may be needed at all. Narrations can be done in picture form as well. Try to mix oral narration,

written narration, and artistic narration, which can help avoid redundancy. As a child ages, longer and more detailed narrations, essays, journal entries, and presentations can be added. For a deeper understanding of narration, you might read Karen Glass' book, *Know and Tell: The Art of Narration*.[20]

Give directions once:
Before giving kids instructions, we can make sure we have everyone's attention, so we only have to say things once. Then let them come to us, or fail, before providing directions again.

Say in one sentence:
The idea is to not repeat the same message. Try to speak clearly in one sentence instead of overstating.

Be comfortable with silence:
Rather than giving the answer or helping or directing, we need to hold our tongue until we know it is necessary.

Move on:
If a child has worked long enough on a subject, whether it's finished or not, or completely understood or not, shut it off for the day and move on to the next subject. They will often come back to it with more energy the next day because their interaction with the material did not completely exhaust them. It also is a more positive interaction because it did not include a fight between the mother and child. Hold a fine balance between asking the child for the right age-appropriate level of perseverance and knowing when they have truly done as much as they can and come to it again tomorrow.

Praise at the right time:
When a child has done an excellent job, they should be told, "Well done." However, when we constantly praise them for everything they do, we steal from our kids the natural God-given reward they experience independent of

us. They learn to do minimal tasks and wait for big grins and rewards versus absorbing within themselves the confidence of all they can and are able to do and challenge themselves to the harder task. Johnny doesn't need to be told "good job" every time he puts his plate away without being asked. The first time will suffice. Then maybe the next time, he'll put his plate away and wipe the table down and see this as simply a part of the responsibilities of getting older. What a wonderful experience when a child discovers he is more capable than he thought.

The Way:

A key piece is the attitude with which we speak to our children. We can be our children's authority while also building a good and amicable relationship with them. The way we do this is by speaking with our authority without simultaneously treating our children like annoyances. There is an art to this. Do we use an angry voice when speaking to our children? Are we often irritated or unhappy, disappointed and disapproving? Do they sense they can never measure up? And does God do this? We are unworthy, but He so LOVED us that His only begotten Son died for us (John 3:16).

Obedience is important and good and protective, and our children need our discipline, but we must also seek to carry our authority with gentleness and not in a degrading manner. If we can do this, it balances the times we must assert authority and the times they need to look to our face for grace and forgiveness. As they get older, they need to ask, "What would my parents want me to do in this situation?" Memories of our voice should stand out as a guiding force when they are tempted to do wrong. But children also need to know, "I can run to my parents when I am wounded, and I can turn to them when I have done something shameful."

This can happen when authority is housed in gentleness and understanding. We and our children are fellow sinners in the journey of this fallen world together. We can make this journey as lifelong friends, starting today. We are not just building their future, but we're becoming true friends for a lifetime. We need to hold fast to our parental authority for now and disciple our children with a voice of humility and love.

Ownership:
When your child is old enough, have them check their schedule, eventually setting their schedule (with your guidance and approval, of course). The right age for this is different for every child. If a child is particularly strong in a subject early, they may be able to take on some independence as young as 9 or 10. But as they age, all children should be handed a good portion of their learning. Save the subjects that are challenging and that bring about meaningful conversation to work on and enjoy together: history, read-aloud stories, Bible, poetry, nature. The hope is these will always be a major part of the memories of a cherished childhood.

Be Scarce:
For many of us who love the sound of our own voice, the best habit is to simply make ourselves scarce. If we can't help but interrupt or make comments, we need to step away. Let the kids narrate to each other, let them struggle with material on their own and come to us when they can't figure it out. Step away so they learn independently to do their best.

Your Care

You enter a room that looks like any room where groups gather for Bible study or book club. A group of women sit in a circle. In one hand they hold a cup of coffee. In the other hand they hold their book study filled with handwritten personal reflections. As you stand at the back of the door and listen, you hear a delightful conversation. One mom shares, "As I get older I feel so much more comfortable in my body size." You notice the woman is not actually being sarcastic. You hear another woman state, "You know, at the end of a long day, I find I like to treat myself with chocolate." It's not that what she said is strange to you, but you notice there is no guilt in her voice. You are a bit surprised at this conversation happening in front of you. Why? Because we are conditioned in our culture towards using statements that revolve around, "I need to change my eating and my body." These habits of thinking and speaking can cause us to place an unnecessary focus on food and exercise.

Please hear me, of course we need to have a balanced diet and consistent daily exercise. We surely cannot eat whatever we want and never move and be healthy in body or mind. Many of us handle food with little self-control and we need to lay it down before the Lord each day. But what I've found to be a core problem is that, in America, we live in the extremes when it comes to eating and exercising. We're either training for a marathon and focused on the newest diet elimination, or we're eating fast food every night and laying on the couch binge-watching. Though we speak of moderation, it is not something we work to attain.

I would like to encourage a new perspective on self-care. The idea is that we learn to slow down and enjoy our food and exercise. How? One, we practice relaxing when we eat. In this way we are more aware of the flavors and appreciate the food and drinks available to us. When we slow down, we tend to eat less. The second idea is to embrace that we are not all created to be the same size. We are not all going to look the same in yoga pants. If we eat a varied diet, do not overeat, and get moderate daily exercise, then perhaps we are the size we are meant to be. The second idea is how we view exercise. Many people love to exercise, whether it be running, cycling, or yoga. Some women choose to get more exercise than others. What we're looking for is consistency. Do you move regularly? Do you spend time outdoors and bike or walk with your family?

SUMMER

If exercise takes up too large a portion of your mind and time, it might be out of balance. Could exercise be a selfish pursuit? Is happiness put off for the day when you lose more weight or get that one extra run in? So, too, in our exercise we need to learn to breathe, pray, use it as a time for gratitude. There is no magic pill that works for each person.

Each of us are individuals with a unique make-up of DNA, family history, medical and emotional issues different from the next person. God knows us down to the root of one very strand of hair, so He provides help and the way to a healthier life. Some of us are tempted by food. Some are tempted by a need to keep to a certain size. Others simply need to stop being jealous.

What is truly healthy should not come from the culture.

What is truly healthy must come from a balanced life that starts with the Lord. As we pray and renew our mind, we make small lifestyle changes toward better health. These changes can have a large impact over the course of time. "I don't have time for the gym, but I can take a walk," or "Instead of that coke, I can have water." I have seen in recent days an obsession that almost edges on the side of idolatry with certain types of eating or exercise regimens. These are often distractions from more worthwhile pursuits.

Again, there is nothing wrong with eating clean or removing certain elements of the American diet from our life because it is healthier. But, if we only feel good at the end of the day because we made "perfect food choices" or if we feel horrible at night because we ate a small piece of cake, we may be allowing food to have more rule over us than it should. There will be times when we must push to do something we don't want to do and, in the end, it will pay off. For example, we may need to take a daily walk. Initially, we don't see the point, but after a couple of weeks when our energy increases, we realize the time spent was well worth it.

As a homeschooling friend reminds me, we must put our efforts into the activities that give time back. For example, when we do that daily walk, though it takes 30 minutes out of our day, we then have the energy to cook better meals and get the laundry done. In this way, the payback is well worth it. On the other hand, if we spend a lot of money on a diet program, then can't seem to follow through with it, our efforts have been wasted.

Overall, if we can slow down and live in the present and simplify our plan, we will enjoy small victories. If we practice slowing down, we might find we're not as stressed, and we won't need to grab an extra slice of pizza. We should be thoughtful and cognizant of our eating and exercise, not obsessed. Just as our children are not academic beings only, we are not the sum of our appearance. Exercise and eating should be balanced in our minds and schedules. These are good ideas to ponder as we try to figure out a proper definition of self-care.

Healthy Self-Care

The subject of "self-care" is overwhelming, which seems like an oxymoron. The abundance of information and opinions on what to eat, how to exercise, and whose opinion to adopt is enough to overload the brain. Yet, a complete lack of focus on taking care of oneself is a recipe for disaster.

So, what does healthy self-care look like with all the busyness that is part of homeschooling? It was interesting that many women interviewed thought self-care was vital, while others thought there is too much a focus on "me time". There is a balance, of course. I don't think pioneer women sat around wondering when they'd get their next date night, but we don't live in 19th century either. We live in the days of expanding suburbs, traffic, HOAs, 24-hour news cycles and busy activities; these do create stress.

SUMMER

We're not looking for our next meal, but we are looking for our purpose, our place and how to balance an ever-increasing frenzied lifestyle. We do need time to ourselves. It is not wrong to spend time away from our children. But, "me time" does not fix things that are wrong while we are away. The kids may still argue, we may still struggle with bedtime routines and academic challenges still await. However, "me time" may bring about rest to change my perspective. "Me time" lets our children know that Mom has needs too! So, if "me time" means we get our nails done or have coffee with a friend, that is fine. Time away allows us to breathe and get perspective. A big part of self-care is learning how to take care of "me" in the midst of the struggle and strife.

Learning to be content, slowing down, and making good daily choices about how to take care of ourselves and our family, will reduce the need for so much "me time." How do we find that kind of moment-to-moment contentment? It starts with praise and gratitude to God. It also lies in our ability to realize our complete dependence upon God. Dependence, not just on what we might consider "big" items, but in the daily details. So, we pray for the strength to make a meal when we want to eat out, we pray for the ability to be patient with a child who is struggling in their behavior. When we accept and then act upon our dependence, we are filled with that which only the Holy Spirit can give- wisdom beyond measure. Lastly, we accept our present situation. Then we wait, which is the hardest part. No massage or weekend away can replenish us like a moment with the Holy Spirit in the midst of an average day.

When we learn to have balanced self-care, we serve as an example to our children.

Our children may find themselves depressed or struggling as adults if they have not learned the value of self-care. In many ways this is under the category of what The Bowen Center for the Study of Family would call "differentiation of self".[21] We want our children to know the difference between moments when they need to be selfless and when it's right to have different opinions and needs than other people. We must start with understanding this concept ourselves. We must live it out in front of them.

CHAPTER 9
Your Enjoyment

"If mothers could learn to do for themselves what they do for their children when these are overdone, we should have happier households. Let the mother go out to play! If she would only have courage to let everything go when life becomes too tense, and just take a day, or half a day, out in the fields, or with a favorite book, or in a picture gallery looking long and well at just two of three pictures, or in bed, without the children, life would go on far more happily for both children and parents."[5]

~ Charlotte Mason ~

"Kaboom, crackle, crackle, crackle…" Nothing cuts through mid-summer like the sounds of July 4th. My family and I have the privilege of getting front row seats to an amazing fireworks show every year in Addison, Texas. It's truly one of the events we look forward to each summer.

Last year, due to bad weather, the show started an hour late. We could feel the tension as families with young ones had to decide whether this delayed fireworks show would be worth the potential cranky ride home. But when the first "boom" lit up the night sky with a shower of radiant purples, pinks, and crystal white tinsel, the crowd, with one united group of smiles, said, "Yes!"

SUMMER

As I looked across the faces of my husband and children, everything went into slow motion. The reflection of blue and red lights warmed their faces. I couldn't help but think of how precious this family tradition had become. It was pure joy to know this was one of those moments, one of the family traditions, they'll carry with them for the rest of their lives. And, though my expectations will try to fool me, I know we can't re-create this moment again. Next year or soon after, one might want to spend the 4th of July with a friend or won't be so excited to do "the same old thing." But maybe it will be one of those remembrances they will want to re-create with their own children.

We all know the finale of a fireworks show because a million fireworks go off at once, non-stop, and your ears and eyes can barely keep up. On this night, right in the middle of the finale, I noticed something that always makes me sad. A few people started packing to leave. I understand it is late and people don't want to get stuck in traffic. But, isn't this what we came for? Didn't we sit out in the humid Texas heat with our flag shorts sticking to our fold-out chairs just to enjoy this moment? So, why leave early? Sit back down, take a breath, and enjoy the moment. It's already late. It's okay. Just be.

Slow Down and Enjoy

If we're going to continue this homeschooling journey year upon year, we need to find a way to enjoy it. How do we do this? By enjoying life outside of homeschooling. We cannot allow homeschooling to obsess our entire existence. There must be some things in life that are not housed under our title of "homeschool mother." We must carve out time for purposeful personal growth and ministry. We cannot wait until our children graduate to participate in all the life God has for us.

We need to stop focusing on the end and find purpose in the journey of today. A good start is to step back to consider whether anything we do or read is about our personal maturation. Do we participate in activities outside the home that use our God-given talents? Are we involved in activities that don't directly benefit our children? This may be serving in our church or volunteering in our community. It may mean simply discovering or re-discovering areas of interest that stir our mind. We might find value in reading classical books, educational philosophies, or picking up a musical instrument. It might include social health by joining a Bible study or a book club. Others enjoy gardening. We must regularly make time for activities that nourish us.

Suddenly, these moments of daily personal recreation and study become the refreshing we need to have vigor in our other homeschooling tasks. It doesn't have to take much time out of our day. But it is important to make a daily and weekly schedule of time to read, time to call a friend or family member, time to work on a project. It's important to realize we're still supposed to be learning as adults.

These moments sharpen us and give us new strength for getting back in the game of homeschooling. It's too easy to fill these downtimes with screens, greater focus on the kids, or chores. But daily moments of reinvigoration are generally much more life giving when we choose a walk, a book, or a project that feeds our soul. Pursuing personal interests grows us. When we find value in something new we are learning or in a way we are serving outside our home, we bring joy back into our four walls. It's good for the children to see us being part of God's bigger family.

A simple start to a self-care plan is to write a schedule where we do one self-care activity in the morning and one in the afternoon/evening. We can start with just one a day if that is more practical. Begin with a short time frame of 15-20 minutes.

SUMMER

A Self-Care Schedule

	Monday	Tuesday	Wednesday	Thursday	Friday	Saturday	Sunday
AM	Devotion/ Walk	Devotion/ Bike Ride	Family Devotion/ Walk	Devotion	Nature Day/ Volunteer	Study the Persecuted Church	Church Volunteer
PM	Read a Novel Volunteer	Nature Reading	Read Charlotte Mason	Walk w/ Husband	Bubble Bath	Family Bike Ride	Nap

CHAPTER 10
Your Individuality

*"On Camazotz, we are all happy because we are
all alike. Differences create problems.
You know that, don't you, dear sister?" "No," Meg said."*[22]
~ *A Wrinkle in Time,* Madeleine L'Engle ~

It is freeing to live honestly. We need to be okay with being different from others. It's good to be self-aware and to be authentically the person God designed. You may be poor or rich, wear makeup or not, watch Netflix and exercise at the gym or take nature walks each morning. You might live in the city or on a farm. Be YOU, not some version of what you think a "homeschool mom" should be.

Of all the commandments, there is one I did not quite understand being counted in the company of "do not murder" and "do not steal." That commandment is "do not covet." But recently, I began to realize so much of a woman's deep-seated unhappiness comes from coveting. The wishing, the desiring for that which God has blessed someone else. The longing to have her home, her looks, her intelligence, her peace, her talents, her well-behaved children, her unending blessings, is sinful. God never intended for all to be the same. We see it sculpted by His hands and painted across the colors of His world.

God loves variety, but culture calls us to assimilate.

Last year in our science material, we had the opportunity to learn about animals from all seven continents. What did I notice about these animals? Variety. From the Sahara Desert to Siberia, from the flying squirrel to the lyre bird, God is amazing in His creativity and His love for variety. So why is it as humans, as women and as homeschooling families, we feel the push to be the same?

You may be a woman who loves crafts and can create some exciting art projects for your kids, or you may be a woman who breaks into a cold sweat when she sees a glue gun! Some women love putting together experiments, and others can't seem to get one "to work" correctly to save her life.

Because you are your child's main teacher, you will be faced with the challenge of presenting materials where you excel and others for which you are weak. It is important to find a way to accept who you are, strengths and shortcomings, and present the materials in the best way you can for your children.

Your educational philosophy and materials will mature over time. Even so, you can't "will" yourself to be someone you are not. You can absolutely grow in skill and temperament but ask God to help you become who He wants you to be. Just as you should not compare your child's progress with another child, so you must remember to not compare yourself with other home educators. Trust in God's overarching plan for your child and for you. He called you, not another person, to teach and train your children.

I have watched homeschooling friends teach and discipline their children, and thought, "Wow, that is fantastic, I should do that." Many times, there are nuggets of wisdom I can use to be a better parent and teacher. We should all be teachable. Even so, you are a unique person and God has given you the children you have. Be careful that you don't think you must "be" another person. You have unique gifts and challenges and so do they. Yet, don't be so prideful that you cannot take advice or learn from others. Always be open to learning.

In the same way, remember that your children are different from you. Although they possess some of your DNA and may even look like a carbon copy of you, they are not. Your children may have vastly different personalities and interests than you. It can be a frustrating process for both you and your children if you try to make them just like you. In fact, you can ruin your relationship with them if you try to control and force them into being you.

Of course, there are standards our children will be expected to uphold. At times, we will have to challenge them to take risks to be the best they can be. This must be balanced with the remembrance of loving the child God has given us, challenges and all. In this way, we will spur them on to whatever path God has for them, even though it may not be our chosen path.

CHAPTER 11
Your Failure

"Every day you preach to yourself a gospel of your loneliness, inability, and lack of resources or you faithfully preach to yourself the gospel of the Lord Jesus Christ."[23]
~ Paul David Tripp ~

How do you speak to yourself? To what streets do you let your voice wander and how do you feel when you get there? Does it chain you to a past that won't let you move forward?

We have ALL made terrible mistakes. But one of the worst things we can do is to walk into homeschooling with a heap of guilt about our past mistakes.

The responsibility of teaching your children and managing your home can overload you at times and you may "lose it" now and again. There is nothing wrong with needing a good cry, but you can't stay there. This can be a problem for some more than others, and especially for those just getting started in their parenting and homeschooling journey. One of the best lessons God has given me regarding anxiety or struggle is to no longer see it as unfair. Rather, some anxiety is a part of life and an opportunity or a sign that something needs to change.

SUMMER

If homeschooling is a constant battle, something is probably wrong. Notice, I did not say that homeschooling will always be easy. Materials, routines, activities, attitudes, discipline and sleep may need to be evaluated. It is possible there is a physical or learning problem to be examined. We do live in a culture that believes the first sign of pain or struggle should be treated, medicated, counseled, or silenced! But the truth is, pain and difficulty are often how we learn and how situations improve over time.

Sometimes, struggles are simply part of a season (even a long one) to be prayed through with there being no fix at all. When this plays out practically for me, when things seem to be going awry, I don't seek to escape from it or overanalyze it by asking, "How in the world did we get here?" I lean into it and pray that God would show me what may need to change, or how I should respond. I simply don't have the power to fix everything instantly. As Victor Frankl, holocaust survivor, said, "When we are no longer able to change a situation, we are challenged to change ourselves. Everything can be taken from a man, but one thing: the last of the human freedoms - to choose one's attitude in any given set of circumstances, to choose one's own way."[24]

> *Let go of what did not turn out, end up, or seem fair, and surrender to the Lord's sovereign will.*

Choose peace and joy, choosing Christ Himself each day. It is a grand and glorious pursuit. Take hold and, though your struggles may persist, you persist all the more. Be encouraged that no matter what mistakes you have made, the Lord can show you the way as you seek Him without ceasing.

There are many things in life we can't choose, but we can choose Who we will look to during difficult times. Give yourself time and grace to think through and work toward the atmosphere you want to encourage in your home. It may take a while to feel confident in the path you have chosen. And in the end, change is a constant.

Although we can grow and make better choices, we will continue to fail and make mistakes in one way or another. But that does not mean that we have to fall apart. J.R. Vassar shares in a recent "Tabletalk" article, "So when we fail, we need not be shaken to the core. The gospel says more about us than our failures do. The verdict God speaks over us trumps every other verdict spoken over us by our voices or the voices of others. God uses our failures to wean us off self-righteousness and point us to Jesus, in whom we find a righteousness that is sufficient for our confidence, value, and unshakeable joy…you can grieve the failure, but not be undone by it."[25]

As you step into your homeschool mornings, take a deep breath, ask the Lord to clear your mind from what is behind or even what is ahead, and live in that moment with his unmoving grace. Remember your source. He is your power and strength and stability. He can give you words, silence, and wisdom as you seek Him. Be keenly aware of how you speak to yourself. When you find your mind wandering to worry, turn them into prayers and let the Lord guide your responses to the everyday anxieties that are part of life.

V.A., age 13

CHAPTER 12

Living Stories

What have been some of your struggles in homeschooling? How do you handle a bad day?

Much of what causes a struggle, or a bad day, is attitude (5). At times, homeschooling can seem like a great responsibility, and a bad day comes when we feel we are not doing our best, or when fears arise that we are "messing our kids up."

There was a deep insecurity of "Am I doing enough?" Often when a subject is not grasped or must be repeated, the inner voice sounds something like, "They will never understand this!" or "They are so far behind!" And on some days, we just don't always feel like homeschooling. One mom said the best advice she ever received in homeschooling was to take the word "behind" out of her vocabulary.

For others, the struggles were more behavioral or parental. Issues of discipline and arguments about schoolwork can wear moms down. When a bad day happens what do women find helpful? Four women stated that crying and praying were the best responses for them. Many times, especially if the struggle is due to relational issues, women find they need to have a conversation with their kids and forgive them or ask their kids for forgiveness. Academics had to be put aside for a time to deal with deeper issues of character. This allowed for some closure and the ability to move forward.

The largest group of women (10) stated on a bad day, something had to give. This might look like: taking time out, changing the routine, finding quiet time, adding rest in the schedule, doing something different such as puzzles, reading a book together, or getting outside. Sometimes, everyone needs a new view. We changed our homeschool routine so that Wednesday and Friday look different from the other weekdays. On Wednesday, our reading and writing are focused on nature and we get outside to enjoy it. On Fridays, we participate in a nature study group. The other three days, we hit "the books" as usual. Adding something to the schedule that we all look forward to brings variety to routine.

However if every day, every month, every year is a struggle, something else may be going on. Two women suggested looking into finding out more about learning disabilities or seeking help as necessary. If the daily routine is extremely difficult for your child, there could be a learning difficulty that needs to be addressed. Often though, you need to change your expectations. You may be asking too much of yourself or your children. Funny as this sounds, sometimes in schooling we feel if an argument has not happened, it must be a sign we've not asked for enough work from our kids. A fight indicates we must be working hard. It might be much more beneficial to your home to ask for a little less and have a lot more peace. As one mom stated, "at the end of all this, the worst thing would be for my kid to look back and say that homeschooling was awful."

Everyone will have bad days, even bad seasons. Starting the day with a defeatist and a fearful attitude, getting overwhelmed by your perceived pressure of homeschooling, and letting your curriculum rule instead of the Lord is a recipe for disaster. We must stop letting the culture dictate to us what a successful life entails. If you and your children are not enjoying homeschooling at all, pray about what might need to change and find ways to enjoy each other, because this journey will go by quickly. It's not whether they have all their facts and figures, but it's about the relationship they have with you and other people.

Only one mom identified over activity as a big reason for her struggles. You may not realize, but it's possible the reason you feel stress during your school day is because you have too many other activities to get to or prepare for, so the relaxed and enjoyable pace gets rushed. No one tends to work well when rushed. It might be that you could increase your enjoyment of your homeschool days when you reduce outside responsibilities so you can expand and take on the schoolwork at an easier and more fulfilling pace.

Also, one woman mentioned when she was struggling, she found it important to speak with her husband and other homeschooling friends. We all need to lean on each other. We should not feel embarrassed to be vulnerable with one another. It is more likely than not that your friend has been through something similar and, if not, at least she can pray for you. Although your husband may not always have an opinion on curriculum or understand all the difficulties, he loves you and your children like no one else, and involving him is a wise and valuable idea.

Why do people quit homeschooling?

With the pressure that can be a part of homeschooling, I wondered what pushed a family to the point where homeschooling was no longer worth it. I was amazed at the level of agreement from the group to this question. At some point it was both comical and sad as I found myself placing questionnaires into two groups, "Insecure" and "Overwhelmed."

SUMMER

Most women (14) agreed that either insecurities or feeling overwhelmed was the most likely cause for women to quit homeschooling. "You feel like you might be doing your kids a disservice and others might think the same."

I am sure everyone wonders about quitting at one time or another. Financial and health issues might cause the family to make other educational choices. Sometimes children may verbalize to their parents they no longer want to homeschool. Some women mentioned that a lack of support by their husband or loved ones will cause one to quit.

Overall, it's important to realize the value of taking stock of your thought life. We live in a time of cultural comparisons. We must take our thought life captive and listen to the voice of God. No one curriculum, bad test, or difficult day will cause one to quit homeschooling.

Other than a life crisis, it is more likely the repetitive bad days and bad feelings are what cause families to end their homeschool journey. If day after day, week after week, homeschooling is a miserable experience, something very deep needs to change. This can be discovered through prayer, self-reflection, and help from others. When we tried a university model program and failed miserably, the cause was exhaustion and constant bickering. What was the source for us? Asking way more of my son than he was capable. Also, my internal stressful temperament encapsulated our home. Those things HAD to change if we were going to be able to continue homeschooling.

It might be that, even as I'm writing this, my family does way less work than we should. But I live with a lot of peace. My kids are asked to keep a routine and do the diligent work, but possibly a lot less than their peers. I don't know. I guess at this point, I don't care. I hope that doesn't sound too abrupt. You shouldn't care either. You should care about keeping a balanced schedule, a balanced life, a lovely life, with your arms wrapped around these little persons. If it doesn't look like that right now, it's okay. With God's help, it can.

What one thing has kept you from quitting and continuing with homeschooling when it gets difficult?

The answers to this question varied with four women stating God alone has enabled them to continue with homeschooling. Both His strength and knowing this was His plan for their family was sufficient to kept them going. Equally, four women stated the alternatives to homeschooling were simply not an option, and that was a big factor for them in choosing to homeschool. For some, their children could pursue higher academics and interests at home. For others, the issue was the culture of institutional schools. Four other women stated their main reasons for homeschooling was family. Building relationships with each other and with other people was their main reason to homeschool. Two women stated their husbands' support and encouragement was their main reason to keep homeschooling. One person simply stated, "Freedom." One other woman said she continues to homeschool because, "When I finally realized there was no perfect curriculum, I stopped changing curriculum and I simply learned to persevere and follow the path. As I did this, I saw some progress and it helped me realize we each find our own program and way and, as we keep on the path, we grow in experiencing a better homeschooling life."

Once you find a rhythm and keep coming to it diligently (though it is imperfect), you will see some progress and you can get the confidence to press on.

SUMMER

How has your relationship with the Lord changed since homeschooling?

Many women who homeschool have been Christians their whole lives. Others came to faith later. Each phase of life: school, work, marriage, motherhood, homeschooling, has its own share of heartaches and joys with the hope of always being a place of growth towards a closer relationship with God.

I wondered how women felt their relationship with God had changed since they began homeschooling. Six out of the 19 women used the word "dependence." Many of their answers included ideas such as, "I have to daily relinquish my plan to His." "I need Him every moment." "He breaks my pride and I'm reminded I can't do this without Him."

In fact, multiple women spoke of the Lord breaking their pride. "Before, I thought I knew how to do this. I was homeschooled myself. But I'm reminded often that I don't know, and I need the Lord to do this through me." I thought one woman put it well, "Living and schooling day in and day out with those closest to you tends to reveal your true heart, it tends to shake the sin out. You realize very quickly how sinful you are and that there is no way you can do this without God's intervening."

Nine other women stated their relationship with the Lord had grown much closer since homeschooling because they simply spend more daily time in the Bible and teaching their kids about God, "I've learned so much more about God because I needed to learn to answer my kids' questions. We're learning together." "We're able to spend more time focused on God because we have the time at home and stay a bit outside of the cultural influences." "I'm reminded that academics are important, but we're training their hearts, which puts our focus on God." Another mom stated, "Each year is different from the one before, with new challenges. I'm often reminded to put the Bible at the center."

One woman had a great way of stating God's role in her homeschooling day by saying that prayer and faith were naturally woven throughout their day, not only when they focused on Bible study. Four other moms also specifically stated their prayer life and dependence on prayer had grown since homeschooling. Other women feel they are on a journey and each homeschooling year is a part of this path, "I have faith in His process," "The Lord honors me, and He has put us on this path and our job is to put Him first." "He has me on a journey and He has taught me that I'm learning just like my son, and I have to be careful not to be legalistic." Two other women agreed with this by saying they've learned teaching the Bible and about God cannot simply be about curriculum. It's about modeling the Christian life for their kids.

Above all, the theme seemed to focus on understanding we are not in control, and we must lean daily, in fact, moment-by-moment, on God through prayer. This seems to be not only for the strength to physically do the educating of our children, but for the right attitude in how to go about it and to give up knowing how it's going to turn out.

Perhaps these changes are part of a Christian woman's journey as a mother, whether she homeschools her children or not. However, we have the special joy (as one mom put it) to choose to focus our learning days more on Him, to teach our children of His goodness, and to depend on Him through daily prayer because we are with our children in a very special atmosphere. In the end, the thing about prayer and dependence on God is it changes us, not our children or our circumstances. There are times in my homeschooling journey where I've felt I was flailing about without a compass. This is when God shows me, once again, that I'm trying to be self-reliant when I know I can only do "all things" in His strength. (Philippians 4:13).

SUMMER

Do you take care of yourself? What are some of the ways you do this?

Sixteen out of the 21 women had the opportunity to answer this question. Out of those responses, 11 said, "Yes, or at least, I'm working on it," and five said, "No ." Of those women that said "no," some of the responses included, "The kids are older now, so I should be able to, but I haven't taken responsibility to do it yet." "I don't do a great job, I'm still learning what self-care looks like." "I would like to focus on it more, but I just keep putting it off."

The final two women discussed they're not sure they're fitted for needing "me time" or "self-care." These women believed their focus should be on spiritual renewal. The final person in this group summed it up by saying, "There's probably a difference between putting yourself first and taking care of yourself."

It may be good for us to accept the difference between what might be called "cultural" phrases such as "me time" or "needing a break." As some of the women said, it's more about showing our children the importance of taking care of ourselves spiritually and physically. We need to model it for them. This plays out when we look at the explanations from women who answered "yes" to this question. There are times in motherhood when just getting a bath is considered self-care. However, all 11 women who said they are working on self-care listed these similar ways: healthy diet, exercise, time with the Lord, reading, time to pursue interests, finding balance in their schedule including fewer activities, and time with husband and good friends. We can all agree these forms of self-care are about better health and connecting with God, family, and friends. When we take even small steps to improve some of these areas, it truly can make us more peaceful and healthy women.

Remember to take time to step back, pray, and discover what those self-care options might be for you and put them into practice. In doing so, you might find your attitude and abilities improve in how you treat your loved ones in your home.

~ PONDERING SUMMER ~

Consideration for deeper reflection

Before answering these questions,
please take time to pray so you can thoughtfully walk through this process.

<u>Who are you?</u>

1. Who are some of the people and what are some of the events that have defined you as a person?

2. Do you need to seek professional counseling or a trusted mentor to work through anything from your past that may be currently causing you some problems?

<u>Your Advisers:</u>

1. Who do you go to for advice and counsel?

2. Are there outside influences you need to remove? Which ones, and how will you remove them?

3. Are there godly people in your life that can support you in your homeschooling journey? Who are they? How will you allow these advisers to support you on a regular basis?

4. Do you put yourself down? What are some ways you can change your negative thoughts about yourself to more positive ones? How can you live with more gratitude?

Your Need to Know:

1. List the anxieties you have about homeschooling. List the anxieties you have about your child's future. Pray about them.

Your Friendships:

1. Make a list of your two to three closest friends. Pray for them and thank the Lord for them.

2. Do you struggle with being critical? Pray that God will help you to be more careful in the way you think about others and what you say about and to people.

Your Boundaries:

1. Have you set good boundaries with the people in your life? If not, what steps do you need to take to set better boundaries or to learn about setting boundaries?

Your Helicopter/Your Voice:

1. What are some ways you struggle with being a helicopter parent? What are some steps you can take to change?

2. Take a moment to think through how and when you speak with your children throughout your day. What strategies can you put in your current routine to change the amount or volume of your voice?

Your Care/Your Enjoyment:

1. What are you currently doing to take care of yourself? List some simple activities you can add to your current daily routine to

take better care of yourself physically, emotionally, socially, or intellectually. Write out that routine below.

2. Are you currently volunteering in any organization? Is there a reasonable place for you to begin serving?

Your Individual/Your Failure:

1. List at least five positive qualities you see about yourself:

2. As you look back at your parenting/home educating, list some of the areas where you feel you have failed. Pray over these areas and seek freedom so you can move forward. After you pray, scratch through each one of the failures. Begin fresh and anew!

SECTION IV

~ To Nancy: for always believing, even when the rest of us couldn't. ~

It will be a chilly fall morning. I can almost feel it now. That tipping point when you feel the final heat of summer fading away with the dawn of a sudden cool morning. It will be so quiet. Everyone else will be asleep. Maybe it would be best to wrap the pumpkin bread in some aluminum foil. I'm not sure when I'll see him next. (I'm believing for it now even though, at this very moment, he's asleep and still dreaming young boy dreams.) A duffle bag will be packed, and the door will make that creak you only notice in early hours, those hours visited solely by the fellowship of weary soldiers and nursing moms. Except for the Watchman, He never sleeps.

I remember when the boy and I lived in those early morning moments. That seemed like some kind of war. And I cannot see his face. But I know it's all going to be okay. His dad and I stand together, arms linked. I can see the back of that beautiful brown hair, the hair everyone was always jealous about, now attached to a man. I don't remember a graduation party or caps and gowns. I don't know whether this dream has those kinds of celebrations. But, as he

FALL

walks away, I know somehow, it's deeper, bigger and holier than any regular path, because God saved that little baby from death.

> Every day of our lives, the struggles, and the beautiful
> daily rhythms have gone by in a flash.
> Each one of those days was working towards something. And, he'll fly!

B.C., age 9

CHAPTER 1
Full Circle

Be diligent. Be excited. Finish strong.

Just a few weeks ago, the sunflowers came back, spurring me to keep writing. They speak to me in the breeze as I drive by with the windows down. "Keep writing, keep going, the seasons are changing! It's time to head to the finish line."

It's hard for me to think that someday this homeschooling journey will end. These three wildflowers blooming in our home will grow and be planted in their own fields. I pray so much that the soil they were rooted in allows our relationships with one another to grow deeper, no matter the distance. And though right now I'm sitting in the heat of summer, I know fall is coming. It's my favorite season!

Autumn is the time for reevaluating the routine. It's also a great time to reevaluate where we plan to put our energy for the coming year. Though we may be weary at times, we seek God's strength to be consistent with the activities and work we've chosen. We think about what materials will fit into this year and what will not make the cut. It's what makes homeschooling unique. There's stretching room to pick new materials or alter how and when they will be presented in the day. We take notice of how each child has grown. A reviewing of materials we hoped to finish that we're still working on and we process how we might need to move forward. It's time to get excited about new books and subject matters. We look forward to a sharpening of minds, hearts and pencils and to the new season the LORD has for us. That's the beauty, if we will grasp it.

Traditional school calendars have never quite fit in perfectly to a homeschooling lifestyle, not the one I'm suggesting anyway. This is our life. This is how we live it together. The season of fall is simply the next phase of our learning journey. We certainly will never accomplish all we would like to in our "school" year. But we can accomplish many wonderful things. Some of these moments are even unplanned as we diligently wake up each morning and place ourselves, children, and materials before the Lord. Some discussions, stories, and experiments will be so good that the memory will be added to our mental journal of the joys of homeschooling for that year. Some will be tougher. But, all of it is used.

Autumn is a fabulous time to think about our educational philosophy and review expectations of each academic day. And, there is need for faith like a drop of amber sunflower oil, because we are called to trust. We are reminded of Who is in charge of each day and where our strength comes from to follow through with our schedules. Finishing a 36-week curriculum or level six math book feels great, but if it was all done in a harsh and stressful atmosphere, what have we shown our children of the purpose of education?

So, before the fall arrives, I look to the sunflowers again and they tell me one more thing. "Keep your eyes on the sun!" For it's so easy to turn to the left or right and to look down in despair.

But the sunflowers keep their eyes to the sun, east to west, east to west. Only then do they grow, just as they should.

One day, there won't be another fall season for homeschooling. So, for now, take each day and use each educational resource bit by bit. And, do not give up. Each day, we will find our purpose, meaning, and place.

We are to be diligent to our teaching and materials. But mostly, we are to be diligent by turning our eyes to God, placing this new "school" year in His hands. Like one leaf in a large elm tree that cannot quite be seen amidst its brothers and sisters, so this year fits into the bigger plan. In His hands, trust that the colors of learning will change in due time. Like the red maple leaf before it flits to the yellowing autumn grass, we'll never get this season with them again. So let's be excited about the coming year and trust in God's mighty hand!

CHAPTER 2
Philosophy

Step back and think about the values and needs of your family.

Often what differentiates one homeschool family from another is curriculum. In conversations with other homeschoolers, it's inevitable questions will arise as to what curriculum you use and why you chose it. Some people can become almost idolatrous in their dedication to a specific method. Others have simply picked what's easiest. One family might change curriculum year to year because they haven't quite figured out what fits their learning style, or they may be captivated by what's new. I suggest simply stepping back and thinking about your values and family needs before choosing a curriculum path.

Discovering our educational philosophy is extremely important. I did not start out with any kind of philosophy in homeschooling other than knowing I wanted us to read great books. My entire educational experience as a child was in public school. I had no clue there were different educational philosophies.

A lot of folks begin homeschooling by picking a curriculum after doing some online research, by attending a homeschool convention, or by following the

FALL

recommendation of their friends. Sometimes, a beautifully laid out plan or guide grabs us and gets us excited.

> *No matter how beautiful or organized a curriculum may be, it will not work if it does not fall in line with your family goals.*

I did not come to embrace a homeschooling educational philosophy until we'd been homeschooling for about two years. Those other years were not wasted, they were part of the process. Discovering an educational philosophy was freeing. I found that holding to a philosophy helped me persevere with the materials I'd chosen when faced with a multitude of resources that all looked good. It also helped me feel more comfortable with why we might do things differently than other families. Our family philosophy made me find "home" for us and sit comfortably in it.

"Educational philosophy," speaks specifically to our views of what education is and how education should be carried out in our home. Our educational philosophy is where our family priorities and our method come together. Philosophy is not curriculum. Philosophy is what guides how we interact with our curriculum and what curriculum we choose.

So, how do we figure out our educational philosophy? We pray and we take time to diligently study the different methods of homeschooling that are available to us. We think honestly about ourselves and our children's strengths and challenges. We consider the atmosphere of learning we would like to have in our homes.

The first step is figuring out your family's priorities. This is what you did when you wrote your letter in "Winter." If you have not had a chance to write your letter, this would be a good time! Step two is studying different methods in homeschooling so you can connect with one whose philosophy matches yours. Step three is picking the materials and activities that help you train your children in the fear and admonition of the Lord.

Sadly, at times, homeschoolers can feel like an old tumbleweed changing one year to the next, looking for the perfect curriculum. If you can step back and figure out what you value most and what methods you connect with, then you can more easily pick your curriculum and stick with it. This allows you to feel a sense of accomplishment as you steadily interact with meaningful subjects and complete materials.

As we study different methods, we generally get a sense of which one might fit our style and goals. On the following pages, I have included a Homeschool Methods Table. Before reviewing it, I have a few thoughts:

For those who are already happy with the method and materials you use, it might be beneficial to read this Table to understand other philosophies and methods. In addition, there may be some resources or history for which you are unaware. Hopefully, this Table will encourage you that you have chosen the right style for your family.

Many families who are new to homeschooling start with a more "school-at-home" approach because it is a method that most resembles public or private school and it seems most comfortable. As some time passes, you may find one of the other methods better fits your children's learning and your philosophy. This is all a part of the normal changes that take place with a homeschool family. Some folks find a great method right away and never change. But, more often, the case is families make some adjustments along the way. However, giant changes in philosophy and method too often should be avoided. Changing a math curriculum a few times can be adjusted but changing from the Classical model to Charlotte Mason to Unit Studies and back to Classical will not allow for contentment and progress in your child's educational journey.

We must be perseverant with our chosen method. This is why I feel this process is so important. If you have never thought about your educational philosophy and simply took on someone else's curriculum, it seems wise to pull back and make sure you've chosen the path that fits. This Table can help you navigate some of the more popular homeschooling methods. This list includes origin, philosophy, strengths, limitations, as well as an inclusion of resources and specific curriculum for each of the most popular homeschooling methods.

Remember, no method is perfect. In no way is this list exhaustive, but I feel it can give a starting point to narrow your field of search. Whichever method you choose, do so prayerfully!

Terminology in Homeschooling Methods

When we begin to study homeschooling methods, we see terms that are unfamiliar. As some of these terms are in the following Table, here are a few definitions.

Textbooks refers to both printed and online material that follow a regular institutional school schedule and style. These books are generally focused on the presentation of facts and figures for one subject matter and may include comprehension questions and/or tests regularly.

Living Books refers to books that present facts within a story. These books are narrative or conversational in style and are usually written by a person who has a passion for the subject.[1,2] If we were to compare a textbook to a living book on the subject of birds, for example, the textbook would contain facts about bird species, geographic location, and beautiful pictures showing the differences between a variety of birds. The living book version would be something like *The Burgess Bird Book* by Thornton Burgess.[3] In this book, we find Peter Rabbit scurrying through the orchard holding discussions with various birds as they come home from winter. In this way, a child learns about different birds through Peter's adventures.

Classic Books refer to books of excellence that have stood the test of time.

Co-ops is another term used by homeschoolers to describe a gathering of homeschooling students to study a topic together. These co-ops are generally parent taught. Co-ops can be started by any group of families that want to support each other in their homeschooling endeavors. Some are small and meet in homes while others are large and meet in churches or other buildings and are run more organizationally, perhaps with paid teachers. Many co-ops focus on extracurricular subjects such as art, nature, and physical education. Some study specialized subject matters and topics that are important and possibly tough to teach in a home setting. Children also get to experience a different atmosphere of learning by joining a co-op.

HOMESCHOOL METHODS TABLES

"Traditional At-Home Method" | Origin

The "Traditional At-Home Method" organically arose from more parents choosing to homeschool their children. It features curriculum created in the hopes of taking the best of current institutionalized teaching styles, materials, routines, grading, and testing into the home environment.

A secondary group has emerged under traditional schooling, which is the group using online programs. Parents may use these for one subject or for the entire curriculum. In this case children may have online teachers versus parents, and all material is completed online.

"Traditional At-Home Method"			
Philosophy	**Strengths**	**Limitations**	**Resources/Support**
Bringing the conventional classroom home.

"Essentialism" in the thought that there is one right course of study for all children.

Generally, more textbook/workbook approach whether paper-based or online, though many Christian pre-packaged materials provide living books and a Christian worldview. | Standard scope and sequence of material.

Clear milestones of accomplishments (testing and grading built into the material).

Ease of use, parent does not have to sift through material; the year is laid out and children simply follow the schedule.

Follows traditional educational expectations in the event a child may have to go to an institutional school at some point and prepares them for a more traditional college-type classroom.

Some top-tier pre-packaged curriculum available.

Generally, align with federal and state learning standards. | Because curriculum is pre-packaged or consumables, this model can become expensive.

At times creating a conventional learning environment at home can be difficult for parents and cause burn out.

Inflexible, rigid schedule.

Time consuming consisting of long days.

Geared towards an average learner, does not consider learning differences.

Teacher-directed, Information transmitted through artificial learning experiences. | Often uses pre-packaged materials.

Programs may use living books or classical materials in addition to a modern/school at home approach or schedule; therefore, you may see some of these curricula listed under other methods. One curriculum may vary greatly from another. Where they are similar is in the sequence of "school-type" schedule and all materials for an entire grade year is provided. Many of these full-packaged programs offer some subjects separately, for example: a family may choose to use one of these curricula for their year of history only versus using the curriculum for every subject covered.

Some examples:
Abeka, Saxon, Houghton Mifflin Homeschool, Sonlight, Rod and Staff Bible Based Curriculum, Institute for Excellence in Writing (IEW), K12.com
Christian Liberty Academy, My Father's World, BJU Press Homeschooling, Alpha and Omega, Christian Light, School of Tomorrow. |

"Classical Method" | *Origin*

The "Classical Method" is historically minded, and language based. The modern proponent of the Classical Model was British writer and medieval scholar Dorothy Sayers. As the Nazis came to power in the 1930s, Sayers felt children could be easily influenced by tyrants. To combat this, Sayers proposed reinstating the classical form of education used in the Middle Ages.

The focus is teaching children to "think" for themselves. It borrows the wisdom of time-tested educational practices dating from as far back as Ancient Greece and Rome. In the case of the Biblical-Classical model, the roots trace back even further, to Hebrew concepts in the Old Testament. Typical classical homeschools employ "Great Classical Books."

"Classical Method"			
Philosophy	Strengths	Limitations	Resources/Support
"Perennialism": The core body of knowledge that children need has remained constant for hundreds of years. Based on medieval European curriculum, the Classical Method follows the Trivium 3 stages: Grammar (early elementary) learning facts, memorizing, and knowledge gathering; Dialectic or Logic (about 5th grade): when reasoning and logic begin to be applied to the knowledge, and Rhetoric (about 15 years of age): building skills of wisdom and judgment. The final stage seeks to produce students who can both write and speak persuasively and gracefully. Often includes the study of Latin and/or other languages. Historically Chronological order to the schedule.	Is adapted to stages of child development. Teaches thinking skills & verbal/written expression. Creates self-learners. Proven educational style for over hundreds of years and has produced great minds throughout history. Emphasis on Biblical worldview training. Focus on Great Books, Classical students are typically well-read and familiar with key works across the history of western civilization. Classical education reinforces one of the life skills most often neglected in formal public, and even private schools: logic. It can incorporate some parental liberties while retaining a strong academic rigor and systematic scope. Because the method is so popular there are lots of ready-to-use curriculum and networks of support.	Reading requirements can be cumbersome and challenging; students who struggle with reading may become overburdened by the amount of reading. For students who excel in other subjects, those strengths may suffer due to the lack of time available due to a rigorous reading schedule. Generally, less flexible due to the chronological and trivium order of learning. Typically, more desk work, rote learning than other homeschooling methods. Some parents may feel time spent on languages such as Latin could be better spent on other subjects more aligned with modern life.	Susan Wise Bauer and Jessie Wise, *The Well Trained Mind: A Guide to Classical Education*, 3rd ed. (Norton, 2009) WellTrainedMind.com ClassicalChristianHomeschooling.org Dorothy Sayers, "The Lost Tools of Learning," [Speech] Oxford Univ., 1947 ClassicalCurriculum.com PeaceHillPress.com MemoriaPress.com VeritasPress.com Progeny Press.com Institute for Excellence in Writing Classical Conversations: classicalconversations.org. Many families join "CC's" which meet once a week and provide support, socialization, and group learning. Oliver Demille Thomas Jefferson Education: Teaching a Generation of Leaders for the 21st Century. TJedOnline.com 2009

"Charlotte Mason Method" | *Origin*

Based on the philosophies of British educator and pioneer Charlotte Mason CM (1842-1923). Her belief was children should have a wide and generous education. She trained teachers and others working with young children. She opened the "House of Education" in Ambleside England. She co-founded the PEU (Parents Education Union, deemed PNEU) "Education is an atmosphere, a discipline, a life." Focus is on living books. Known for coining the term "twaddle": inferior materials which speak down to the listener often insulting the intelligence; not inspiring the spirit and mind nor sparking virtue.

| "Charlotte Mason Method" ||||
Philosophy	Strengths	Limitations	Resources/Support
CM believed all children are persons, not empty vessels to be filled but possessing full abilities for learning and knowledge and capable of understanding the world around them, "the souls of all children are waiting for the call of knowledge to awaken them to delightful living." Focus on how all creation works together before narrowing a field of study: "Education is the science of relations." Focus on how learning impacts virtue not simply knowledge for knowledge sake. Attention to habits, short appropriate lessons, narration to teach the child to think clearly, dictation to teach spelling and grammar. Other subjects include art and music. Motto: I am, I can, I ought, I will… Generally harder academic work kept for the mornings, afternoons free for outdoors, handicrafts, other areas of interest. Time outdoors and nature study is a hallmark where the CM model differs from other methods.	Exposed to living objects and books rather than artificial. Eliminates meaningless busywork. Focus on beautiful and classical words which inspire good writing and virtuous thoughts. Stresses good habits and character development. Students use journals and portfolios more than quizzes and tests. Lower-cost materials, downloadable, or sometimes free. Well-suited to non-professional teachers. Solid biblical model and training in materials. Developmentally appropriate. Works well for whole family study.	Not as many options of prepared material as some other methods. May neglect higher level studies because of its emphasis on art, literature, and nature study. May become too eclectic. Some families have found they must outsource to non-CM materials to fill in some gaps. This method can seem neutral on intermediate and advanced studies in math and science. To address this, parents may use a more eclectic model for these areas. Fewer publishers producing modern CM material.	A six volume book series on CM educational philosophy is available. A free version of these volumes may be found at Ambleside Online.org, which also provides free and full CM curriculum guides. CM Curriculum/Books: SimplyCharlotteMason.com LivingBooksPress.com ADelectableEducation.com CharlotteMasonHomeschooling.com AGentleFeast.com CM Philosophy: CharlotteMasonInstitute.org Books: *Consider This* by Karen Glass *For the Children's Sake* by Susan Schaeffer Macaulay *A Charlotte Mason Companion* by Karen Andreola Habits: *Laying Down the Rails* by Sonya Shafer Other Curriculum: Science/Nature: Nicole Williams: SabbathMoodHomeschool.com Writing: Julie Bogart: BraveWriter.com Support: CharlotteMasonInCommunity.com

FALL

"Unit Study Method" | Origin

Unit Studies do not have a specific origin; they are more of a method which has come to the forefront as a form of how a family might present material for homeschooling.

"Thematic"- Children can focus on one overarching theme and all their subjects can be combined under this theme.

"Unit Study Method"			
Philosophy	Strengths	Limitations	Resources/Support
The theme for a family's unit study can be a historical event, a holiday, a location, a person, among others. For example, a unit study on birds could be offered as part of nature study, sketching, essays, reading textbook or living books, biographies on famous naturalist or ornithologist and writing about them (Reading, Writing, Art). Studying the parts, functions, and life cycles of birds and perhaps even the aerodynamics of flight, determining the migration paths, habitats, (Science and Math): and ecological/sociological impact of birds (Social Studies) and building bird houses or feeders (Hands-on activities). A common approach is picking a time in history and following the same idea. For example: Ancient Egypt might be covered by maps of Egypt in geography and living books on the history of Egypt. Art could cover hieroglyphics, the book of *Exodus* in reading, and Bible theories of human origins and early transportation or food preparation in science; ancient pyramids for geometry in math.	Families with multiple ages can all learn together A family's interests can be pursued deeply, students get the whole picture. Curiosity and independent thinking are generated. Knowledge is interrelated so is learned easily and remembered longer. Makes learning fun, can be interactive, making learning come alive Student-directed This method can partner well with other methods such as: Eclectic or Unschooling.	Some Unit Study curricula might skip over whole subject areas, thus leaving the parent to anticipate and compensate for educational gaps. Similarly, in subjects like math where knowledge must be built one step on another, thematic shifts may leave gaps in knowledge. Some parents who use unit studies adjust by using a more traditional method for math while using unit studies for other subjects. Hard to assess/record the level of learning occurring. Prepared unit study curricula are expensive. Do-it-yourself unit studies require planning and lots of creativity from the parent which may cause burn-out. Subjects that are hard to integrate into the unit may be neglected such as Math and Science. Without a strong educational philosophy behind its methods there is no unified set of ideas explaining the "big picture" for this approach.	Valerie Bendt's, *Unit Studies made Easy*, (Bendt Family Ministries, 2004) Lori Pickert, *Project Based Homeschooling: Mentoring Self-Directed Learners* (CreateSpace, 2012). Interest-Led Learning Evan-Moor science units Teacher Created Materials units. Weaver units Homehearts – The Unit Study Approach UnitStudies.com Unit Studies by Amanda Benet Konos.com DIY Homeschooler free Unit Studies Eclectic Homeschool Online – create your own unit studies Donna Young – Unit Study Planner Gail Kappenman, "What is a Unit Study?" (Crosswalk.com, 2009).

"Eclectic Method" | *Origin*

Like Unit Studies, in that this category is not so much based on a philosophy but more of a method in which families choose what they see as the best of different approaches and philosophies to meet different subjects or children's needs. The longer a family homeschools, the more likely they may find themselves as eclectic homeschoolers.

After trying many methods and curricula with many children, moms discover what fails and what succeeds regarding routine in their home. They may discover they don't need to worry so much about following one specific curriculum or set schedule and can use multiple resources for different children's needs at different times.

"Eclectic Method"			
Philosophy	Strengths	Limitations	Resources/Support
The belief that different methods fit for different subject matters and different children. Using multiple methods: An eclectic family may choose classical materials for their study of history and language, then use standard textbooks or workbooks for math, science, handwriting and spelling, a CM approach to nature study, a traditional curriculum for language arts, and simply use an online list for readers and read alouds. A less curriculum-based example: An eclectic family might have children simply read a chapter from any book they like and read more classic and living books together for history and read aloud time; writing might be focused on journal writing, letter writing and creative writing; math might be completed through an online program and science through a local co-op.	Most flexible homeschool model. Most resources and material available as families can pick from any style they feel fits best for a child or subject they plan to cover. As the parent, you take charge of the education of your child, finding the balance of sticking with the material you know fits, and then not feeling shaken by picking other sources when one method does not work. In addition, you feel freer to reevaluate and change material when something doesn't work which may reduce burnout and stagnating. Developmentally appropriate as you pick material that fits with your child for any given season. Strong support networks and availability to choose many homeschool community groups in which to participate. If a child excels in one subject area but is deficient in another a mom can pick curricula that meets both needs.	The availability of all the methods can feel too open-ended and overwhelm you with choices. May feel a sense of lack of progression if too many changes in material are made too often. Not all homeschool materials and methods mix well together which may confuse teacher or learners. Mixing too many different materials or philosophies could leave you with not understanding any of them well, versus getting the best of them all. Might run the risk of only skimming good curriculum that might need long-term dedication to experience the full benefit.	EclecticHomeschool.org Eclectic-Homeschool.com TheHomeschoolMom.com – Eclectic Method Jeanne Faulkner, "Instead of Curriculum" (TheHomeschoolMom.com, 2013) Amber Oliver, *The Relaxed Art of Eclectic Homeschooling* (Self-published, 2012). Kelly Crawford, *Think Outside the Classroom: A Practical Approach to Relaxed Homeschooling* (CreateSpace, 2014). <u>Curricula and Teaching Materials</u> A2Z Homes Cool Learning Style Test Time4Learning – Eclectic Homeschool Page The Great Courses Eclectic-Homeschool.com – Reading List

"Unschooling Method" | Origin

John Holt, a 20th century educator who believed that the normal modes of schooling destroy both the desire and curiosity of learning. Wrote "Teach your Own" where he concluded what children need is not better curriculum but more real-world experiences. They need time to ponder. With advice, guidebooks, and road maps, they will figure out what they need to know when they need to know it.

"Unschooling Method"			
Philosophy	Strengths	Limitations	Resources/Support
"Child-led learning" the parent is the facilitator.

"Wholism": although unschoolers may use many books, they focus on a richer learning experience by including hands-on life activities as a major part of the child's learning experience (based on the child's interests.)

We are naturally curious, and children don't need to be forced to learn. Learning is all-day every day, and we follow our interests. Parents do their best to create an environment of natural learning.

Generally, no use of formal curriculum. Unconventional, Individualistic. Children get to academically pursue their own passions. Large priority on experiential, activity-based, and learn-as-you-go education. Though parents may teach the basics. | Takes little planning. Children may learn from real world experts and plenty of time and space to figure things out on their own.

Children are less likely to become academically frustrated or "burned out."

Children can delve into a subject as deeply or as shallowly as they desire. Provides a discipleship model of learning. Encourages a love for learning and self-learners.

Each student is seen as a unique and creative individual.

Because a parent must get to know a child's individual gifts and interests it teams well as an educational aspect to the parenting relationship. | Some subjects may get neglected. Hard to assess level of learning. Lacks the security of a clearly laid out program Is extremely child centered. Difficult to explain to others. May be overly optimistic about what children will accomplish on their own.

Seen as reactionary, as if backing away from the mistakes of other methods will keep you from mistakes in the other direction. Some traditional forms of education have stood the test of time, and unschooling can seem to to suggest all such formal methods must be thrown out. Some students may need more structure and rigor. Can be sporadic and unsystematic in covering content leaving large gaps in core competencies

A good change from mechanical educational systems, but it can become too "free-form" in which some parents might say "kids have to learn subjects they aren't always interested in." By generally rejecting traditional schooling parents may find themselves trying to reinvent topics or subjects that have already been answered appropriately with traditional means. | UnschoolRules.com
JohnHoltGWS.com
John Holt & Pat Farenga, *Teach Your Own: The John Holt Book of Homeschooling*, 1st Paperback Ed. (De Capo Press, 2003)
Clark Aldrich, *Unschooling Rules: 55 Ways to Unlearn What We Know About Schools and Rediscover Education* (Greenleaf Book Group, 2011)
Mary Griffith, *The Unschooling Handbook: How to Use the Whole World as Your Child's Classroom*, 2d ed. (Three Rivers Press, 1998)
The Master List of Unschooling Resources by WeedemAndReap
JohnHoltGWS.com –
List of Unschooling Blogs
Support:
Family Unschoolers Network
Unschoolers.com
Unschooling in the World |

Resources guiding the creation of the preceding Homeschool Methods Tables include:

- Homeschool Legal Defense Association. "Common Homeschool Learning Approaches." 2018. www.hslda.org.

- The Homeschooling Mom. "Homeschooling Styles: What's the Difference?" 2018. www.thehomeschoolmom.com.

- David Ferrer. The Quad. "Homeschooling: Which Model is Right for You?" 2017. www.thebestschools.org

- Homeschooling.com, The Original Homeschooling Community. "Different Methods of Homeschooling." 2018. www.homeschool.com.

CHAPTER 3
Schedules and Routines

As a seasoned homeschooler once told me,
"The material is not your master; you master the material."

Schedules and routines are easy to create but hard to keep. Why? On a piece of paper, we create beautiful columns and tables with dates and times and matching subjects, and the plan looks lovely. But the day-to-day carrying out of what we place on paper takes perseverance and steadiness. So, it's important to take the time to create a thoughtful and realistic school schedule. What are some things we need to consider as we create the right pace and right atmosphere for learning?

Routine / Speed

"Never hurry and never worry!"
~ Charlotte's Web, E.B. White *~*

There is a "just right" feeling to your day. You want to be efficient without being stressed. Often the frantic pace is because we struggle to enjoy being in the moment of this one school day. If we rush through everything, we will become annoyed and not have a peaceful atmosphere. Try to enjoy the material you are teaching. The goal is not just to get done. Enjoy learning with your children. Each season there are exciting subjects for which we engage. When we rush though our days, we're also rushing our children to grow up.

This morning, I was thinking about how Jesus did not come to earth as a full-grown man. He spent nine months in Mary's womb. Jesus spent years growing as a boy under the tutelage of His parents. He didn't begin His ministry work until He was in His 30's. If that was God's design for His own Son, why are we in such a hurry to "raise" these children?

As Susan Schaeffer Macaulay states in *For the Children's Sake*, "And so, over-entertained, pushed, pulled, and tidied up, often the child of today has the rich creative play response crushed out. Sometimes the only thing his dulled eyes focus on is a premature adolescence which will release him from childhood."[5]

Routine / Rhythm

The timing of when it is right to move from one subject to the next is of great importance in keeping a more enjoyable school day. "The child has been doing sums for some time and is getting unaccountably stupid: take away his slate and let him read history, and you find his wits fresh again. Imagination, which has had no part in the sums, is called into play by the history lesson, and the child brings a lively unexhausted power to his new work. School time-tables are usually drawn up with a view to give the brain of the child variety of work; but the secret of weariness children often show in the home school room is, that no such judicious change of lessons is contrived."[6]

If we offer our child a broad education, we will have many subjects to cover that need good attention. And we all have a limited amount of attention we can give to each of these topics. We should offer age appropriate amounts of time to work on each topic.

If math is taking our child over an hour and he can't seem to get it all done, set a timer for 30 or 45 minutes and call it done for the day so he can focus on other subjects. Of course, some children can and should handle more in their routine than others. However, with long, drawn out lessons, does a child have a chance to sit and ponder or process any of the information? Do they have the energy to put towards their other pursuits? The quick read and cheerful discussion could leave them wanting more. But attention wanes when we push to get through one more chapter. Mom becomes irritable! Arguments ensue.

At other times, we are so captivated with a story we might read two or three extra chapters. This is the reason we must always keep the full days schedule and responsibilities in the back of our mind. In this way, we know when we can be spontaneous and when we can't. Sometimes we can get more in and sometimes we just shouldn't.

We are like lifeguards who oversee the whole picture. We only intervene or "blow the whistle" when redirection is needed to keep all of the different activities moving along appropriately.

Routine / Planning

Some people prepare their academic school goals months in advance, some plan a week at a time, and some pull material out the night before. In general, we want to take time each weekend to look over the week ahead and get a sense of what we will cover.

Some materials, like read alouds, do not take preparation time, but we may still want to consider how we will have the children respond to the read aloud. Will it be a family discussion or a drawn or written response? Especially if we have an experiment coming up, we don't want to pull out the materials only to find we didn't have all the items needed. Indeed, we might want to try the experiment ourselves beforehand. We will always feel better when we've reviewed the routine for the week, and handouts are ready for map work, or bags are already packed for a nature day. Preparing our mind and materials ahead of time will save time in the long run. But don't make the mistake of letting the preparation take longer than it should.

For a period of time, I would set a 20-minute timer at night to allow preparation for the next school day. When time was up, I made myself stop and turn my mind to other pursuits. I'm in this lovely phase of homeschooling now where the material takes care of itself and my children are independent enough that I don't have to prepare as much as when I first started. As children get older, they most likely will be able "to own" the routine.

No matter how you prepare, make sure to allow yourself time, at the end of each day, free from thoughts about your children and their education. Spend time with your husband! Don't neglect that most important relationship. Also, put energy into the self-care opportunities we spoke about earlier to help you grow.

If we do not have time to do anything else in our day other than think about and cover academic subjects, it's likely we have too much on our plate, "If you have more to do than time to do it in, the simple fact is this: some of what you are doing isn't on His agenda for you."[7]

Routine / Guidebooks

Many homeschool curriculum guides provide an outline for what we should accomplish each school week. We may need to make some alterations to that schedule so we're accomplishing a reasonable amount of material for our family. We are allowed to do this! Often well-meaning curriculum gives so much work to cover that halfway through our day, we still haven't gotten to all the subjects planned. This will cause burnout. Even the best of materials must be taken in appropriate chunks for your family.

How can we recalibrate the amount of work? When the lessons instruct reading two chapters, we might reduce it to one. This allows attention and time for meaningful discussion. As a family, instead of reading history every day, we might read it three days a week and simply take longer to get through the material. If the curriculum says something should be finished in 12 weeks and it takes us 16, that might be fine. If the spelling book says our child should be at level 4, but he's at level 3, that may be perfectly appropriate for that child. The opposite is also true. If our child is zooming through a subject, it might be time to let them jump ahead. We may decide to join some type of co-op or organization where there is a timeline we must keep. We will figure out if this is an ally to our educational goals or adds stress.

I am not saying we should not have a rigorous schedule. I am not saying we should not finish material. What I am trying to say is that it must be balanced for your home.

Not getting to every book or every educational level will not thwart God's plan for our children's lives.

Routine / Cheerful
I have found, if we have the right fit, even the youngest child can do most of their work on their own with minimal instruction. This allows mom to put her energy toward the family subjects or harder subjects. If ALL of it is hard, you will not last.

The overall idea is to keep a nice pace to the day, engaging in your material. If our children are coming to the material diligently and our home has a cheerful atmosphere, what more can we ask?

When we look over our routine once it's down on paper, and what we feel is peaceful and excited, we know we are on the right track. If what we feel is a sense of overwhelm or, "I don't think there will be enough hours in the

FALL

day to do this," listen to that voice. Maybe something needs to come off the schedule. What we eliminate may be an activity, a subject, or the amount of time we spend on a subject or activity.

Routine / Evaluation

If we have a reasonable routine and yet still aren't *ever* getting to all of our work, then perhaps an evaluation is overdue. One thought Sarah Mackenzie brings up in *Teaching from Rest* is the importance of regularly evaluating our routine. This does not mean we make huge curriculum changes, but it's simply a conscientious observation of the routine. She encourages this type of evaluation about every six weeks.[7]

Ask yourself questions such as, "Are we getting to all the material we'd like to?" "Are we getting to all of our priority areas?" For example, we may find that we're getting to all our academic work, but have not volunteered as a family, or spent much time outside. Does this need to change, wait for another season, or can it be paired with another activity? For example, why not pair reading time with the outdoors, or pair history reading with lunch. Other questions might include, "Would it be good to change our location or the order in which we cover material?"

If all things are working well, we may not need to change anything. There is a balance of being diligent to the plan, knowing whether some things simply take perseverance, or whether it's time for a change.

No amount of alterations in the routine will make child training easy, but it can be more peaceful. We may have to sit with a child and walk slowly through some subjects. But sometimes a slight change in the routine does help! It's good for our brain to be stimulated in new ways, whether through a change of scenery or direction. It is important these changes not be made too often, or they could lose their impact. Suddenly, no one knows what the routine is, and the schedule becomes more frazzled and disjointed than it needs to be.

Routine / Large Changes
What would be the cause of a more dramatic change in our schedule? Maybe it's a change in curriculum or the addition of a new subject or activity. Maybe it's a new educational philosophy.

At least once a year, go through the process in "Winter" again and rewrite your letter. It can seem like a lot of evaluating, and we might wonder if the time is worthwhile? I've done these evaluations for a few years, and they have breathed life into our homeschool.

Each year is set apart as its own special "moment in time." It's unreasonable to think the routine we start when our children are young will stay the same as they get older. Remember, if we make changes to the routine that don't seem to be working, step back and evaluate if we just need to give it more time, or if it was a bad call. It is okay to say, "This isn't working, so we're going back to how we were doing it before."

Understand, some subjects or materials you were excited to try just don't work out. A seasoned homeschool educator once told me about "twenty percent of homeschooling materials are wasted." That is just the nature of trying different options. Not everything is a good fit. But if we are throwing out 30% or more of our material every season, something in our priorities, routine, or method probably needs to change.

Routine / Unplanned
There are times when we must accept that some parts of the day, or even the year, do not go as planned. Children (and parents) get sick, a concept is forgotten, a child's interest wanes on a once beloved topic. These experiences tend to test our sense of security and success. But we must live one day at

a time. We need to show our children that our peace and patience does not go out the window if we must backtrack on schoolwork, or if we had to take a week off because of a stomach virus. Our faith is in God's grand plan and design, and we cannot expect each day to go exactly as planned. Our joy cannot be tied to everyone always obediently following our perfect routine!

There are wonderful experiences that can happen in those unplanned moments. A child suddenly begins reading better and a question is asked about God that had never been considered before! We may have to take time to correct a child's misbehavior and spend some time working through the problem. Yet, continue to be diligent to the important academic aspects of your home education schedule. It's important your children learn this discipline. It will spur us on when we see our educational goals coming to fruition. But we should not let our lack of self-control go haywire when things are not fitting into our expectations.

Routine / Siblings

If we have children of varied ages, they should help each other! An older child can read to the younger or vice versa. Send two or more children to work on a chore. Have children take turns reading during family Bible time. Have them spend time outdoors, riding bikes or taking a walk together. Those connections will be valuable to their relationship as adults.

Routine / Music

Don't overlook the beauty of music in your school day. Music can be an assistant to atmosphere. While working on writing or art, why not have beautiful music playing in the background? Calming or worshipful music can also slow us down to be in the moment. Hymns and songs of praise can refocus our hearts and remind us that our strength is found in God alone.

Routine / Food & Drink

Food preparation and presentation was something I rushed through in my day. It took years to realize food is something we are supposed to enjoy. In order to do this, we must slow down. The need for food weaves through many parts of your day when we are caring for growing children. While enjoying meals together, we can also enjoy poetry or read alouds.

After finishing schoolwork, there is nothing wrong with enjoying lemonade and cookies as a reward for work well done. Some tend to get a bit legalistic and worry this might appear to be rewarding food for work that should be done naturally. However, in moderation, special treats can add to the joyous environment and give a bit of extra motivation to get the work done. One home educator always included coffee and chocolate with her math lessons. That sounds good to me! Our nature co-op offers cookies and lemonade during our poetry time. Not overdone, food adds to the atmosphere of great learning.

Our children need to learn how to cook and bake and prepare healthy meals. They can begin learning this skill by serving snacks to each other, helping set the table, and cleaning up after a meal. Later, they can help cut vegetables or mix batter. Much learning can take place in the kitchen.

Routine / Ordering

A lot of home educators have found that putting the more difficult academic subjects on the schedule earlier in the day is a great help to the flow of the routine. So, as you set your routine, keep this principle in mind, "It follows that the hours for lessons should be carefully chosen, after periods of mental rest -sleep or play, for instance - and when there is no excessive activity in any other part of the system. Thus, the morning, after breakfast (the digestion of which lighter meal is not a severe task), is much the best time for lessons and every sort of mental work; if the whole afternoon cannot be spared for out-of-door recreation, that is the time for mechanical tasks such as needlework, drawing, practicing."[5]

Routine / Expectations of the Young

We expect too much academically and too little in the way of habits in young children. If there is one thing I could redo, it would be waiting to start "schoolwork" until my children were older. I would have reduced how much time we spent on lessons when my kids were ages 4-8. I would have focused more time on developing good habits, outdoor time, good books, and family chores. This is not because children can't do the work, it's because when we start the work so young, they are generally missing out on other skills needed first.

Again, it is too easy to get stuck in our thinking about what the general public has to say about early childhood education. But you will save yourself much grief by starting out slow and waiting until they are ready for studious book learning.

Because every child is different, there is not an exact age litmus test of when to start "school". Instead, be aware of your child and what his or her capabilities are at each learning stage. Don't feel the need to push your children ahead. Let learning happen naturally and reasonably.

Don't be held captive by the worry they are missing out on what other children are doing at their age level. It might be they will experience a book or a subject content at a deeper level if they interact with it at an older age. If our children seem behind their peers, it's a fine response to say, "This is something we're still working on" or "We plan to start that type of work a bit later."

Routine / Expectations of the Older
As our children get older, we slowly hand off some of the schedule to them. Better yet, have them make their own schedules and help them be disciplined to keep to their plan.

I have found in conversations with many homeschoolers that an understandable but grave shift happens as youth begin high school. Though your child may be college-bound, be thoughtful that the planning of credits does not outweigh your time preparing your child for a healthy adult life. In other words, as children begin years 9-12th grade, review your schedule and make sure subjects like Economics and Trigonometry don't outweigh learning to budget, cook, volunteer, or hold a job. We look at each of our children as individuals and make adjustments with the whole person in mind.

Routine / Children with Challenges
Because I have a child who, at varying points, has dealt with dyslexia, anxiety, and OCD, I'd like to share a few thoughts on their routine.

Children with anxiety need to be outside as much as possible. Their technology must be reduced. They need to be slowly walked into places of independence in a steady and deliberate manner. This must be a part of the routine; it is likely more important than academics. We must be careful to teach them to understand their emotions yet, if they are always being overanalyzed, problems often become bigger than what they are. Be patient, yet keep moving forward. Pray and fast for these children.

OCD is a kicker for me. It's complicated. For us, it comes and goes. It shows up boldly then disappears. It's humorous at times and then it's simply weird. For some its debilitating. What we've tried to see over the years is where it can be viewed as a positive. These children have deep interests. They keep well to a good routine; keeping a daily schedule is a bonus. Issues come up when change happens. We do our best to keep to our schedule and not overload. If we add one activity, another must come off his plate. As he gets older, we allow for spontaneity in small bits because we all know that life is unpredictable, and they need to be able to adjust.

Be patient with dyslexic children or those with slow processing disorder. These children will generally need to be exposed to material and study habits many more times to "get" a concept or skill. Share reading by letting them read a few pages and you read a few pages. Allow them to listen to audiobooks and complete written or oral narration afterwards. Often these children can understand, and are interested in, material beyond their reading capability so have lots of read alouds as a family! In regard to writing, offer many opportunities for free writing that will not be corrected and deliberately pick one or two papers to correct together each week. We will faithfully expect their spelling and writing to improve with time.

Keep writing and reading activities short with multiple opportunities throughout the day versus long periods of sitting with heavy reading and writing requirements. Consistent copywork can be a huge help to these children. I've also found as my child ages that keyboarding has also been a great assistant to both reading and writing skills. Increase these with time.

Help them understand how to verbalize their differences to others. Although these children may need to work on material a year or two behind their age level, find areas where they can work at or above level such as history or geography or music. They need to understand they are good at many things! The goal is mastering material appropriate to their learning level. The work should challenge but not freeze these children.

I have found that if you are going to seek outside help, it is generally better to find centers that work on underlying brain development and connections versus tutoring. Programs that strengthen their brain. Shoving more information in will not work if the brain cannot receive or process appropriately.

Routine / Summer

Some families find it helpful to homeschool throughout the year and not take a "summer break". It allows for one to stretch out the timing of a traditional one-year curriculum. Others like to work hard during the other three seasons of the year and take the summer off. In the high-school years, the summer can be used to cover a subject needed for college entrance that could not be peacefully fitted into the other months.

The summer is also a great time to challenge children in non-academic areas such as going to a summer camp, working at a job, or participating in volunteer work. It's fine some years to take the summer off and, in other years, we may find it's better to keep working through our normal school schedule. Either way, we find God is always teaching, even when we are at rest.

Routine / Strength

If we suddenly feel stuck and have lost our joy in homeschooling, we must check ourselves. Are we receiving our strength from the Holy Spirit, or are we working in our own strength? Re-read your "Winter" letter. Daily pray about your schedule and routine. Ask for a willingness to change or go with the flow as needed. Stay daily connected to the Lord and His purposes for your family.

Routine / Time Off

Until this year, I tended to feel guilty when we took any time off from our academics. But a beautiful aspect of homeschooling is taking off a week or two to help a friend in need or take a last-minute trip. We should take advantage of the freer options provided in homeschooling.

FALL

When COVID-19 began, my mother was preparing to get married. As many families experienced, our plans had to change. I spent time in prayer asking for the Lord's guidance. The initial plan was a simple trip to Mississippi. What God organized instead was a two-week drive, the kids and I, through Arkansas, Tennessee and Alabama to retrace the Civil Rights Movement. We traveled to Florida and back seeing sites we had read about in books but never imagined we would see in person.

We took part in my mom's beautiful, sunny wedding day to a godly man! My kids played with cousins, learned to usher, and helped with last minute wedding details. They played ukulele with my amazing aunt! We sunk our toes in the sand, filled out pockets with shells, and jumped waves. On the way home, a sudden backroad in Louisiana brought us to the spot where Texas Rangers ambushed Bonnie and Clyde. All of this because we were willing to let go for a bit.

Be prayerful about when you need to let go of the routine to take advantage of your life, and adventure. Now and again, let God bring you some beautiful spontaneous moments. Go!

Routine / Dinner

I finally found the words this year, at 43, to say, I don't like to cook. I see value in it, I want to teach it to my children, and I do cook, because it's a necessity of life. You might love to cook. But, if you don't, it's okay. Many women told me cooking can become difficult because so much of their energy goes toward homeschooling and activities that meals became a secondary priority. Often after a long and studious day, the stress of "what's for dinner?" can be exhausting.

It may be an extremely worthwhile project to streamline your meal routine. Whatever we can do to get it off our mind and keep it simple can eliminate stress from our day. Some women do this by picking one day a week to meal plan and then order groceries online. Others simply go to the grocery store the same day each week. For others, it's important to put on their calendar some planned "meals out." For me, I cook almost the same thing every week. My meal plan is: brinner (breakfast for dinner), pork, fish, pasta, pizza night, chicken, dinner out. We do not have food allergies or sensitivities which certainly simplifies meals. I try to make sure we have one vegetable at dinner. My kids often make their own breakfast and lunch, but they must have one fruit or vegetable. You may need much more variety and enjoy cooking and that is wonderful. For me, simplification works better. Take time to think about what kind of meal prep, grocery schedule, and cooking routine will be best for your season of life.

It's too easy to fall into this habit of eating out if we don't have a meal plan. It should be seen as a part of our school schedule. When our children are old enough, we have a duty to teach them about healthy meal planning and preparation. Be reasonable. Save yourself time and money by planning and cooking but leave yourself room in the schedule for "pizza nights" or Sundays at a restaurant where you enjoy a meal out together. Be balanced.

As children age, we should also slowly hand over meal preparation and cooking duties to them. Why not have our teenager take charge one night a week in cooking the family meal? It's easy to focus on the academic education of our children and forget that a huge part of growing is life education. We might be a great artist or a talented scientist, but how much more time will be spent cooking meals for our family? We do our children a disservice when our need for a clean kitchen, or a meal done without fuss, keeps us from better preparing them for the realities of being a responsible member of their future family.

It is true they can learn these skills as adults, but it will be much harder and more stressful for them. This does not have to be done all at once. Taking slow steps, we hand over cooking regularly to our children.

FALL

Inviting friends into our home for a meal is also a great opportunity for our kids. The children get a model of hosting and they observe us care for and enjoy dear friends. Try to hold on to family dinner time. It makes common sense that, due to activities and responsibilities, it cannot always be possible. But using family dinners to stay close and evaluate the day, to laugh together and share stories, is of extreme value to a warm and generous home.

Routine / Affection

Take moments every day to hug, pat on the back, and have a conversation with your children. Although we want to encourage our children towards independence and a life apart from us, don't miss out on those sweet times. Tell them you love them. Try to embrace the truth that you do not always have to be in "teacher mode." Don't forget these are the babies we carried in our womb. These are the toddlers we read bedtime stories to at night and tiringly disciplined. These are the children we cheered at soccer games and watched at piano recitals. They are the teenagers that want to have conversations at midnight, and we must gently walk with them through relationship difficulties. We will watch them drive down the road to a life away from our arms. Remember to enjoy time together by playing and just being a family that lives together under one roof.

Routine / Humor

Always try to keep your sense of humor. Many of the things we get all worked up over don't matter when it comes to eternal life (as my mother would tell me). None of us know ahead of time about the struggles and successes our child may have in their lifetime. Life can be difficult, and our children will discover this. But in your home, while they are under your care, enjoy them! Laugh as much as possible, even when things seem a mess. Always remember the goodness of God and rest in His sovereignty.

Routine / The Bible Alone

In the end, no matter how easy school is for your child or how great a curriculum you choose, all children will face inevitable sufferings and difficulties. Only one material was designed to prepare us for that, the Bible. There are many beautiful and moving books that we are so blessed to hold in our hands. Wonderful writers take us to faraway places and teach us amazing lessons. I am grateful to these authors that span decades and teach us about subjects from geology to physics and culture to astronomy. Books can make us laugh until our belly hurts. Books can make us cry because we feel deeply what the character feels. But, the foundational book for our lives is the one that will guide us through the ups and downs of life - Scripture alone. Make the practice of personal and family Scripture reading a treasured time in your home!

> "I want to know one thing, the way to heaven: how to land safe on that happy shore. God himself has condescended to teach the way; for this very end he came from heaven. He has written it down in a book! Oh, give me that book! At any price, give me the book of God! I have it: here is knowledge enough for me. Let me be: 'A man of one book.'"[8]
>
> ~ John Wesley ~

CHAPTER 4
A Sample Schedule

Putting together a family schedule is like painting or writing an essay.
It calls for brainstorming, creativity, and stepping away for a while to reassess.

Draft One: Priorities

Look over your priority list. Gather your preferred medium for working through a schedule: computer, phone, blank piece of paper. Fill in your weekly schedule beginning with your top priorities and moving to your least priorities. You do not need to mark the "time" you will spend on these subjects yet, just how many days or which days you'd like to focus on these areas. Some of what you might consider the "basics," such as math, reading and handwriting, may not have been listed on your priority list. Don't worry, these will be added in the second draft.

Draft Two: Basics

Place the basics in the schedule. What are the basics? These are subject you know you need to cover that were not already listed in your priorities. Possibly: math, science, reading, history, handwriting, spelling etc. The basics are usually covered most days of the week, but not necessarily all.

Now, in each day of the week, order what you want the flow to be between priorities and basics. How will you move from harder to easier subjects?

What is the best time of day for a subject? Be thoughtful toward subjects that will be covered together or subjects/time period in the day when older kids will be on their own. To keep your schedule from getting into a rut, have at least one day that looks totally different from the others. Remember, you're the lifeguard here!

Draft Three: Activities

Add your extra-curricular activities. If music was on your priority list, it's likely you've already put music lessons on the schedule. But if art lessons have not been put on the schedule yet, look at the shrinking time and see if it can be reasonably added. This is where you may struggle to create a balanced schedule. Step back and get a feel for the schedule. Is it reasonable to add the extra activity? Is there space?

Final / Curriculum

Look over the completed schedule one more time. Be thoughtful as to whether you are giving too much or too little emphasis to priorities and non-priorities. Finally, go back through the schedule and remove one item. When we first make a routine, we put everything in! We think, "We'll find the money, or a way." If this is the case, then the subject or activity would be lovely to include, but this is not the season. Remove it from the list.

Now, with your educational philosophy and schedule in mind you begin looking for the curriculum you want to use to present your subjects. Some of these are listed in the earlier table. You might also want to look at "Living Stories" at the end of this section where the women I interviewed shared what curriculum they use. Once you have curriculum in your hand you might see where some final refining of your schedule may need to occur. You will now be able to decide how much time is reasonable for each child and each subject.

You may not need to say, "We will always start math right at 9:00 a.m. and always start reading right at 10:00 a.m." But you may need to realize, to be able to keep a peaceful schedule through the day, everyone needs to wake up by 8:30 a.m., then flow from one subject to the next in a reasonable time frame. I often simply plan what I feel we should accomplish before lunch and what we can do in the afternoon or evening.

Overall, we will need to try out the schedule for a week or so and make some adjustments when you see the reality of how your schedule plays out. Each day will look slightly different because you are real people and some days material is grasped easily and sometimes material is harder. Be diligent and trust the Lord.

Riffe Family Sample

Next is a sample of our family's schedule from last year. Your priorities will differ from ours, so your schedule will likely look quite different. The point here, is to see if you can connect how our family's priority list for 2019/2020 (shown in Winter) is represented in this weekly schedule.

FALL

Sample Family Schedule
Monday through Friday

Monday	Tuesday	Wednesday (Nature Day)	Thursday	Friday
Individual Bible	Individual Bible	Morning Together	Individual Bible	Nature Study Co-op
Individual Exercise Oldest Child	Individual Exercise Oldest Child	Hymn	Individual Exercise Oldest Child	
Math	Math	CM motto/ Church Creeds	Math	Nature Walk
Family Outdoor Exercise	Family Outdoor Exercise	Park/Nature Walk/Nature Journal	Kids Outdoor Exercise without mom	Nature Journal
History Reading (oral/written narration)	History Reading (oral/written narration)	Nature Lore Reader (oral/written narration)	History Reading (oral/written narration)/VOM videos	Nature Reading
Readers (oral narration)	Readers (oral narration)	Science (oral/written narration)	Readers (oral narration)	Artist/ Composer Study
Handwriting/ Spelling	Handwriting/ Spelling	Cursive	Handwriting/ Dictation Language Arts	Poetry
Keyboarding	Keyboarding	Spelling/ Copywork	Keyboarding	Narrations
Lunch (Family Read aloud)	Lunch (Family Read aloud)	Lunch (Nature Reading)	Lunch (Culture Reading)	
Family Poetry (sharing/ memorize/ sketching)	Language Arts Game	Piano Practice	Dry Brush Lesson/ Dry Brush Nature Object	
Piano Practice	Piano Practice	Piano Lesson	Horseback Riding	Movie Night
Chores/Rest/Free Time	Chores/Rest/Free Time	Chores/Rest/ Free Time	Chores/Rest/ Free Time	
Dinner (AHG/ Trail Life)	Handicrafts	Dinner (Geography reading with Dad/Map Work)	Dinner (Family Free Read or History)	
Oldest Child dinner/Individual Study	Dinner (Bible with Dad)	Evening Reader		
	Evening Reader		Evening Reader	

Sample Family Schedule
Saturday and Sunday

Saturday	Sunday
Family Exercise/ Yard Work/ Mowing	Church/ Serve
Chores	Family Reading
Piano Practice	Piano Practice
Possible Family Read aloud	Lessons with Dad once a month
	Scripture Memory
	Dinner (Bible with Dad)

As I stated in "Winter," at the end of each season I review the schedule and see if any areas need to be altered. Once a year, usually summertime, I go through the process anew. Check in with your schedule at least once a month to make sure you are sticking with what you planned. It's normal to have some natural swaying in the schedule.

CHAPTER 5

Saplings

> "But I wanted to do it for you," Mr. Murry said. "That's what every parent wants." He looked into her dark, frightened eyes. "I won't let you go, Meg. I am going." "No." Mrs. Whatsit's voice was sterner than Meg had ever heard it. "You are going to allow Meg the privilege of accepting this danger. You are a wise man, Mr. Murry. You are going to let her go."[9]
> ~ *A Wrinkle in Time,* Madeleine L'Engle ~

Years go by in our journey at a quickened pace as our children get older and our concerns seem greater. The thoughts filling our minds change from, "Will my child read?" or "What activities should they join?" to, "Should they date?" and "Are they prepared to leave home?" The seconds empty faster than we can fill them. The road that once looked so far away fast approaches. That sapling stands tall, yet we know their trunk is still bare and easily bendable.

The later years of homeschooling bring their own joys, questions, and even sorrows. A grieving and a celebration of sorts are mixed into one, and maybe we're left feeling a bit confused. These years bring questions of relationships, independence, work life, college and spiritual independence. It's a special blessing to be home with our children as they transition through these years. Yet, how do we navigate them in healthy ways under the same roof? Much

FALL

of the peace of these years lies in keeping our heads on straight about our role as parents.

As Paul Tripp states in his book on raising youth into young adults, "It is vital for us to confess that the struggle of the teen years is not only about teen biology and teen rebellion. These years are hard for us because they expose the wrong thoughts and desires of our own hearts."[10]

This is the age of keeping our minds thoughtful and prayerful before we speak, maybe more than ever before. According to the Bible, our words can bring peace and healing or great disaster,

"For we all stumble in many ways. And if anyone does not stumble in what he says, he is a perfect man, able to bridle his own body. If we put bits into the mouths of horses so that they obey us, we guide their whole bodies as well. Look at the ships also: though they are so large and are driven by strong winds, they are guided by a very small rudder wherever the will of the pilot directs. So also, the tongue is a small member, yet it boasts of great things. How great a forest is set ablaze by such a small fire! And the tongue is a fire, a world of unrighteousness. The tongue is set among our members, staining the whole body, setting on fire the entire course of life, and set on fire by hell" James 3: 2-10 ESV.

In these fast-moving years, we must ground ourselves and be more thoughtful with when to speak and when to be quiet.

We must pause to know when to let our children fall and when to step in with guidance. Often, we simply need to remember to be kind and gentle and wise when we want to be irritated. We may be offended because we might feel our authority is being threatened. We may fear for their future and who they will become. So, we may react in ways that are hysterical at worst and unhelpful at best.

These are the years of asking questions before we respond hastily. Why are these years so challenging for us? In her article, "Independence or Rebellion" featured in Focus on the Family, Jan Kern says, "Our influence isn't slipping away, our role is shifting."[11]

Accepting that our role as a parent and as a homeschool educator is changing is key to embracing these years. This does not mean these years have to be full of discontent, but we must ride the waves, not fight the changing tide. It is God driven and God designed and, if we can first accept the changes, not fight every step of the way, it will be a much smoother ride.

In the early years we were exhausted, but we were in control to a large degree. Now, our arms flail wildly around as we try to figure out what to do with ourselves in this new place. We are perhaps physically needed less, but emotionally and spiritually needed more. So, we ourselves, once again, must be deeply connected to God and Scripture and we must be prayerful over our children with great haste and great perseverance.

How does this change our daily homeschool routine? Often this means handing over more of the routine and schoolwork to our children. It means expecting them to be away from home more as they volunteer, work, and find interests of their own. Some of us love this because it reduces our work a bit. Others dislike it because we so much love the time spent with our children. We don't want to let that go.

A Healthy Balance

There is a healthy balance. For example, your child of 14 gets up and makes their own breakfast, throws a load of laundry in and completes his reading and writing for the day. You meet to check his math and then he finishes other writing and music practice on his own. Perhaps, he is in charge of reading to a younger sibling. The afternoon includes personal interest work in art or language or sports. Perhaps there is an online class. Yet, whether it be the middle of the day or the evening, the family reads together and covers the topics of history, geography, Bible, and a favorite family read aloud. These family-focused times keep communication intact. If we don't give them freedom from hovering over their work, they don't take on independence or learn to deal with their own mistakes. We must give them opportunities to fail. Yet, if we hand all of it over, we break the memory building and family conversations that tie them to home. They can hide struggles easier. It can also create selfishness.

In addition, we may find it important to find new ways to connect with them during these years. That boy who once sat down and played Legos with you may now need you to connect by going camping or fishing or volunteering at church together. Whether in the car or hanging out late at night before bed, there are opportunities to connect, not simply to hand out lectures. During these years, they may already feel sensitive and insecure, so hammering them about how they don't get every detail right, whether in chores or academic pursuits, is not going to be particularly helpful to our relationship or build confidence. They need a mentor to help them process life in healthy ways. We are that mentor - not disciplinarians only. Don't leave all the important conversations to be had with the youth pastor! You have far greater opportunity to listen and converse with your child than anyone else. If you keep turning them off because you are tired or irritated, they may stop trying.

Spiritual Development

We enjoy reading the Bible and praying with children, but we also encourage them in their own personal pursuit of God. We give them a framework for personal prayer and set aside time for those pursuits in their daily routine.

We don't do the spiritual work for them, but we can discuss theology and answer the questions they might have about God. We trust in God as we provide good materials and a homelife that will nourish their souls. We challenge them to a deeper understanding of the faith so they can stand firm when faced with their own doubts and objections by others. We provide important apologetic materials when the time is right, and we daily focus on the goodness of God and help them "work out their faith." "Always be prepared to give an answer to everyone who asks you to give the reason for the hope you have. But we must always do this with gentleness and respect" (1Peter 3:15 NIV).

Sadly, statistics show that many young people from Christian homes leave the faith after leaving home. J. Warner Wallace compiled an insightful literature review of the many books and articles regarding the reasons young people walk away from the church and their faith.[12] One factor is that young people do not understand why they believe what they believe and have trouble articulating it. Therefore, they become easily swayed by non-Christian classmates and professors.

One study by Ligonier Ministries and Lifeway Research in 2015 discovered, when asked questions about Christian doctrine, young people held consistently heretical views compared to older respondents.[13] These findings piggyback on earlier studies published in the book: *Soul Searching: The Religious and Spiritual lives of American Teenagers* (2005), in which they found a large percentage of teenagers are incredibly inarticulate about their faith and have what the authors call "Moralistic Therapeutic Deism": a God exists who created and orders the world and watches over human life on earth. God wants people to be good, nice, and fair to each other as is taught in most world religions, and the central goal of life is to be happy and become good people who go to heaven.[14]

We see this played out on a grander scale when young people stop going to church. In the 2007 book *"Unchristian,"*[15] The Barna Research Group found that Christians in their twenties are "significantly less likely to believe a person's faith in God is meant to be developed by involvement in a local church." Their results indicate this life stage of spiritual disengagement is not going to change. Shockingly, only 33% of churched youth say the church will play a part in their lives when they leave home.

So, how is it these children who grow up attending Sunday School and Wednesday night youth group find themselves without room for church in their early twenties? Perhaps more disturbing is some have completely discarded basic Christian truths. An older but important study in 1997 called *Why Kids Leave the Faith* found four main reasons, including: troubling unanswered questions; their faith was not "working" for them; other things took priority, and they never personally owned their faith.[16]

The Work of Faith

We cannot leave the work of our children's Christian faith upon the overburdened shoulders of church workers and Sunday morning services! We must own these opportunities at home to teach and train our children in the fear and admonition of the Lord and lead them into relationship with our Lord and Savior Jesus Christ! We must start when our children are young with a big understanding of a big God who created the world and all that is in it. (Genesis 1:1 and Psalm 24.)

As children grow, and particularly in the years before they leave home, we must help them answer the hard questions, give them opportunities to grow in their faith, and work through the hard questions. We must share stories of courageous missionaries and martyrs. We must not only wait for the questions to come, but we must make time to discuss topics in our homes such as, "Is Jesus the Son of God?" "Was Christ resurrected?" "Do you believe God sends people to hell?" We must address the cultural accusations that may come strongly at them at college and in the workplace, "You only believe because of where you grew up." "The Bible is a bunch of made up stories and only uneducated people would believe them." "You are closed minded and hateful to believe that homosexuality is a sin." "You are being controlled by a misogynistic church that tells you that you are not in charge of your own body."

These statements must be well addressed at home if we expect our children to understand the hope they live by and to stand by it in the face of a culture that is increasingly aggressive. It is a special art to teach our children how to stand for truth with grace and love. The spirit of these conversations cannot be dogmatic lectures, but an opportunity to help them understand the reality of the faith, the truth of the gospel, the facts that hold true.

Prayer and Faith

In the end, it doesn't matter how much they study, it is all clanging cymbals if they do not have a personal commitment to Jesus Christ. If the heart is not changed, if their faith is not drenched in love for their Savior and for His people, it's all to no avail. And this is the spot where we may feel the rub! We cannot love Jesus for them! It is faith alone that saves, and THIS is where our hope rests, "Faith shows the reality of what we hope for, it is the evidence of things we cannot see" (Hebrews 11:1). If our children do not love Him, nor want to live for Him, no amount of apologetic study and application will matter.

This, of course, is the hardest part. We cannot force our children into the faith. But remember, God Himself is all powerful! We must not only pray diligently, but fast and pray, so that we can beseech His intervention on

FALL

behalf of our children. I do not yet pray for my children as often as I should. This must change. It is, after all, the most important thing I can do for them.

Overall, the teenage years are a fantastic time to provide essential experiences to help them prepare for adulthood as a firm believer in His church. It may be that our children's future in church looks different than what we experienced. Our children might attend a home church, help with a church plant, or attend a large church. They may have grown up in a non-denominational church but join a more traditional Presbyterian congregation or the other way around. But we do need to teach them questions to ask of any church they might want to attend so they will not be misguided into error and heresy.

We must not add to the cynics who say there is no place for the church in this postmodern world. Let's help them love the church, support it, and make it an essential place to grow, learn, and serve. We start this by the way we define it in their years of growing up at home.

In a recent conversation with a youth pastor, I asked about college-aged kids leaving the church. He brought up a very insightful thought. He said many parents in those later years become so focused on the academic and practical side of getting kids to college they often forget some of the valued conversations that need to happen about church involvement. Sadly, discussions about dorm rooms and signing up for a college major trumps the conversations that could help their young student connect with a new church near their school.

In addition, we must remember that simply attending Bible College or a Christian university will not keep your child secure from the culture. You may choose certain Christian schools over secular ones because they take steps to encourage opportunities for young people to continue in their pursuit of Christ. But we would do well to remember that simply attending a Christian school does not guarantee our adult children will seek the Lord. As they approach these teen years, it's important to help our children look at their path realistically and practically, taking both academic, family-life, and spiritual pursuits into account. No matter where they end up going to school or working, God has a community of believers for them to connect with and the work of the church should not become some side-item that they will fit in as time permits.

CHAPTER 6:
College

College has become a microcosm of the rapid changes going on in the philosophy and practices in our culture.

College Preparation

There is much to be said about the changes that have taken place in recent days on our college campuses. If we plan to send our children to college, it is particularly important they are prepared.

While you review the accommodations, financial implications and academic standing of the schools you are interested in, you will also need to get a sense of the philosophy, politics, and student groups on campus. Unfortunately, many young homeschoolers are not prepared for the onslaught to their worldview that takes place on many modern college campuses. Universities which were once a place for open dialogue are no longer so. Where there used to be civil discourse, there is now public shaming. You may have to close the door to some schools you would have considered in the past due to these truths.

We find ourselves between a rock and a hard place. We want to prepare our children for the quality aspects of college life that could provide excellent experiences and opportunities. Yet, how can we best equip them for all they will see and hear without an absolute shock to their system?

First, we must do our research and understand what is happening at the college they might choose to attend. Much of the changes we now see in the college environment are simply a culmination of what has been going on in communities across America.

The powerful book, *The Coddling of the American Mind,* by Greg Lukianoff and Jonathan Haidt states, "We argued that many parents, K-12 teachers, professors, and university administrators have been unknowingly teaching a generation of students to engage in mental habits commonly seen in people who suffer from anxiety and depression. We suggested that students were beginning to react to words, books, and visiting speakers with fear and anger because they had been taught to exaggerate danger, use dichotomous (or binary) thinking, amplify their first emotional responses, and engage in a number of other cognitive distortions." They go on, "At some schools, a culture of defensive self-censorship seemed to be emerging, partly in response to students who were quick to "call out" or shame others for small things they deemed to be insensitive-either to the student doing the calling out or to members of a group that the student was standing up for. We called this pattern vindictive protectiveness and argued that such behavior made it more difficult for all students to have open discussion in which they could practice essential skills of critical thinking and civil disagreement."[17]

So, we have children growing up in homes and schools where they are taught words are equal to violence, and different opinions are to be feared. Safety trumps all other concerns. Experiences that used to be considered part of the normal, unfair human life, are seen as avoidable, at all costs. We somehow believe we are in a utopia where no one should ever disagree, have their feelings hurt, or not be included. We are not raising children who bounce back anymore. Are we raising children who overanalyze their every feeling or emotion?

Teaching Self-Evaluation

It is good to help our children with some self-evaluation. We ask them to consider the other person and be thoughtful in their decisions and with their words. But we seem to be going to the extreme and teaching our children that disagreeing with someone and verbalizing this is paramount to violence against that person. Then we put all these children on a college campus and tell them not to do exactly what college was intended for; to be a place of free thinking, where peaceful disagreements are welcomed.

Colleges are no longer the place for intellectual ideas to be shared and varied points of views to be heard. The place we thought we were sending our students to grow into capable adults and to prepare them for a career seems to be focused on changing their worldview instead. What compounds the problem is, even when we want to raise confident, empathetic, and resilient children, the culture as a whole has embraced this "me and my feelings first" philosophy.

We live in a very reactionary culture that jumps to extremes with great rapidity. People attack others who disagree with them. They don't discuss the merits of an idea. Truth has no place. Rather, personal attacks are seen as acceptable or unacceptable depending on one's personal view and perspective. Slight errant words or a momentary lack of sensitivity are given the status of trauma. Instead of resilient children who are ready to face the challenges of the world, many are creating what the Coddling book calls "fragility", "Beliefs about their own and others' fragility in the face of ideas they dislike will become self-fulfilling prophecies. Not only would students come to believe that they can't handle such things, but if they acted on that belief and avoided exposure, eventually they would become less able to do so. If students succeeded in creating bubbles of intellectual "safety" in college, they would set themselves up for even greater anxiety and conflict after graduation when they will certainly encounter many more people with more extremes views."[17] We are encouraging a victim mentality.

> *Your children do not need to apologize for being Christians and thinking differently than the culture around them.*

While our children are at home, we must be a strong voice encouraging them and bolstering their boldness. We also must not exacerbate situations that are not that bad. Some situations are simply an uncomfortable part of life. They will unfortunately run into hateful and ignorant people. We must stop rescuing them and magnifying the impact of small life squabbles. Teach them about true humility and gentleness. When to stand, and when to walk away. In this way, when a true trauma and true evils are witnessed, our children can give them appropriate reactions.

We want to have many conversations with our students about what they might hear in the classroom or see in the dormitory and how to best respond in those difficult situations. But they are still young and impressionable. Therefore, some parents are choosing specific colleges they know will not work towards the brainwashing of their children.

College Educators

What about professors? Whereas college professors have always generally tended toward being liberal in their views, statistics show the differences are even more prominent today, and this is also skewing the potential benefits of college, "The loss of political diversity among the faculty has negative consequences for students, too, in three ways. First, there's the problem that many college students have little or no exposure to professors from half of the political spectrum. Many students graduate with an inaccurate understanding of conservatives, politics, and much of the United States."[17]

We should not hold to the standard our children should never be taught by a professor with different views. However, if they ALL do, and have an agenda with our child, this is a difficult environment for a 19-year-old to hold firm. When these modes of thinking are pressed in on our young adults' day in and day out, we Christian parents wonder if they will succumb to the pressure? Can our homeschool graduates make any impact at a secular college?

Indeed, we are to reach out to the lost and the lonely by holding out to the world the true Word of Life (Philippians 2:16). Our children must be ready and know how to discern truth from error and know how to humbly articulate disagreements with their professors who are much more seasoned at debating. How can they possibly do this? The last year prior to college, we can role-play these scenarios with our children. In addition, we need to remind our children that God is their strength and it's not their job to change anyone else's mind. But the truth should be upheld even in the face of humiliation or various types of persecution.

What is a Christian parent to do? Is it okay to send your child to a secular college or must you send them to a Christian college? There is no simple or single answer. You can scour the internet and find testimonies of Christian youth who have thrived in secular colleges as well as those whose lives were impacted in extremely negative ways. A school's reputation cannot give you peace that your student is going to become a stronger Christian in their college years. We can look at many factors including our student's study area of interest, future goals, spiritual maturation and find out as much information about a school as possible. Discuss openly with your homeschool graduate about the positives and negatives of these schools, not just academically. In the end, we must hand it over to God, as we help our youth make the best decision possible.

College Life

Beyond the politics of school life, there are other aspects of college you want to discuss with your kids. There will be underage drinking and sexual immorality on the campus. You may choose to share with them the good and the bad of your own college experience. At this point, you are doing them no favors by pretending you were perfect in college. The Lord knows the right path for your children, even before they were born. College is only one possible path for some, not all. Begin to pray now about how you can best serve the Lord by preparing your child for adulthood.

CHAPTER 7

Adventure

> *"We are plain quiet folk, and I have no use for adventures.*
> *Nasty, disturbing, and uncomfortable things. Make you late for dinner!"*[18]
> *~ The Hobbit, J.R.R. Tolkien ~*

I have written about the challenges of college, but there are also many joys. College can be a wonderful learning experience when you choose the right one.

For me, college was a place of excitement in learning. I was a late bloomer to education, so college was extremely inspiring. I met some of the best friends of my life there and was given opportunities to grow in skill and maturity that make me who I am today. The college experience also required me to grow spiritually.

I remember vividly my college freshman year sociology class and the impact it had upon my spiritual life. In Introduction to Sociology, my professor posed the question, "How much do you think your environment effects what you do every day?" I remember thinking, "I am a Christian, so God guides me, and the environment probably impacts very little." I proceeded to raise my hand and say with great confidence, "A little." The professor smiled and said, "Hmmm, a little…"

He went on, with chalk in hand, to make a laundry list of all the things most people do every day, only because our environment deems it so. He listed everything from brushing your teeth, to how you wear your hair, to what car you drive. That conversation shocked me. I remember walking back to my dorm room in a bit of a fog, sitting on my bed and thinking, "Oh my goodness, am I only a Christian because of the environment where I grew up?"

It hit me hard. I remember calling my mom and talking with her about it. I talked with some close friends to see what they thought. In the end, I came to a prayer I have used often ever since. I got on my knees and said to God, "Please help me to believe who You are and help me to worship You as You truly want to be worshipped." During those early days of college, I learned I had to "own" my faith and no one could do it for me. But I always knew I could call my mom with my confusion and she would guide me.

Our kids need to know the same. By providential grace and trust in God, I was born anew. I was not a Christian because my family said it was so. By faith through grace, I was saved. These are the maturing moments we hope for our children. Though at the time, I felt shaky, God used that professor and those interactions to try my faith and draw me to Himself.

> *Overall, we want to have a broad outlook of how God can use college or other experiences to grow our children into godly men and women.*

College can be an amazing adventure. If God has numbered all of their days, then surely, He knows the right college for them, too.

"Then something Tookish woke up inside him,
and he wished to go and see the great mountains,
and hear the pine-trees and the waterfalls, and explore the caves,
and wear a sword instead of a walking-stick."[18]

~ *The Hobbit,* J.R.R. Tolkien ~

CHAPTER 8
Working Hands

How wonderful to raise a child who can hold down a job and provide for their family while at the same time being an interesting and skillful person.

I have often read that poets make up words to help convey images. So, I decided the current college debt crisis I've become aware of needs a name. I thought *Inundebted* was a good choice, for surely young people are inundated with debt like never before. Although I personally know what it's like to take on debt and the arduous process of repaying, I learned more about the current college financial situation.

According to the documentary, *Broke Busted and Disgusted*, student debt has risen at an alarming rate.[19] The numbers seem almost made up. They are so high! There has been an increase of 511% in student loans since 1999. The current cost of public college is about 80K and private college is 175K.

Why are these huge jumps in cost occurring? The reasons include: the push for everyone to attend college, cultural acceptance of debt as a normal way of life, and students expecting more from the college experience.

Those costs are passed on to students through loans. We pair these factors with young adults who have no concept of how interest works or what the cost of living post-college looks like, and we may be setting them up for major life struggles. Our culture has passed on the idea that as long as one has a college degree, he or she will get a good job and will be able to purchase anything needed. But this is not true. It may take until they retire to pay off these debts! In this way, the debt cycle continues generation after generation. This is one of the reasons many families consider the route of community college, trade school, or apprenticeship. Over 80% of students change their majors in college and even more debt is incurred.

Should we worry if our homeschool graduate chooses not to attend college? I know in my birth home, and with most of us who grew up in the 1980s and 90s, college was the "only" option. And, of course, it is still a wonderful path for many young people (and even older adults!). However, it is freeing and good to remember that college is not necessary for everyone. May we be ever prayerful as we guide our children towards these adulthood decisions.

> "Father, it must be lonely for Brother Klaus to live all by himself in that dark place and just pray all the time." "Perhaps it may be for you, Son," replied father, "but Klaus seems happy. When any one of the mountain folk is ill or without bread, Klaus comes to comfort him. When a woman loses her husband or a mother a child, Klaus is there to pray with her. All men, Walter, do not like to do the same thing. Some like to hunt, others to fight, and still others to till the soil. Klaus is a man of God and I am sure he is happy even if he lives alone in that dark cave yonder."[20]
> ~ *The Apple and the Arrow*, Mary and Conrad Buff ~

Many children are suited well for a skilled job. Sadly, as a society, too many believe the "rite of passage" must include college. Train your children in the truth. "Success" is not about a title or owning a huge house. It's about working as unto the LORD.

A second problem seems to be we are raising children with a lack of interest in work. "Forty years ago, even thirty years ago, there was no shame in a young man choosing a career in the trades. Beginning in the early 1980s and, particularly with the publication of the 'Nation at Risk' report in 1983, a consensus grew in the United States that every young person should go to college, regardless. 'Vocational education' lost whatever prestige it had… principals and superintendents began to see classes in auto mechanics or welding as expensive diversions from the school's core mission of ensuing that every student would go to college."[21] The end result is that finding a good craftsman is tough these days, and children who once found great pleasure and purpose in a trade, find themselves lost in college and under mounds of debt.

As journalist Charles Murray states in an article in the Wall Street Journal in 2007, "The spread of wealth at the top of American society has created an explosive increase in the demand for craftsman. Finding a good lawyer or physician is easy. Finding a good carpenter, painter, electrician…is difficult. Master craftsman can make six figures. And the craftsman's jobs provide wonderful intrinsic rewards that come from mastery of a challenging skill that produces tangible results. How many white-collar jobs provide nearly as much satisfaction."[22]

One way we are working on this in our home is to set time aside in our schedule for the children to work with my husband to learn some of these skills. Not every family has a "handyman," but asking others within your family or community to help train your children in these areas is well worth your time. Finding a mentor who can work with your child to teach them a trade could be a very vital part of your child's educational experience.

If your child excels tremendously in mathematics and wants to be an engineer or shows a great interest in animals and wants to be a veterinarian, the college route may be a perfect fit. For some, the college route is still the only path to their chosen career, but they should understand all its obligations. And, others may want to learn a trade or craft, start a business, join the military or serve with the church fulltime. This certainly doesn't mean they don't have academic interests!

As a homeschooling parent, we still expose them to history, literature and the arts for a well-rounded education. We want them to be well-rounded people. They may be great at math and seek to use it in the fields of technology, electrical work, or carpentry. They may choose not to get a degree in music, but still play for the church orchestra or band or give piano lessons. Consider well the financial impact of these educational options and decisions.

Success is not about how other people look at you because you hold a degree or not. We are not all fitted for the same path. Exposing our children to a variety of skills and opportunities benefits all along the way.

CHAPTER 9

Reviving the Renaissance

*Remember, we are about the blessing of growing people,
not the tinkering of wooden toys or the programming of little robots!*

I remember sitting with my children and looking at a picture book about the Renaissance. Perusing various characters playing music, studying philosophy, languages, and beautiful works of art stirred my heart. To watch these same characters learn skills of horsemanship and fighting was an interesting combination. The kids and I looked at each other and said, "We're a Renaissance Family."

Well, I'd say we're not quite there, but something in that book resonated with us. From man to machine, from virtue to productivity, a grave shift has occurred over the years in our secular educational system that teaches there is no Creator. Our culture has detached education from character. "Only within the past several generations has education become entirely divorced from moral development, and we see the results around us every day."[23]

Those who have children in public school, especially in the elementary grades, have seen a large shift towards test taking. The daily classroom experience has tilted less towards being exposed to great material and more towards techniques to help children move to the next grade. With a change in moral focus and the increase of testing and technology in the culture, there has been a move away from valuing a liberal arts education. Some of this has occurred because a liberal arts education at the college level will not always transfer to the job market, and we wonder if such a degree will help our kids pay the bills. If your daughter comes to you and says she wants to get a degree in music or sociology, you may see the value but, you may inwardly cringe because you wonder how she will pay for graduate school and what kind of job she can obtain?

Liberal Arts Education

Many universities in the United States still consider themselves liberal arts schools. In addition, a majority of those homeschooling their children are providing a liberal arts education. We should then not be surprised when our children want to follow those pursuits into adulthood. Liberal arts were foundations of classical learning in ancient Greece and Rome. In this sense, I am using the term liberal arts to also describe the modern academic or college degree model which traditionally includes topics such as fine arts, music, performing arts, literature, philosophy, religious studies, social sciences and even mathematics.[24] In addition, a liberal arts education is a broad education and includes how one analyzes and interacts with educational materials, "A liberal arts education is meant to get the student thinking critically about the world around him and is intended to prepare him for a variety of positions within society."[25] So, the value of a liberal arts education is more than the exposure to many topics, it's also the way a person learns to think, evaluate, and even debate various important topics.

There is a move away from the "arts" in recent years. Why has this happened? The rise of technology has indeed impacted both the skills needed and jobs available. We've discussed the cost of college, and therefore, how can we expect our graduates to obtain a degree in the liberal arts and have a salary to match the debt payments and cost of daily living?

Coming out of school with a degree in psychology, I had no option but to attend graduate school. But the financial load was a heavy burden upon our family. Parents are now strongly encouraging children towards a technical, engineering or business degree and devaluing a liberal arts education because they are concerned about their futures. Of course, these areas of study and the careers that follow are an exceptional choice for many students, but they certainly cannot be the path for everyone. But, the payoff between debt incurred and salary earned no longer weigh out in the minds of many families. This is very understandable. However, we must be more cunning in finding ways for the liberal arts to continue to flourish. Why? Because we are attempting to raise empathetic and well-rounded adults, and certainly just as some youth are fitted for the trades or for engineering, some are certainly fitted to continue their studies in the areas of liberal arts.

The college experience for those in a liberal arts degree is also unique because generally these schools are smaller, and they are exposed to much more in the field of humanities.

Science Technology Engineering and Math

The American educational system is concerned about our standing amongst the world educationally, and this is also to some degree understandable. The response has been programs focused on STEM (Science Technology Engineering and Math). Often, summer camps and after school programs have this term alongside their advertising. We can absolutely appreciate the increased interest and focus upon STEM. However, it is a different push than we've had before in our educational system in the United States. Historically Asia has never embraced a liberal arts philosophy in education.

However, even for Asia, change is in the air. "Hong Kong and some other Asian countries are embracing everything from art history to sociology as necessary components of undergraduate coursework."[26] Why? "Just as the U.S. begins to move away from traditional liberal arts programs and turn to specialized online programs, Asia is discovering there is benefit in the creativity and well-rounded perspective that comes from a liberal arts education," says Chester Goad, Ph.D., who sits on the Journal of Postsecondary Education and Disability. "Seeking to break away from their own traditionally homogenized and rigidly specialized educational system, Asian countries began in recent years to find inspiration from our system."[27]

Will we, as an American society, have a generation of adults whose only knowledge base is technical in nature? "There is some irony in the fact that at the very moment the liberal arts model of education is under attack in the West as impractical and irrelevant, it is being embraced in Asia. Places that routinely posts the top international test scores in math and science- the likes of Singapore, Hong Kong, Japan, and South Korea as well as India and China have moved to create new undergraduate liberal arts programs or colleges, adopting the broad-based education that defines some of the US' finest institutions…in the US, many have concluded to prevail in this competitive, globalized world, the liberal arts are an expensive luxury that must be replaced by more technical training and skills. However, policy makers in other parts of the world, looking at the same forecasts, have come to the opposite conclusion and view the liberal arts as essential to the task of training young people."[28]

It is too easy to not think for ourselves or pray and ask God to guide us as we make educational decisions for our children. It may be that your child will be an amazing hymn writer, philosopher or teach a language. My fear is these positions will be in even greater need and more on the decline because too many have stopped seeing the value of a liberal arts education.

> *Our culture has stopped teaching responsibility and virtue alongside knowledge.*

Loads of debt is like shackles laying on top of many as they move into adulthood. It is just as unfortunate to be a person who makes good money but has a poor understanding of God's truth and His working in the world through art, history and literature.

Why is it today we see so many young people supporting a socialistic society? Is it because they have not learned the history of what living in these societies will do to their personal liberties? Have they not been told the pattern of dictatorship which has played out on the world stage over and over again? Are they depressed because they've never looked at items of beauty or never seen the value of stretching their limbs out on the lawn without a phone?

These are just some of the questions and concerns I have as I ponder the future of education and ask, How are we as home educators to prepare our students for choosing their future paths? There is no simple answer. We must consider our own family and financial situations and not allow others to dictate to us what defines a valuable degree or college education.

If a private liberal arts post-secondary education is probable for our graduates, we need to make some different choices with how we spend our money now, so we can save for these future opportunities. We might have to forego an expensive vacation or the newest purchase, because we're going to try to prepare for their future schooling. If a private liberal arts education is not going to be a wise financial choice, we might send them to community college for the first couple of years or they might find a part-time job or volunteer in an area of interest. They might be able to take online classes. Regardless, there is nothing wrong with encouraging them during these primary and secondary years to pursue these beautiful areas of life.

Whether our daughter is an electrician, or our son comes home to read Tolstoy, or they decide to work in business together or one or more plays the guitar at church on Sunday, it all has value! Be encouraged! No matter what schooling they have or vocation they choose, their lives have purpose beyond where they go to work each day.

Their Future Pursuits

These days of homeschooling will be a part of who they are and who they become. Your teaching and training will mold their perspectives and the way they analyze the world and how they treat others. As your children get older, these are conversations to have with them about their future pursuits.

Some of our children may get married and start a family right away, others may go off to college, and still others may go into the military service, vocational, or missionary work. Some homeschooling parents tend to get stressed about school as their teens hit high school, as though what they had been doing all along had no value.

Of course, you will want to look at requirements for college or a training program. But that does not mean you have to plan every moment of the next four years. I'm telling you, if you do that, you will likely make yourself sick. Parents suddenly feel a rush to get "serious." They feel they must now assimilate into the cultural norm when they early on chose to teach and train their own children differently for a reason.

A close homeschooling friend shared a conversation she had with another homeschool friend. The friend stated she had been building this home from its foundations like a mansion, every year with the beauty of homeschooling and, "was she now at the end to put an aluminum foil roof on the top?" What she was saying is that after all these years, is she now to jump right back into what everyone else is doing just because her child is college aged?

Continue to ask God to prepare your children each moment, each year, and know that beauty in your teaching has a purpose and God will not let it go to waste. You are growing people, not the tinkering of wooden toys or the programming of little robots!

CHAPTER 10
Seasons Beyond

"A comfort zone is a wonderful place, but nothing ever grows there."
~ Unknown ~

When you're in the midst of the everyday routine of homeschooling, you probably don't think much about the life you will have when your children grow up and move out of your home. But whether your road is easy and smooth or crooked and hilly, at some point you will no longer be "schooling" your child. It may seem strange, especially if you have very small children, to consider these seasons beyond. It will be a major transition. But there are some steps you can take to make sure it's a bit smoother. In fact, if you can implement some of these steps along the way, it will likely make you a healthier and more mature parent.

As you go through your day-to-day routine, you want to remind yourself that you are not *just* a "homeschooling mom." You are God's daughter! Your innate value does not come from a title. There is nothing wrong with enjoying your role as a homeschool mom! But, in this day and age, where our value is attached to what we "do," we want to be careful that we remember who we are.

FALL

God does not love you more because you homeschool, He would not love you less if you did not homeschool. Be thankful for these homeschooling days but keep an eye to the fact that one day you will not be a full-time home educator. God will have other roles for you to fill. Just because your homeschooling time ends, does not mean your teaching and training will end! Our grown children and grandchildren will need us in various ways. They will need your wisdom, care, prayers, and time. You will always have a role in your children's lives. The gift and challenge of mothering will never end. But, it may also be that God has new roles for you to fulfill in other places which you could not do when you were homeschooling full time.

Before having a family and homeschooling, you probably filled your time with other activities. Are you an artist, a teacher, a scientist, or business owner? While you are homeschooling, especially as your children age, it's important to pray about when and how these talents, or new ones, can be used for the benefit of your family, friends, church, or community. It may not be that you go back to a "job," but there will certainly be other places and open doors where you can serve the Lord. What's amazing is how the Lord built these skills during the course of your homeschooling journey, and He will now use to bless others. For example, if you worked as a teacher in public school before coming home, you can continue to teach at home, church and in the community in various ways. Perhaps, during your homeschooling journey you found a love for nature. This may be something you did not enjoy before homeschooling.

As your children get older, you might take classes at local gardens or museums and get a Master Gardener certification. You might go back to school and be trained in a new field. There are, of course, a myriad of ways the Lord might open doors for you. Each season, as you evaluate your homeschooling routine, also evaluate where you are, what skills you have, and where God wants you to serve and grow.

Making the Most of Time

It's not uncommon to find that after many years of working hard, when time is given back to us, we squander it. There is a real longing for comfort in the American life that can easily seep into the way we choose to use our time, especially when we have more of it.

My husband and I have often had the conversation about the kind of people we "want" or "don't want" to be when we retire. Observation has shown that if a person does not decide what they will do with their time, it will simply fly away. What you think you are able to do will shrink. Suddenly, someone who worked full-time and volunteered at church finds it a huge ordeal simply to make it to the grocery store once a week! Certainly, I am not saying that in your older years you must fill every moment, but you will need to have forethought into how you plan to spend your time.

When our kids are grown and gone, we hope to have ample opportunity to serve, work, create, give back, learn as our health allows it. Others need us to do this. God has called us to do this. We must choose to set boundaries around comfort and use our time in a way that may cost us something.

In financial circles, they use a term called "forced scarcity," which means an artificial limitation you put on something to prevent things from getting out of control. Often, it is used in regard to financial matters. As our means increase, our spending increases. So, we must choose not to buy that extra outfit, even though we know we can afford it, as an act of self-control, and because we want to save our money. In a way, we must use this same mindset when it comes to comfort. Instead of sleeping in, we wake up early and have a devotional time. Rather than simply attending church every Sunday, we volunteer to teach a Sunday School class. Instead of binge-watching shows, we go outdoors, or paint, or write a poem, or pray. We find people who need God's love and we share the gospel of grace with them because of the good work God has done in our own lives. There are younger mothers who need words of encouragement and wisdom.

In these later years, seek God for where he would call you to use your time and talents. Ask him how to best steward and share the resources He may have given you. I am in awe when I read stories of people like George Mueller, Gladys Aylward, and Amy Carmichael. These people did not stop serving God as they aged. In our own life at any season, surely God still has much for us to do and accomplish for the benefit of the next generation.

Never Let Go

We never really let our children "go" into some vast, chaotic world in which we now have no role. Now we step in as their advocate in prayer, fellow Christian, and friend. We let them go into the hands of a mighty and sovereign God, who is the only One who ever had control! They will have their own life, their own burdens to bear, and their own choices to make. As we let them go, we must hold onto faith and trust they will never be alone. There might be trials, distance, disagreements, and disappointments.

This letting go is to accept the cycle of life that God created, and our hope, desire and prayer is that they will move into adulthood and will continue to lean into Him fully. So, when it's time, find your way and let them go. Let them know clearly that you are always there. You may laugh, cry, celebrate, grieve, and embrace the truth that this beautiful life of home together was an irreplaceable treasure! But now, you won't need a phone call for every decision or an invite to every party or even the knowledge about every decision.

And, even though we don't want to contemplate it, or even utter it, some children may stray. So, we steadfastly pray that those sheep will come back to the fold. "Women received their loved ones back again from death" (Hebrews 11:35).

Hold fast to the knowledge that you chose home as the best place to teach and train them and, every day, you steadfastly pointed them towards the King of Kings, the Lord or Lords! Well done, good and faithful servant!

CHAPTER 11
Living Stories

What curriculum or method do you use?

I found during my interviews that there was an almost even split between families who used what would be considered Classical curriculum and those who used more Traditional curriculum. Seven women mentioned using a specifically classical approach which was guided by their involvement in Classical Conversations. A few mentioned Veritas Press. However, many of these women said, though their foundation was Classical, they might also use curriculum from BJU Press or other online sources for various subjects. Eight women focused on a more Traditional method using one or more of the following Christian options: Sonlight, My Father's World, Abeka, and Christian Liberty Academy. Some home educators followed a mostly eclectic model by choosing from the materials they felt best in each season from a variety of sources. Several women's philosophy and materials were inspired by Charlotte Mason's teachings and the materials that have been developed using her methods. Specific math programs mentioned during these interviews included: Teaching Textbooks, Math U See, Horizons, and Saxon. Specific writing, handwriting, and reading programs mentioned included: Handwriting without Tears, IEW, Brave Writer, Explode the Code, and All about Reading.

Interestingly, no matter what method women followed, the majority said that they used different curriculum in different seasons. Materials they used when their children were young changed as they got older. Some of this was simply due to the fact that children no longer needed certain materials, such as reading helpers and handwriting basics. No matter their main philosophy, they all found materials from a variety of sources helpful.

In addition, many women mentioned the importance of living books and reading together as a family, no matter what method was followed. As I mentioned earlier, the one question that almost every woman answered the same was, "What is your favorite part of the school day?" Without fail, every woman said, "Reading aloud," "Sharing books," "Sharing conversation about the Bible or books." Please don't fail to remember how valuable and beautiful these moments are together!

Why did you decide to join Classical Conversations or a Co-op? What are the benefits and/or downside of being involved in these groups?

A large number of the women interviewed participated in either CC or a Co-op. Six women stated they were currently involved in a CC group, while nine suggested they were involved in a Co-op. The benefits mentioned included: inspiration and motivation, discovering a community of like-minded friends, being accountable to others, prepares children for a classroom environment, opportunity to be taught by another parent, friendships, the provision of help in subjects that are more challenging like advanced science, art, PE, and languages.

Some of the difficulties listed in regard to participation in these groups included: difficulty preparing and teaching other people's children. Other challenges included staying on someone else's schedule, not having much relationship outside of group meetings, lack of flexibility, breaks the flow of the home routine, can be tiring and intense, and normal group experiences such as cliques. Overall, some families find these groups an extremely important guiding force in their homeschool life, while others join for a season.

How does homeschooling change from elementary through teenage years?

Thirteen women had children in the teenage years who responded to this question. Six had answers which related to the joy of greater independence on the part of their student, "they begin to own their education," "they self-regulate more and take on more responsibilities," "greater focus on life skills," and "they become self-teachers." One mother said it's quite wonderful to sit back and be able to say, "Wow, we did it" by watching their children take the routine and material for themselves and not be at their elbows. Along with this idea, one mother said you have more experiences such as, "Here's your stuff, go and do it," yet you still have to find time for family engagement which can be a challenge.

Other women mentioned these are the years of deeper lessons as their children are being prepared for adulthood. There are more conversations where we can help them process situations. Two mentioned this is the age where peers have more influence. They are exposed to more, so we must find a balance of giving them more freedoms while also making time for conversations to help them on a variety of issues. The overall idea was that these years can sneak up on you and between activities, schoolwork, and jobs or volunteer work, you want to make sure you prayerfully hold firm to making time for family connections and conversations.

FALL

How do you feel your children transitioned to college life?

Only four women interviewed had children in college. However, their answers gave some insight into what seemed to help the transition to adulthood. One major theme was preparing children and teens with life-skills before they leave for college. The general idea was, if you have taught your children academic independence and a good work ethic, this will pay off in college. However, if they do not have the life skills of cooking, cleaning, washing their clothes, changing a flat tire, balancing their budget, they may find these years a bit harder.

A couple of the women mentioned community college was a great start to the college experience for their family. In this way, their graduate could take a bit more time to figure out their interests, get their college basics covered, and spend far less money. One mother stated, no matter how much exposure you give to your children, they may generally have a period of being shocked when they step into the college classroom full-time.

These mothers said that you must "release yourself" from your duties as home educator and realize you have done enough, and now is the time to pray even more! A final comment one mom mentioned is, even as your children move out of your house, you may feel guilty. Could you have done it better, had more patience, covered just one more topic? But in the end, we must release them to God knowing their future is in His hands and continue to pray.

Anything I missed?

I left a final question and asked these home educators to share anything else that came to their mind during our discussion.

- "There is no perfect formula to homeschooling or to disciplining. There is no "If you do it just right, this will be the result.""

- "People assume in larger families everything is perfect and everyone helps each other. It is a special situation, but it is not perfect."

- "Talk to your kids about God's perspective on sexuality early in an age-appropriate way."

- "It's important for children to observe us taking care of ourselves. We are not to be at their every beck and call."

- "It's important to respect other families who do things differently."

- "Our schooling should be well-rounded. Expose children to many topics."

- "We must make our husbands a priority! It's too easy to leave him out of the daily decisions. In addition, we need to make time to simply be a married woman, not always mom and teacher!"

- "Stay in your own lane and be true to what God has called you and your family to."

- "Be thoughtful about extra-curricular choices."

- "Keep your sense of humor."

- "Don't be critical."

- "Now and again, have a 'girls' night out."

- "Have a healthy balance, the children cannot be your only world."

- "It's messy, it's real, and it does not usually go as planned. But you will never regret being the major influence in your children's lives. He entrusted them to you, He even uses our failures."

- "Develop a community. Isolation makes homeschooling bigger than life, overwhelming."

- "Allow free unstructured play."

- "Be with like-minded people who allow you to let your guard down and just be yourself."

- "Each age with your children has joys and difficulties."

- "God fills in the gaps."

- "There is no mistake that He can't redeem."

- "I will not make or break them from this one decision."

- "Make choices out of love, not fear."

CHAPTER 12
The End

In this book writing journey, I've realized my life has been lived all over the state of Texas. Every city where I have lived, God used for amazing purposes and has left nothing to waste. Being a home educator is not what I first envisioned for my life, but it's been so much richer than I could have imagined!

As I come to the close of this book, I've been thinking on eternity. When I was in my 20s, I worked in Galveston, which is full of history and, for all its reputation for not offering the best beaches, there are beautiful flowers in abundance. I used to take the long way to work in spring because of the mixes of hot pink and light pink oleanders in full bloom, stretching out over the main road.

One day as I was going that route, I noticed an old cemetery. It was the most beautiful thing I had ever seen. The cemetery was completely covered in wildflowers. An abundance of yellow wildflowers! Little did I know, this was a well-known secret held by the folks who grew up in Galveston. It's one of the oldest cemeteries there, hosting the graves of those who died in the 1900 hurricane that almost wiped Galveston off the map. The cemetery sits off Broadway. While people are filling their cars with gas and dropping their children at the local school, this amazing symbol of eternal life sits in front of them. It was a daily reminder of how, every spring, I should ask the Lord to keep my heart on eternity while my eyes are on today.

I'm reminded of this often by one of the ministries our family is connected with, The Voice of the Martyrs.[29] This organization supports persecuted Christians around the world. A great reminder that we receive every time we read a story about these brothers and sisters around the world is how their focus is on the eternal.

I'm convicted about how often I'm not focused heavenward. I know we must each live today in this somewhat crazy secular American culture where we were born and raised. This culture has stretched us mentally, physically, and emotionally, more often than we might realize. Yes, we are teaching and training our children in the here and now, and as much as I would sometimes like, I can't escape it. However, I will not let this world overtake me or hold me in a catatonic state of fear. For I know the One who has overcome the world. I can live well, being salt and light, and I will not let the American standards be my master. I am grateful for the freedoms I have in this land and thankful for the many who have fought and died to make it so. I will try to not be cynical about living in suburbia or in a consumer driven culture. Yes, the United States has its problems, but it also has immense strength and freedom, and it's why so many around the world still want to live here. I can use my material wealth for the good of others and I must resist excess. I can seek beauty! For it is there to be found, if I choose it. I thank the Lord for the beauty found in nature and the lovely found in His people. It is true that life often seems uncertain, but it always has been difficult throughout history. We don't know what governments will change hands and if our daily life will continue the way we know it.

Just as I was drafting this section of the book in the spring of 2020, the COVID-19 crisis began. I write these words having no idea what life will look like tomorrow, or in a month, or next year! Will life go back to the way it was? What an opportunity to embrace the truth that we are limited creatures yet, we can be refined and clarified in a call to stand for what is right.

I'm thankful to know the One who holds all things together. When I wake each morning, I put my life, family and country in His hands. As Christians, we must keep our adoration and our affections toward Him. We often hold on too tightly to this world. We cling, white knuckling this hot Earth when it truly is not our home. So, when we use the terms "home" school, we would do well to remember where our true home remains, with Him in eternity. Home is not really under these streetlamps and brick and mortar structures of Texas. Home is with Him. One day, all of us who believe, will gather to be with Him. We will be closer than ever to this glorious God whom we spoke about with our children in barefoot backyard moments, around the family table, and during our nighttime prayers. Whenever we called upon His name and lifted up prayers and cried for help, He was there. All this homeschooling stuff, it is all about Him! We will soon see Him face to face, and we will be reminded that He was with us from the very beginning.

> "Then Frodo came forward and took the crown from Faramir and bore it to Gandalf; and Aragorn knelt, and Gandalf set the White Crown upon his head, and said: 'Now come the days of the King, and may they be blessed while the thrones of the Valar endure!' But when Aragorn arose all that beheld him gazed in silence, for it seemed to them that he was revealed to them now for the first time. Tall as the sea-kings of old, he stood above all that were near; ancient of days he seemed and yet in the flower of manhood; and wisdom sat upon his brow, and strength and healing were in his hands, and a light was about him. And then Faramir cried: 'Behold the King!'"[30]
> ~ *The Lord of the Rings: The Return of the King*, J.R.R. Tolkien

FALL

We will gather as a fellowship of all believers. That day is coming even though it may seem far off to us. So, keep an eye always on the eternal when this Earth seems like more than you can bear and when the little worries come and try to whisper your name. Remember that You know the One to Whom it all belongs and to Whom your children belong and you, too," Little Wildflower," never forget in Whose garden you grow! "The grass withers and the flower fades, but the Word of the Lord stands forever" (Isaiah 40:8).

Harvest Home by Henry Alford (1844) [31]

Come, ye thankful people, come, Raise the song of harvest-home:
All is safely gathered in, Ere the winter storms begin;
God, Our Maker, doth provide For our wants to be supplied:
Come to God's own temple, come, Raise the song of harvest-home.

All the world is God's own field, Fruit unto his praise to yield;
Wheat and tares together sown, Unto joy or sorrow grown:
First the blade, and then the ear, Then the full corn shall appear:
Lord of harvest, grant that we Wholesome grain and pure may be.

For the Lord our God shall come, And shall take his harvest home;
From his field shall in that day All offenses purge away;
Give his angels charge at last In the fire the tares to cast,
But the fruitful ears to store In the garner evermore.

Even so, Lord, quickly come To thy final harvest-home;
Gather thou thy people in, Free from sorrow, free from sin;
There forever purified, In thy presence to abide:
Come, with all thine angels, come, Raise the glorious harvest-home.

~ PONDERING FALL ~
Considerations for deeper reflection

Before answering these questions,
please take time to pray so you can thoughtfully walk through this process.

Philosophy/Method:

1. If you are new to homeschooling, what philosophy/method is of most interest to you?

2. If you are already homeschooling, what philosophy/method have you been following:

3. Are you happy with the method you have chosen or do you feel you need to make some changes?

4. After reading the Homeschooling Methods Table what stood out to you?

Routine/Schedule:

1. Take time to work on the drafts of your homeschool routine:

Saplings:

1. How is your relationship with your teenager?

2. What steps can you take to improve your relationship or make more time for them?

3. Write a schedule for how you will pray daily for your teenager:

FALL

Example:

Monday	Tuesday	Wednesday	Thursday	Friday	Sat./Sun.
Their relationship to God.	Their future spouse.	God's plan for their future college/ work.	Their relationship with you and your spouse.	For their theology.	Make time small or large to personally connect with your teenager over the weekend.

4. What quality apologetic or spiritual material can you provide your teenager in the high school years to prepare them for the adult life of a Christian?

College/Work Life:

1. When your child reaches high school, you do not need to plan every moment. However, this is an important time to begin discussing with your teenager their future goals. In this way, together, you can begin looking at a realistic path. It's time for some conversations.

2. Are there any life skills you believe your child needs to work on this year? Make sure these are placed in your homeschool schedule.

3. Do you plan on sending your children to college? How will you today, financially begin to plan for this?

4. Is your child fitted for a trade? What are some options for your child in regard to training?

5. Do you believe your child might want to pursue a degree/career in the liberal arts? How do you feel about this?

6. Before speaking with your teenager about future goals, make sure you and your husband are on the same page as to what is possible. Be prayerful in these conversations.

<u>Seasons Beyond:</u>

1. Before having children, what were some of your interests?

2. Are you still interested in these areas or have you found new ones?

3. If you are getting close to the "seasons beyond," ask the Lord to show you where you can move forward in training, education, or volunteering in this new phase of life.

E.W., age 9

ABOUT THE AUTHOR

Emily and her husband Darren live in North Texas with their three children. She received her Master's degree in Health Education and Promotion from The University of Texas Medical Branch at Galveston. Prior to homeschooling, Emily worked as a Tobacco Treatment Specialist.

Alongside homeschooling, she volunteers in Girl Leadership for a local American Heritage Girls Troop. Every Friday you will find her in mud boots out on a nature trail with her dear friend Deven co-leading a Nature Study Homeschool Co-op.

Her educational philosophy has been rooted in Charlotte Mason. She continues to study deeply and learn more of these methods each season. Other areas of interest include: Christian martyrs, technology and society, apologetics, and butterfly gardens. Her favorite book is *The Magician's Nephew* by C.S. Lewis. Her favorite wildflower is the Indian paintbrush.

To contact the author:
emily@raisingyourwildflowers.com

NOTES

Preface and Winter

1. Sanchez, Anita. *The Teeth of the Lion: The Story of the Beloved and Despised Dandelion.* McDonald & Woodward. 2006. Ch. 1.
2. The Associated Press. (2009, Jan.) *Extraordinary Perception Permeates Painter's World.* Bangor Daily News. https://bangordailynews.com/2009/01/17/news/lsquoextraordinary-perceptionrsquo-permeated-painterrsquos-world/
3. Lewis, C.S. *The Chronicles of Narnia: The Lion, The Witch, and The Wardrobe.* Harper Collins. 2001.
4. Ambleside Online Annotated Charlotte Mason Series, *Vol 1. Home Education*, 2003. www.amblesideonline.org. Accessed 1 Jan. 2016. pg. 3-6
5. *Westminster Shorter Catechism.* Westminster Assembly. Assembly at Edinburgh, July 28, 1648. Sess. 19. Q. 1.
6. Swindoll, Chuck. "A Successful Man Ruined by Pride." Stonebriar Church. Frisco, Tx., 8 Sept. 2019. Sermon.
7. AZ Quotes. Thomas Fuller Quotes. https://www.azquotes.com/author/5233-Thomas_Fuller. Accessed on 21 Jan. 2019.
8. Oswald, Chambers. *My Utmost for His Highest: 30 Day Edition.* YouVersion Bible App. Version 8.14. 2017.
9. Becker, Joshua. *Inside Out*: *Life-Changing Keys to Your Most Important Relationships.* Self-Published. 2011.
10. Becker, Joshua. Simplicity: *7 Guiding Principles to Help Anyone Declutter Their Home and Life.* Self-Published. 2014.
11. Kondo, Marie. *The Life Changing Magic of Tidying Up: The Japanese Art of Decluttering and Organizing.* Ten Speed Press 1st Ed. 2014. pg. 117.

12. *Homeschooling in the United States: 2012.* National Center for Education Statistics, 1 Nov. 2016, https://nces.ed.gov/pubsearch/pubsinfo.asp?pubid=2016096rev. Accessed 20 Jul. 2016.
13. Louv, Richard. *The Last Child in the Woods.* Algonquin Books. 2013. pg. 44.
14. Ray, Brian D. Ph.D. (2004). *Homeschoolers on to College: What Research Shows Us.* The Journal of College Admission,185.
15. Neufield, Gordon. *Hold onto Your Kids: Why Parents Need to Matter More Than Peers.* Ballantine Books, Reprint. 2006. pg. 15
16. Basham, Patrick G., Merrifield, John, Hepburn, Claudia R. *Home Schooling: From the Extreme to the Mainstream.* The Fraser Institute, October 2007. www.fraserinstitute.org. Accessed on Nov. 2016.
17. *Spanglish.* Directed by John L. Brooks, Columbia Pictures, 17 Dec. 2004.
18. Fisher, Dorothy Canfield. *Understood Betsy.* Republished Independently. 2019. pg. 102
19. Sax, Leonard. *Boys Adrift: The Five Factors Driving the Growing Epidemic of Unmotivated Boys and Underachieving Young Men.* Basic Books. 2016. pg. 197.
20. *The 10 Weirdest Facts About Venus.* Space.com, https://www.space.com/15988-venus-planet-weird-facts.html. Accessed 10 Sept. 2019.
21. Homeschool Legal Defense Association. *Curriculum,* 2019, www.hslda.org. Accessed April 2019.

Spring

1. Shafer, Sonya. *Spelling Wisdom, Book One.* Exercise 16 "Trust the Creator" a quote by Ralph Waldo Emerson. (2006).
2. Sax, Leonard M.D., Ph.D. *Boys Adrift: The Five Factors Driving the Growing Epidemic of Unmotivated Boys and Underachieving Young Men.* Basic Books. 2016. pg. 46.
3. Meililo, Robert. *Disconnected Kids.* TarcherPerigee. 2015. pg. 72.
4. Clarkson, Sally. *Different: The Story of an Outside-the-Box Kid and the Mom Who Loved Him.* Tyndale House Publishers, Inc. 2017. Introduction.
5. Mackenzie, Sarah. *Teaching from Rest: A Homeschooler's Guide to Unshakable Peace.* Classic Academic Press. 2015.

6   Garis, Howard R. *Uncle Wiggily's Story Book*. Platt and Munk. 1987.

7   Ambleside Online Annotated Charlotte Mason Series, *Vol 1. Home Education*, 2003. www.amblesideonline.org. pg. 43-45.

8   Louv, Richard. *Last Child in the Woods: Saving Our Children from Nature-Deficit Disorder*. Algonquin Books. 2008. Ch. 5.

9   Payne, Kim John. *Simplicity Parenting: Using the Extraordinary Power of Less to Raise Calmer, Happier, and More Secure Kids*. Ballantine Books. 2010. Ch. 3.

10 Simply Charlotte Mason: www.simplycharlottemason.com

11 Sabbath Mood Science: www.sabbathmoodhomeschool.com

12 Louv, Richard. *Last Child in the Woods: Saving Our Children from Nature-Deficit Disorder*. Algonquin Books, 2008. Kindle Version, Loc. 2079.

13 Wild and Free: www.bewildandfree.org

14 Johnson, James Weldon. "Deep in the Quiet Wood". 1871-1938. https://poets.org/poem/deep-quiet-wood. Accessed on 2019 April.

15 Pant, Paula (Producer). (2019, February 4). Digital Minimalism with Cal Newport [Audio podcast]. https://affordanything.com/cal-newport/

16 Swindoll, Chuck. sermon citation "Epochal Events Nobody Expected – The Magnificence of a Closed Door." Stonebriar Church. Frisco, Tx., 29 Sept. 2019. Sermon.

17 Shafer, Sonya (2018, March). *Top Three Habits for a Homeschool Mom*. https://simplycharlottemason.com/blog/top-three-habits-homeschool-mom/

18 Van Allsburg, Chris. *The Wretched Stone*. Houghton Mifflin. 1991.

19 Almond, Steve (2013, June). *My Kids are Obsessed with Technology and It's all my Fault*, NYT Magazine. https://www.nytimes.com/2013/06/23/magazine/my-kids-are-obsessed-with-technology-and-its-all-my-fault.html

20 American Academy of Pediatrics (2019). *Media and Children Communication Toolkit*. https://www.aap.org/en-us/advocacy-and-policy/aap-health-initiatives/Pages/Media-and-Children.aspx

21 *Common Sense Media (2019). The Common Sense Census: Media Use by Tween and Teens*. https://www.commonsensemedia.org/research/the-common-sense-census-media-use-by-tweens-and-teens-2019

22 Ratcliffe, Shawn (2018, March). *More Than 2 Hours of Screen Time May Affect Kids Brains*. Healthline. https://www.healthline.com/health-news/more-than-2-hours-of-screen-time-can-hurt-kids-brains

23 Domonoske, Camilla (2016, May). *For First Time In 130 Years, More Young Adults Live With Parents Than With Partners.* National Public Radio. https://www.npr.org/sections/thetwo-way/2016/05/24/479327382/for-first-time-in-130-years-more-young-adults-live-with-parents-than-partners

24 Quoctrung, Bui (2017, July). *Why Some Men Don't Work: Video Games Have Gotten Really Good.* New York Times. https://www.nytimes.com/2017/07/03/upshot/why-some-men-dont-work-video-games-have-gotten-really-good.html

25 Sean, Craig (2017, August). *Turns out action video games really can harm your brain, says Montreal study.* Global News. https://globalnews.ca/news/3654662/turns-out-action-video-games-really-can-harm-your-brain-says-montreal-study/

26 Tumbokon, Ronaldo (2019, December). *Raise Smart Kids: 25 Positive and Negative Effects of Video Games.* www.raisesmartkids.com

27 Influence Central (2020). *Kids and Tech: The Evolution of Todays Digital Natives.* http://influence-central.com/kids-tech-the-evolution-of-todays-digital-natives/

28 The NOVUS Project (2020). http://thenovusproject.org/resource-hub/parents

29 Chen, Brian X. (2016, July). *What is the Right Age for a Child to get a Smartphone?* The New York Times. https://www.nytimes.com/2016/07/21/technology/personaltech/whats-the-right-age-to-give-a-child-a-smartphone.html

30 Weisberg, Elizabeth (2015 April). *Some Parents Say "No" to Phones for Teens.* USA Today. https://www.usatoday.com/story/tech/2015/04/09/pew-mobile-phones-smartphones/25493215/

31 Gabb Wireless: www.gabbwireless.com

32 Grothaus, Michael (2017 December). *Your Digital Detox: 17 Smartphone Apps to Delete in 2018.* https://www.fastcompany.com/40503317/your-digital-detox-17-smartphone-apps-to-delete-in-2018

33 Engel, Renee Ph.D. (2019, May). Does Social Media Use Really Cause Depression in Teen. Psychology Today. https://www.psychologytoday.com/us/blog/beauty-sick/201905/does-social-media-use-really-cause-depression-in-teens

34 Twenge, Jean M. (2017, September). Have Smartphones Destroyed a Generation? The Atlantic. https://www.theatlantic.com/magazine/archive/2017/09/has-the-smartphone-destroyed-a-generation/534198/

35 Adams, Nick (2016, December). Not so Merry and Bright: Teen Mental Health During the Holidays. Sovereign Health. https://www.sovteens.com/mental-health/merry-bright-teen-mental-health-holidays/

36 Ciaccia, Chris (2017, November). *Former Facebook exec Sean Parker says 'God only knows what it's doing to our children's brains'.* FoxNews. https://www.foxnews.com/tech/former-facebook-exec-sean-parker-says-god-only-knows-what-its-doing-to-our-childrens-brains

37 Sorbo, Sam (2017, November). *Our culture is experiencing a hostile takeover. We must stop rejecting God if we ever want it to end.* FoxNews. https://www.foxnews.com/opinion/our-culture-is-experiencing-a-hostile-takeover-we-must-stop-rejecting-god-if-we-ever-want-it-to-end

38 Becker, Josh (2019). *Reducing Social Media Usage.* www.becomingminimalist.com

39 Cocoon, www.cocoon.com

40 Sunday TODAY with Willie Geist (Episode on 2019, 29 December). *Statistics on the number of people who use Facebook even though they don't trust it.* Today Show, NBC.

41 Pene du Bois, William. The *Twenty-one Balloons.* Puffin Books. 2005.

42 Srigley, Ron (2019, December*). I asked my students to turn in their cell phones and write about living without them.* MIT Technology Review Humans and Technology. https://www.technologyreview.com/contributor/ron-srigley/

43 Mohler, Albert. *We Cannot Be Silent.* Thomas Nelson. 2015. Ch. 7.

44 *The Detrimental Effects of Pornography on Small Children* (2017, 19 December). www.netnanny.com

45 MacMillan, Amanda (2017, May). *Why Instagram is the Worst Social Media for Mental Health.* TIME. https://time.com/4793331/instagram-social-media-mental-health/

46 Murray, David (2016, October). *Digital Theology.* Tabletalk Magazine. Ligonier Ministries.

47 Mackenzie, Sarah. *Read-Aloud Family.* Zondervan. 2018. pg. 49.

48 The Church of the Firstborn. The Online Library of T. Austin-Sparks. https://www.austin-sparks.net/english/books/003328.html. Accessed on 2020 June.

49 Hanegraff, Hank. The Christian Research Institute, www.equip.org

---

Summer

1 Heidi Thomas, & Syd Macartney. (2017). Season 6 Episode 8, *Call the Midwives*. London: British Broadcasting Company.

2 Lewis, C.S. *Chronicles of Narnia: The Lion, The Witch, and the Wardrobe*. Harper Collins, Reprint. 2008.

3 McKeown, Greg. Essentialism: *The Disciplined Pursuit of Less*. Currency. 2014. Ch. 3.

4 Davidson, Margaret. *I Have a Dream: The Story of Martin Luther King Jr*. Scholastic, Inc. 1986. pg. 18.

5 Voskamp, Ann. *One Thousand Gifts: A Dare to Live Fully Right Where You Are*. Zondervan. 2011.

6 Ambleside Online Annotated Charlotte Mason Series, *Vol 1. Home Education*, 2003. www.amblesideonline.org. Accessed 1 Jan. 2016. pg. 10, 147, 155.

7 Jethani, Skye. *With: Reimagining the Way You Relate to God*. Thomas Nelson. 2011. Kindle Version, Loc. 953.

8 Lucado, Max. *You Are Special*. Crossway. 1997.

9 Shurden, Nate (2017, January). *Worldly Success*. Tabletalk Magazine. Ligonier Ministries.

10 *Quotes by Elisabeth Elliot:* https://www.goodreads.com/author/quotes/6264.Elisabeth_Elliot?page=4. 2020.

11 Pietzker, Mary Ann. *Miscellaneous Poems*. Griffith and Farran, London. 1872.

12 Cloud, Henry and Townsend, John. *Boundaries: When to Say Yes, How to Say No to Take Control of Your Life*. Zondervan. 2017. Kindle Edition, Loc. 231.

13 Cloud, Henry. (2020 January 14) *Codependency*. YouTube. https://www.youtube.com/watch?v=AQDGD9LC_U0

14 Wikipedia. (2020 April 11). *Codependency*. https://en.wikipedia.org/wiki/Codependency

15 Ambleside Online Annotated Charlotte Mason Series, *Vol 3. School Education*, 2003. www.amblesideonline.org. Accessed 1 Jan. 2016. pg. 10, 147, 155.

16 Wikipedia. (2020 April 10). *Helicopter Parent.* https://en.wikipedia.org/wiki/Helicopter_parent

17 Skenazy, Lenore. (2008-2018). *Free Range Kids.* www.freerangekids.com

18 Ulutas, Ilkay, & Aksoy, Belgian Ayse (April 2014) *Helping or Hovering? The Effects of Helicopter Parenting on College Students' Well-Being.* Journal of Child and Family Studies, Volume 23, Issue 3, pp 548–557.

19 Glass, Karen. *Consider This.* CreateSpace Independent Publishing Platform. 2014.

20 Glass, Karen. *Know and Tell: The Art of Narration.* CreateSpace Independent Publishing Platform. 2018.

21 *Eight Concepts, Differentiation of Self.* The Bowen Center for the Study of the Family. https://thebowencenter.org/theory/eight-concepts/. Accessed on 2020 June.

22 L'Engle, Madeleine. *A Wrinkle in Time.* Square Fish. 2012.pg. 130.

23 Tripp, Paul. Quotes by Paul David Tripp. https://www.goodreads.com/author/quotes/123576.Paul_David_Tripp. Accessed on 2020 June.

24 Frankl, Victor and Winslade, William J. *A Man's Search for Meaning.* Beacon Press. 2006.

25 Vassar, J.R. *When I Don't Feel Successful.* Tabletalk. Ligonier Ministries. 1 Jan. 2017.

Fall

1 Wikipedia contributors. (2020, June 4). Living Books. In *Wikipedia, The Free Encyclopedia.* Retrieved 21:38, June 5, 2020, Retrieved from: https://en.wikipedia.org/w/index.php?title=Living_Books&oldid=960625685

2 Shafter, Sonya (2019 February) Simply Charlotte Mason. *What is a Living Book?* https://simplycharlottemason.com/faq/livingbook/

3 Burgess, Thornton W. *The Burgess Bird Book.* Dover Children's Classics. 2003.

4 White, E.B. *Charlotte's Web.* HarperCollins. 2001.

5 McCauley, Susan Schaeffer. *For the Children's Sake.* Crossway. 2009

6. Ambleside Online Annotated Charlotte Mason Series, *Vol 1. Home Education*, 2003. www.amblesideonline.org. Accessed 1 Jan. 2016. pg. 24.
7. Mackenzie, Sarah. *Teaching from Rest: A Homeschooler's Guide to Unshakable Peace*. Classic Academic Press. 2015.
8. Wesley, John. (1703-1791) A Man of One Book. https://www.bartleby.com/209/750.html. Accessed on 2020 June.
9. L'Engle, Madeleine. *A Wrinkle in Time*. Square Fish. 2012. pg. 180.
10. Tripp, Paul. *Age of Opportunity: A Biblical Guide to Raising Teens*. P&R Publishing. 2001. Kindle Edition, Loc. 360.
11. Kern, Jan. (2011, January). *Independence or Rebellion?* Focus on the Family. https://www.focusonthefamily.com/parenting/independence-or-rebellion/
12. Wallace, Warner J. (2019, January). *Updated: A Young People Really Leaving Christianity? Cold Case Christianity with J. Warner Wallace*. https://coldcasechristianity.com/writings/are-young-people-really-leaving-christianity/
13. Ligonier Ministries and Lifeway Ministries. The State of Theology. 2015. https://thestateoftheology.com/
14. Smith, Christian and Denton, Lundquist Melinda. *Soul Searching: The Religious and Spiritual Lives of American Teenagers*. Oxford University Press. 2005.
15. Kinnaman, David. *Unchristian*. The Barna Research Group. Baker Books. 2007.
16. Bisset, Tom. *Why Christian Kids Leave the Faith*. Discovery House Publishers (1997).
17. Lukianoff, Greg and Haidt, Jonathan. *The Coddling of the American Mind: How Good Intentions and Bad Ideas are Setting Up a Generation for Failure*. Penguin Book. 2019. Ch. 1, 5.
18. Tolkien, J.R.R. *The Hobbit*. Houghton Mifflin Reprint. 2013.
19. *Broke Busted and Disgusted*, Directed by Calvin Johannsen (2017). https://www.brokebusteddisgusted.com/
20. Buff, Conrad. *The Apple and the Arrow*. HMH Books for Young Readers. 2001.
21. Sax, Leonard M.D., Ph.D. *Boys Adrift: The Five Factors Driving the Growing Epidemic of Unmotivated Boys and Underachieving Young Men*. Basic Books. 2016.
22. Murray, Charles (2007, January). *What's Wrong with Vocational school?* The Wall Street Journal. https://www.wsj.com/articles/SB116900815084478640
23. Glass, Karen. *Consider This*. CreateSpace Independent Publishing Platform. 2014.

24 Wikipedia contributors. *Liberal arts education. Wikipedia, The Free Encyclopedia*. Wikipedia, The Free Encyclopedia, 6 Jun. 2020. https://en.wikipedia.org/w/index.php?title=Liberal_arts_education&oldid=961109527

25 Bowen, Ronda (2011, January). *Build a Well-Rounded Liberal Arts Home School Curriculum*. Bright Hub Education. https://www.brighthubeducation.com/homeschool-curriculum-reviews/104777-putting-together-a-complete-liberal-arts-homeschool-curriculum/

26 Wildavsky, Ben (2016, March) *The Rise of Liberal Arts in Hong Kong*. The Atlantic. https://www.theatlantic.com/education/archive/2016/03/the-rise-of-liberal-arts-in-china/474291/

27 Klebnikov, Sergei (2015, June). *The Rise of Liberal Arts Colleges in Asia*. Forbes Education. https://www.forbes.com/sites/sergeiklebnikov/2015/06/03/the-rise-of-liberal-arts-colleges-in-asia/#47bfeb637e3c

28 Craig, Trisha (2016, February). *World Insight: Banging the drum for liberal arts in East Asia*. Times Higher Education Magazine. https://www.timeshighereducation.com/blog/world-insight-banging-drum-liberal-arts-east-asia

29 Voice of the Martyrs, www.persecution.com.

30 Tolkien, J.R.R. The Lord of the Rings: The Return of the King. HarperCollins. 2001.

31 Henry Alford (1810-1871), "Harvest Home" Retrieved from Ambleside Online: https://www.amblesideonline.org/HolidayThanksgivingPoems.shtml

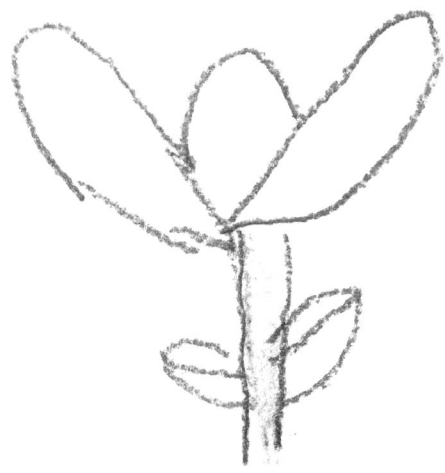

P.A., age 9

WORKS CITED

Adams, Nick (2016, December). Not so Merry and Bright: Teen Mental Health During the Holidays. Sovereign Health. https://www.sovteens.com/mental-health/merry-bright-teen-mental-health-holidays/

Almond, Steve (2013, June). *My Kids are Obsessed with Technology and It's all my Fault*, NYT Magazine. *https://www.nytimes.com/2013/06/23/magazine/my-kids-are-obsessed-with-technology-and-its-all-my-fault.html*

Ambleside Online Annotated Charlotte Mason Series, *Vol 1. Home Education*, 2003. www.amblesideonline.org. Accessed 1 Jan. 2016. pg. 3-6, 24, 43-45.

Ambleside Online Annotated Charlotte Mason Series, *Vol 3. School Education*, 2003. www.amblesideonline.org. Accessed 1 Jan. 2016. pg. 10, 29, 33, 147, 155.

American Academy of Pediatrics (2019). *Media and Children Communication Toolkit*. https://www.aap.org/en-us/advocacy-and-policy/aap-health-initiatives/Pages/Media-and-Children.aspx

AZ Quotes. Thomas Fuller Quotes. https://www.azquotes.com/author/5233-Thomas_Fuller. Accessed on 21 Jan. 2019.

Basham, Patrick G., Merrifield, John, Hepburn, Claudia R. *Home Schooling: From the Extreme to the Mainstream*. The Fraser Institute, October 2007. www.fraserinstitute.org. Accessed on Nov. 2016.

Becker, Josh (2019). *Reducing Social Media Usage*. www.becomingminimalist.com

Becker, Joshua. *Inside Out: Life-Changing Keys to Your Most Important Relationships.* Self-Published. 2011.

Becker, Joshua. Simplicity: *7 Guiding Principles to Help Anyone Declutter Their Home and Life.* Self-Published. 2014.

Bisset, Tom. *Why Christian Kids Leave the Faith.* Discovery House Publishers (1997)

Bowen, Rhonda (2011, January). *Build a Well-Rounded Liberal Arts Home School Curriculum.* Bright Hub Education. https://www.brighthubeducation.com/homeschool-curriculum-reviews/104777-putting-together-a-complete-liberal-arts-homeschool-curriculum/

Broke Busted and Disgusted, Directed by Calvin Johannsen (2017). https://www.brokebusteddisgusted.com/

Buff, Conrad. *The Apple and the Arrow.* HMH Books for Young Readers. 2001.

Burgess, Thornton W. *The Burgess Bird Book.* Dover Children's Classics. 2003.

Chen, Brian X. (2016, July). *What is the Right Age for a Child to get a Smartphone?* The New York Times. https://www.nytimes.com/2016/07/21/technology/personaltech/whats-the-right-age-to-give-a-child-a-smartphone.html

Ciaccia, Chris (2017, November). *Former Facebook exec Sean Parker says 'God only knows what it's doing to our children's brains'.* FoxNews. https://www.foxnews.com/tech/former-facebook-exec-sean-parker-says-god-only-knows-what-its-doing-to-our-childrens-brains

Clarkson, Sally. *Different: The Story of an Outside-the-Box Kid and the Mom Who Loved Him.* Tyndale House Publishers, Inc. 2017. Introduction.

Cloud, Henry and Townsend, John. *Boundaries: When to Say Yes, How to Say No to Take Control of Your Life.* Zondervan. 2017. Kindle Edition, Loc. 231.

Cloud, Henry. (2020 January 14) *Codependency*. YouTube. https://www.youtube.com/watch?v=AQDGD9LC_U0

Cocoon, www.cocoon.com

Common Sense Media (2019). The Common Sense Census: Media Use by Tween and Teens. https://www.commonsensemedia.org/research/the-common-sense-census-media-use-by-tweens-and-teens-2019

Craig, Trisha (2016, February). *World Insight: Banging the drum for liberal arts in East Asia.* Times Higher Education Magazine. https://www.timeshighereducation.com/blog/world-insight-banging-drum-liberal-arts-east-asia

Davidson, Margaret. *I Have a Dream: The Story of Martin Luther King Jr.* Scholastic, Inc. 1986.

Domonoske, Camilla (2016, May). *For First Time In 130 Years, More Young Adults Live With Parents Than With Partners.* National Public Radio. https://www.npr.org/sections/thetwo-way/2016/05/24/479327382/for-first-time-in-130-years-more-young-adults-live-with-parents-than-partners

Eight Concepts, Differentiation of Self. The Bowen Center for the Study of the Family. https://thebowencenter.org/theory/eight-concepts/. Accessed on 2020 June.

Engel, Renee Ph.D. (2019, May). Does Social Media Use Really Cause Depression in Teen. Psychology Today. https://www.psychologytoday.com/us/blog/beauty-sick/201905/does-social-media-use-really-cause-depression-in-teens

Fisher, Dorothy Canfield. *Understood Betsy.* Republished Independently. 2019.

Frankl, Victor and Winslade, William J. *A Man's Search for Meaning.* Beacon Press. 2006.

Gabb Wireless: www.gabbwireless.com

Garis, Howard R. *Uncle Wiggily's Story Book.* Platt and Munk. 1987.

Glass, Karen. *Consider This*. CreateSpace Independent Publishing Platform. 2014.

Glass, Karen. *Know and Tell: The Art of Narration*. CreateSpace Independent Publishing Platform. 2018.

Grothaus, Michael (2017 December). *Your Digital Detox: 17 Smartphone Apps to Delete in 2018*. https://www.fastcompany.com/40503317/your-digital-detox-17-smartphone-apps-to-delete-in-2018

Hanegraff, Hank. The Christian Research Institute, www.equip.org

Heidi Thomas, & Syd Macartney. (2017). Season 6 Episode 8, *Call the Midwives*. London: British Broadcasting Company.

Henry Alford (1810-1871), "Harvest Home" Retrieved from Ambleside Online: https://www.amblesideonline.org/HolidayThanksgivingPoems.shtml

Homeschool Legal Defense Association. *Curriculum*, 2019, www.hslda.org. Accessed April 2019.

Homeschooling in the United States: 2012. National Center for Education Statistics, 1 Nov. 2016, https://nces.ed.gov/pubsearch/pubsinfo.asp?pubid=2016096rev. Accessed 20 Jul. 2016.

Influence Central (2020). *Kids and Tech: The Evolution of Todays Digital Natives*. http://influence-central.com/kids-tech-the-evolution-of-todays-digital-natives/

Jethani, Skye. *With: Reimagining the Way You Relate to God*. Thomas Nelson. 2011. Kindle Edition, Loc. 953.

Johnson, James Weldon. "Deep in the Quiet Wood". 1871-1938. https://poets.org/poem/deep-quiet-wood. Accessed on 2019 April.

Kern, Jan. (2011, January). *Independence or Rebellion?* Focus on the Family. https://www.focusonthefamily.com/parenting/independence-or-rebellion/

Kinnaman, David. *Unchristian*. The Barna Research Group. Baker Books. 2007.

Klebnikov, Sergei (2015, June). *The Rise of Liberal Arts Colleges in Asia*. Forbes Education. https://www.forbes.com/sites/sergeiklebnikov/2015/06/03/the-rise-of-liberal-arts-colleges-in-asia/#47bfeb637e3c

Kondo, Marie. *The Life Changing Magic of Tidying Up: The Japanese Art of Decluttering and Organizing*. Ten Speed Press 1st Ed. 2014. pg.117.

L'Engle, Madeleine. *A Wrinkle in Time*. Square Fish. 2012. pg. 130, 180.

Lewis, C.S. *The Chronicles of Narnia: The Lion, The Witch, and The Wardrobe*. Harper Collins. 2001. pg. 131.

Ligonier Ministries and Lifeway Ministries. The State of Theology. 2015. https://thestateoftheology.com/

Louv, Richard. *The Last Child in the Woods*. Algonquin Books. 2013. pg. 44.

Louv, Richard. *Last Child in the Woods: Saving Our Children from Nature-Deficit Disorder*. Algonquin Books, 2008. Kindle Version, Loc. 2079.

Lucado, Max. *You Are Special*. Crossway. 1997.

Lukianoff, Greg and Haidt, Jonathan. *The Coddling of the American Mind: How Good Intentions and Bad Ideas are Setting Up a Generation for Failure*. Penguin Book. 2019. Ch. 1, 5.

Mackenzie, Sarah. *Read-Aloud Family*. Zondervan. 2018. pg. 49.

Mackenzie, Sarah. *Teaching from Rest: A Homeschooler's Guide to Unshakable Peace*. Classic Academic Press. 2015.

MacMillan, Amanda (2017, May). *Why Instagram is the Worst Social Media for Mental Health*. TIME. https://time.com/4793331/instagram-social-media-mental-health/

McCauley, Susan Schaeffer. *For the Children's Sake*. Crossway. 2009

McKeown, Greg. Essentialism: *The Disciplined Pursuit of Less*. Currency. 2014. pg. 18.

Meililo, Robert. *Disconnected Kids*. TarcherPerigee. 2015. pg. 72.

Mohler, Albert. *We Cannot Be Silent*. Thomas Nelson. 2015. Ch. 7.

Murray, Charles (2007, January). *What's Wrong with Vocational school*? The Wall Street Journal. https://www.wsj.com/articles/SB116900815084478640

Murray, David (2016, October). *Digital Theology*. Tabletalk Magazine. Ligonier Ministries.

Neufield, Gordon. *Hold Onto Your Kids: Why Parents Need to Matter More Than Peers*. Ballantine Books, Reprint. 2006. pg. 15

Oswald, Chambers. *My Utmost for His Highest: 30 Day Edition*. YouVersion Bible App. Version 8.14. 2017.

Pant, Paula (Producer). (2019, February 4). Digital Minimalism with Cal Newport [Audio podcast]. https://affordanything.com/cal-newport/

Payne, Kim John. *Simplicity Parenting: Using the Extraordinary Power of Less to Raise Calmer, Happier, and More Secure Kids*. Ballantine Books. 2010. Ch. 3.

Pene du Bois, William. The *Twenty-one Balloons*. Puffin Books. 2005.

Pietzker, Mary Ann. *Miscellaneous Poems*. Griffith and Farran, London. 1872.

Quoctrung, Bui (2017, July). *Why Some Men Don't Work: Video Games Have Gotten Really Good*. New York Times. https://www.nytimes.com/2017/07/03/upshot/why-some-men-dont-work-video-games-have-gotten-really-good.html

Quotes by Elisabeth Elliot: https://www.goodreads.com/author/quotes/6264.Elisabeth_Elliot?page=4. 2020.

Ratcliffe, Shawn (2018, March). *More Than 2 Hours of Screen Time May Affect Kids Brains.* Healthline. https://www.healthline.com/health-news/more-than-2-hours-of-screen-time-can-hurt-kids-brains

Ray, Brian D. Ph.D. (2004). *Homeschoolers on to College: What Research Shows Us.* The Journal of College Admission,185.

Sabbath Mood Science: www.sabbathmoodhomeschool.com

Sanchez, Anita. *The Teeth of the Lion: The Story of the Beloved and Despised Dandelion.* McDonald & Woodward. 2006. Ch. 1.

Sax, Leonard M.D., Ph.D. *Boys Adrift: The Five Factors Driving the Growing Epidemic of Unmotivated Boys and Underachieving Young Men.* Basic Books. 2016. pg. 197.

Sean, Craig (2017, August). *Turns out action video games really can harm your brain, says Montreal study.* Global News. https://globalnews.ca/news/3654662/turns-out-action-video-games-really-can-harm-your-brain-says-montreal-study/

Shafer, Sonya (2018, March). *Top Three Habits for a Homeschool Mom.* https://simplycharlottemason.com/blog/top-three-habits-homeschool-mom/

Shafer, Sonya. *Spelling Wisdom, Book One.* Exercise 16 "Trust the Creator" a quote by Ralph Waldo Emerson. (2006).

Shafter, Sonya (2019 February) Simply Charlotte Mason. *What is a Living Book?* https://simplycharlottemason.com/faq/livingbook/

Shurden, Nate (2017, January). *Worldly Success.* Tabletalk Magazine. Ligonier Ministries.

Simply Charlotte Mason: www.simplycharlottemason.com

Skenazy, Lenore. (2008-2018). *Free Range Kids.* www.freerangekids.com

Smith, Christian and Denton, Lundquist Melinda. *Soul Searching: The Religious and Spiritual Lives of American Teenagers.* Oxford University Press. 2005.

Sorbo, Sam (2017, November). *Our culture is experiencing a hostile takeover. We must stop rejecting God if we ever want it to end.* FoxNews. https://www.foxnews.com/opinion/our-culture-is-experiencing-a-hostile-takeover-we-must-stop-rejecting-god-if-we-ever-want-it-to-end

Spanglish. Directed by John L. Brooks, Columbia Pictures, 17 Dec. 2004.

Srigley, Ron (2019, December). *I asked my students to turn in their cell phones and write about living without them.* MIT Technology Review Humans and Technology. https://www.technologyreview.com/contributor/ron-srigley/

Sunday TODAY with Willie Geist (Episode on 2019, 29 December). *Statistics on the number of people who use Facebook even though they don't trust it.* Today Show, NBC.

Swindoll, Chuck. "A Successful Man Ruined by Pride." Stonebriar Church. Frisco, Tx., 8 Sept. 2019. Sermon.

Swindoll, Chuck. sermon citation "Epochal Events Nobody Expected – The Magnificence of a Closed Door." Stonebriar Church. Frisco, Tx., 29 Sept. 2019. Sermon.

The 10 Weirdest Facts About Venus. Space.com, https://www.space.com/15988-venus-planet-weird-facts.html. Accessed 10 Sept. 2019.

The Associated Press. (2009, Jan.). *Extraordinary Perception Permeates Painter's World.* Bangor Daily News. https://bangordailynews.com/2009/01/17/news/lsquoextraordinary-perceptionrsquo-permeated-painterrsquos-world/

The Church of the Firstborn. The Online Library of T. Austin-Sparks. https://www.austin-sparks.net/english/books/003328.html. Accessed on 2020 June.

The Detrimental Effects of Pornography on Small Children (2017, 19 December). www.netnanny.com

The NOVUS Project (2020). http://thenovusproject.org/resource-hub/parents

Tolkien, J.R.R. *The Hobbit*. Houghton Mifflin Reprint. 2013.

Tolkien, J.R.R. *The Lord of the Rings: The Return of the King*. HarperCollins. 2001.

Tripp, Paul. *Age of Opportunity: A Biblical Guide to Raising Teens*. P&R Publishing. 2001. Kindle Edition, Loc, 360.

Tripp, Paul. Quotes by Paul David Tripp. https://www.goodreads.com/author/quotes/123576.Paul_David_Tripp. Accessed on 2020 June.

Tumbokon, Ronaldo (2019, December). *Raise Smart Kids: 25 Positive and Negative Effects of Video Games*. www.raisesmartkids.com

Twenge, Jean M. (2017, September). Have Smartphones Destroyed a Generation? The Atlantic. https://www.theatlantic.com/magazine/archive/2017/09/has-the-smartphone-destroyed-a-generation/534198/

Ulutas, Ilkay, & Aksoy, Belgian Ayse (April 2014) *Helping or Hovering? The Effects of Helicopter Parenting on College Students' Well-Being*. Journal of Child and Family Studies, Volume 23, Issue 3, pp 548–557.

Van Allsburg, Chris. *The Wretched Stone*. Houghton Mifflin. 1991.

Voice of the Martyrs, www.persecution.com.

Voskamp, Ann. *One Thousand Gifts: A Dare to Live Fully Right Where You Are*. Zondervan. 2011.

Vassar, J.R. *When I Don't Feel Successful*. Tabletalk. Ligonier Ministries. 1 Jan. 2017.

Wallace, Warner J. (2019, January). *Updated: A Young People Really Leaving Christianity? Cold Case Christianity with J. Warner Wallace.* https://coldcasechristianity.com/writings/are-young-people-really-leaving-christianity/

Weisberg, Elizabeth (2015 April). *Some Parents Say "No" to Phones for Teens.* USA Today. https://www.usatoday.com/story/tech/2015/04/09/pew-mobile-phones-smartphones/25493215/

Wesley, John. (1703-1791) A Man of One Book. https://www.bartleby.com/209/750.html. Accessed on 2020 June.

Westminster Shorter Catechism. Westminster Assembly. Assembly at Edinburgh, July 28, 1648. Sess. 19. Q. 1.

White, E.B. *Charlotte's Web.* HarperCollins. 2001.

Wikipedia contributors. (2020, June 4). Living Books. In *Wikipedia, The Free Encyclopedia.* Retrieved 21:38, June 5, 2020, Retrieved from: https://en.wikipedia.org/w/index.php?title=Living_Books&oldid=960625685

Wikipedia contributors. *Liberal arts education. Wikipedia, The Free Encyclopedia.* Wikipedia, The Free Encyclopedia, 6 Jun. 2020. https://en.wikipedia.org/w/index.php?title=Liberal_arts_education&oldid=96110952

Wikipedia. (2020 April 10). *Helicopter Parent.* https://en.wikipedia.org/wiki/Helicopter_parent

Wikipedia. (2020 April 11). *Codependency.* https://en.wikipedia.org/wiki/Codependency

Wild and Free: www.bewildandfree.org

Wildavsky, Ben (2016, March) *The Rise of Liberal Arts in Hong Kong.* The Atlantic. https://www.theatlantic.com/education/archive/2016/03/the-rise-of-liberal-arts-in-china/474291/